# Gut Holzhausen

# The Second Son

Diana von der Borch-Garden

First published in Australia in 2017
by Diana von der Borch-Garden

Copyright © Diana von der Borch-Garden 2017

All rights reserved. No part of this book may be reproduced or transmitted by any person or entity (including Google, Amazon or similar organisations), in any form or means, electronic or mechanical, including photocopying, recording, scanning or by any information storage and retrieval system without prior permission in writing from the author.

National Library of Australia Cataloguing-in-Publication data:
Borch-Garden, Diana von der, author.
The second son / Diana von der Borch-Garden.
ISBN: 9780648115809 (paperback)

Subjects: Borch, Leopold von der.
George Shotten (Ship)
Nobility--Biography.
German Australians--Biography.
Police--Northern Territory--Biography.
Detectives--South Australia--Biography.
Translators--South Australia--Biography.
Photographers--South Australia--Biography.
South Australia--Genealogy.
Northern Territory--Genealogy.
Germany--Genealogy.

Landscape photograph front cover:
View of the MacKinlay River (1880) by Paul Foelsche
State Library of South Australia B 22211

Cover design and typesetting by Ilura Design
www.ilurapress.com

Printed and bound by Lightning Source Australia

This book recounts the life of the author's great-grandfather, drawing from a vast collection of letters and documents held in family archives, and from news clippings and historical information. For dramatic and narrative purposes, this book contains some representative or fictionalised scenes, characters and dialogue. The views and opinions expressed in this book are those of the characters only and do not necessarily reflect or represent the views and opinions held by individuals on which those characters are based.

*Dedicated to
my mother, Leonie,
whose passion for family history has enriched our lives*

# Foreword

There are a number of people I would like to thank for the important part they have played in helping me to complete *The Second Son*.

My sister, Noushe, who collaborated with me on the book, particularly helping me with research and listening to me read parts of the story as it progressed, no matter what time of day or night. My son, Alexander, who has shown genuine enthusiasm and has encouraged me to follow my heart. As a family, we have travelled vast distances through South Australia and Germany to explore Leopold's world. What amazed us were the distances he travelled on horse, and the isolation he must have encountered.

*The Second Son* would not have been possible if not for the generosity of the current heir to Gut Holzhausen and dear relative, Johann-Friedrich Freiherr von der Borch, who gave permission to access letters written by Leopold between the years 1864–1920. The Australian and German von der Borch families have always maintained contact with each other, and although we knew some of Leopold's life in Australia, the letters, written by Leopold to his brother Alhard and to his father, Carl, revealed a much more exciting and adventurous life than we could have imagined.

I would also like to thank my cousin Jennie Morisset, for contributing her drawing of Gut Holzhausen, which is printed in the front of the book. She is an amazing artist.

The first year of Leopold's life was quite a mystery, until our research led us to Don Elks, a great-grandson of Ernst Pustkuchen. It was an important piece of the puzzle, and we are so grateful to him for sharing the information with us.

I would like to thank Brigitte Schwanitz, a local librarian in South Australia, who was able to transcribe Leopold's letters from Gothic German into English, bringing his letters to life with her knowledge of the language and her studies in graphology. We indulged in too many cups of tea and citrus tarts to count, over the many hundreds of hours we spent at coffee shops.

*The Second Son* was the story I needed to write. From the age of thirteen, I can remember telling my family and friends that I wanted to write a novel when I grew up; I had no idea it would take me so long to begin and then to complete one, nor that it would be about my great-grandfather Leopold. They always say that you need to find a story that speaks to you, and this story did.

When my sister and I were growing up, our mother talked to us about our family, telling us many stories that her father, Erwein, had told her, often on cold nights when he would put his big jacket over her shoulders to keep her warm, while she held a kerosene lantern for him as he pruned the vines that grew in his vineyard.

Erwein, our grandfather, loved his father, Leopold, and felt proud of his heritage, and I think our grandfather tried to recreate a family-style estate in South Australia where his eleven siblings could bring their families. As well as a vineyard, our grandfather had acres of almond orchards, citrus trees and vegetables, and he planned to pass it all on to his sons if they were interested in continuing his work. Unfortunately, the local government wanted the land, and our grandfather was forced to sell it before he could pass it on.

*The Second Son* has been an amazing exploration of my great-grandfather's life and the challenges he met in a new land. My goal was to find him, and to try and understand his journey, both physically and emotionally. I believe I have achieved that goal.

I would also like to thank my great-grandfather for the values he passed down through the family, and for the bond the von der Borch families share with one another.

Finding Leopold's soul has been like finding out a little bit about myself I never knew.

*Men at some time are masters of their fates:*
*The fault, dear Brutus, is not in our stars,*
*But in ourselves, that we are underlings. (1.2.9)*

# One

Leopold held onto the metal handrail of the passenger train, his left hand firmly gripping the stitched handle of his brown leather suitcase. He climbed the metal steps of the Royal Prussian steam train, and walked as fast as he could to his seat by the window. He placed his case on the floor, opened the window and leaned out to wave goodbye to his friends. It was cold, and the snow was blowing into the train, creating a fuss amongst the other passengers. Leopold was aware of the inconvenience to them, but he thought it might be the last time he would see his friends.

He decided he was going to do what he wanted, and waved goodbye to those friends who had been there to support him through the conflict with his father, the same friends that believed his stories when he had tried to explain his situation to his father and to his superiors in the army.

Before Leopold and his brother Alhard entered the army, both young men had been provided with a guardian to ensure they studied, got to classes on time and stayed out of trouble. Alhard came under the guardianship of a fellow by the name of Struckmann, whilst Leopold, who was a bit of a dreamer, was mentored by Lieutenant Otto, who had been recommended by his godfather, Adolf. Lieutenant Otto was thought to be just the man to teach Leopold some discipline, as Leopold's father,

Carl, never thought of Leopold as being creative, but more as being rather impulsive, and reckless, and perhaps, a little too easy going. The one thing everyone agreed on was that Leopold had a passion for life.

The army understood Leopold's situation in Berlin and had been very supportive, indeed pleaded with his father to let him stay with them. However, Leopold's father would not agree. At the time of the alleged forgery, the officers in Berlin had tried to convince Carl that most young men of his age did stupid things at times, and that he would come good, but the baron would have none of it. Leopold had explained to all of them, including his father, that he had indeed not committed forgery and that it was the tailor and the conmen who had suggested that it would be quite alright for him to buy his suit under his father's name. Leopold's mistake had been to trust the tailor and the conmen.

'Leopold has embarrassed the family and will have to suffer the consequences,' Carl had said to the officers. 'He certainly needs to learn to stand on his own two feet,' he continued, 'and not allow himself to be so influenced by those low-lives.'

After the incident, Carl wanted Leopold discharged from the army, but before the paperwork could be signed, the Austro-Prussian war had broken out, and Leopold, like his friends in the infantry, was fighting against the Austrians. It was a brief war, only seven weeks in duration, with the results that several thousand soldiers were killed.

Leopold was distracted by his friends' antics as they began dancing around arm in arm on the station's platform, making funny faces and saluting to him. Leopold could not help but laugh. He planned to apologise to the passengers later and offer them some of the boiled, aniseed lollies that he had bought while waiting to board the train. For now, though, he wanted to farewell his friends. He gave an audible sigh, closed the window, and sat on the seat and started to think about how much his life would be changed.

As a young man of six feet tall, with strong, even features and a neat moustache and blue eyes, he was considered handsome. His hair was parted in the middle and combed back. A piece of wavy, dark-brown hair fell over his brow. It always did. He settled into his seat, looked out of the window, and wondered how much Eighteen sixty-six would change not only his life, but that of the future of Germany.

The engine was ready to make its journey, and at last the painful farewells were over. The train billowed clouds of dirty steam into the air as it snaked its way through the hills that lay blanketed in snow. Pine trees stood tall and silent, and the trunks stood dark against a whitened mist, a veil of snow on the branches. Leopold looked out of the window, out to the dark steely-grey skies and watched as the wind blew the snow against the train windows. Small patches of white slid down the glass and nestled itself into the corner of the wooden window frame.

Leopold leaned forward to offer some more boiled lollies to the couple sitting opposite him. 'I heard the officers speaking this morning about getting early, wet snow, but I had no idea we would get this much of it,' said Leopold.

'Yes. I'm pleased we're going by train. From my experience, when we do get an early snow like this, the weight of the snow breaks some of the smaller branches, and the roads become slushy and dangerous,' answered the older gentleman.

Leopold took the leather glove off his hand and placed his palm on the glass to see how cold it was. His warm hand on the cold glass formed a foggy mark around the outside of his fingers. He liked this feeling: somehow the intense cold made him feel connected to the world. The train chugged along on its journey towards Altenbeken and the snow continued to fall.

Leopold wondered about himself—if he was a rather immature young man of twenty, or just naive. He knew, though, that in spite of his wrong-doing in Berlin, his father would be pleased to see him. His father, Baron Carl von der Borch, was a fine man, well-educated and commanding, a man who honoured the Prussian upbringing. Carl thought young men, especially Noble young men, should set an example to society by entering military school, as he believed the army had the same high expectations as he did. There would be no exceptions, no excuses. If a job needed to be done, it would be done. Although Leopold had not wanted to enlist in the army, the officers in Berlin valued him as a soldier. His older brother, Alhard, had not been keen to enter the army either, but, as the first-born son who would one day inherit the family estates, it made more sense for him to join. Alhard was more disciplined, and understood that it was part of his education: he was more rigid in his thinking than Leopold, had more of what his father expected from a young man, and he knew that the army would provide him with the prestige that was expected of the first-born son.

The von der Borch family had three properties in all: Langendreer, Schönebeck, and Gut Holzhausen.

For Leopold the future was uncertain, especially now. He always saw himself as the stand-in. Not important enough to inherit control of the properties and make decisions but as someone who was just there, waiting, maybe waiting all his life, to contribute to the family, but certainly never the decision maker.

Leopold had shown himself to be a passionate, creative type of person. He was more prone to drifting, yet enjoyed learning. He spoke seven languages fluently, which made it easy for him to discover new places and meet new people.

For as long as anyone could remember, Leopold had always loved to travel by train. The rocking of the train carriages and the clickety clack of the wheels made him feel relaxed and gave him time to think.

Leopold thought back to his earlier years when he would often spend his spare time writing or drawing, sometimes sneaking up into the attic of the Big House when he should have been attending to something else such as spending time with his maths tutor.

When he was a child, his mother, Countess Ludmilla, loved to go for walks in their beech forest. She would set up her easel, canvases and watercolours for herself and the children to paint. Sometimes they would lie down under the beech trees on a blanket and look up through the dappled light that made its way through the light green coloured leaves. They would close their eyes and listen to the various animals scratching in the forest, guessing what animal was responsible for the sounds and laughing out aloud at the ridiculous guesses they made. The children also loved to chase each other. One of the children, usually Leopold, would cover his eyes and yell out all the names of the animals in the forest that he could think of instead of counting from one to ten—deer, porcupine, rabbits—until he reached the tenth animal, and then he would go in search for his brothers and sisters. It was a favourite game of the younger siblings.

When visitors came to stay with them, the children would go out into the meadows and have a picnic. Along the way they would collect wild flowers the colours of orange, pink and yellow to put them in a vase in the guest room. Their mother, Ludmilla, would talk to them about famous writers and musicians, and would tell them stories such as 'The Musicians of Bremen', which was one of Leopold's favourite stories. Their forest was the same forest that the Grimm brothers wandered through for inspiration for their stories. It was a magical place for the children.

Their mother had the heart-shaped face of an angel. Her skin was soft to the touch and her eyes large and twinkly. When she entered a room, she did so in a quiet manner and almost seemed to float across the room in her floor length, beautifully handcrafted dresses. She had a smile that lit up the room, and warm hugs and gentle words for her family. She was loved by all.

The children's favourite game on a Friday night or on cold winter days was called 'Shoot the Eagle', a name Leopold always thought of as being rather odd. It was a fun game that led to them eating lots of chocolate. They would spend hours sitting around the big oak table laughing and chatting while they ate their favourite food.

Therese was usually in charge of setting up the game. She was tall for her age and quite different to look at compared to her twin sister, Amalia. Therese's features were more angular and long like her father's, whilst Amalia had the angelic features of her mother.

Therese would place a large piece of chocolate, wrapped in paper and tied with string, in the middle of the table on a chopping board. Next to it, she would place a knife and fork, a woollen hat, a pair of dice, and a pair of woollen gloves. The first person would roll the dice, and before they could enter the game they had to role a six. The dice went to the next person on the left and so on until a six was rolled. As quickly as possible that person would don the hat, the gloves and the scarf and take the knife and fork and start cutting the string around the chocolate so they could eat some. At the same time, the dice would be handed around until someone else rolled a six, and then it would be their turn to attempt to get into the chocolate. The game would progress, and lots of laughter would be heard as all the children, and sometimes their mother, would try to be the first to open the chocolate.

Leopold felt the chugging of the train beneath his feet. There was a rhythm, a certain predictability in the way the carriage rocked back and forth.

He replaced the glove on his hand and then reached into his leather case that he had placed on the floor next to his feet when he had first entered the carriage. His fingers felt around until he found the rather stiff, linen paper his father had written on and sent to him commanding him to come home. It was well read and crumpled. He made himself comfortable and sat back to read it once again, trying to understand the repercussions that were to follow.

*Dear Leopold*

*It has been brought to my attention by a senior family member that you should learn to stand on your own two feet after your reckless and impulsive behaviour in Berlin. You are a young man with responsibilities and therefore need to be more answerable to the family. You are far too influenced by others and spend money far too quickly!*

*As I have withdrawn you from the army early, it is my legal responsibility to keep you suitably occupied and pay your way.*

*As such, I have written to General Duchene in January this year to see if they were still looking for recruits for the Belgique Armee in Mexico and also to a family friend to see if we could get you onto the Austrian Council. Disappointingly, this was not possible. It is my intention to keep you as far away as I can from those undesirables in Berlin.*

*You must come here no later than December 15th to discuss what it is that I am to do with you,*

*Your loving father*

*P.S. I am still waiting for your discharge papers from the army!*

The steam train continued to weave its way through the hills, stopping occasionally at a station for others to board.

Leopold looked at the letter again and wondered which of the senior members of his family had been advising his father.

Leopold stared out into the distance to the dark skies that pervaded the day, and thought back to his day in court, or at least snippets of it. The courtroom was lined with wooden panelling and wooden bench seats for everyone to sit on: his father dressed in a suit made by Herr Schneider sitting quietly and looking at Leopold as he gave evidence to the judge.

Before Leopold entered the courtroom, one of the conmen pulled him aside and threatened him. If he gave evidence he would be looking over his shoulder for the rest of his life.

Leopold's father had convinced him otherwise, saying that

the conmen were well known to the police and that they had told him that, if Leopold gave evidence, they could lock up the conmen for years. Carl was a little unsure if his son was telling the truth about buying the suit.

Once the trial had concluded, and Carl had heard all the evidence including Leopold's, he had second thoughts. Carl could not understand how Leopold could have been so influenced by those men.

'You were raised in a traditional aristocratic household and were well educated,' Leopold could hear his father say. 'Why then did you listen to these conmen? Why were you so influenced by these low-lives?'

A sudden jolt of the carriages distracted Leopold.

It would be another thirty minutes to reach Altenbeken, so Leopold folded the letter and put it back in his bag. He danced his fingers along the other things in his bag, looking for a book to read. He slipped his fingers on either side of the binding and lifted out *Winter Notes on Summer Impressions* by Dostoyevsky, an account of Dostoyevsky's trip to Western Europe.

The book had been given to Leopold to read by one of his friends, a fellow soldier in the Prussian Army. Dostoyevsky was writing at a time before Leopold was born. It was Eighteen sixty-two, and the author had gone abroad for the first time, travelling to places like France and England. He travelled Europe again in Eighteen sixty-three and Eighteen sixty-five. During that period his wife and brother died, and Dostoyevsky had become obsessed with gambling, and was plagued by debts.

Like Dostoyevsky, Leopold had experienced the death of loved ones at a young age. Leopold was twelve years of age when his mother had died quite suddenly, leaving behind ten children, of which the eldest was Alhard, aged thirteen, and the youngest, Kurt, only two years of age and not long out of nappies.

As the second son, he felt somewhat responsible for his younger brothers and sisters, including Therese and Amalia, who were aged eleven. Leopold was especially close to Therese, who was named after his grandmother, Princess Therese Bentheim-Tecklenburg-Rheda, who he cherished.

His sister Therese always made him laugh. Once, when she was only about seven years of age and waiting for *Christkind*, Father Christmas, to come, she looked out through the window of her father's library, out to the fields and the trees covered in snow. The water in the moat had frozen over. She had grown bored with waiting for him, and had been staring out into the night for what seemed like ages, when suddenly Therese saw what she thought looked to be an angel with gold wings standing at the edge of the moat. She almost fell over trying to run fast enough to tell everyone before the angel disappeared.

After Leopold's mother had died, the staff at Holzhausen helped out as much as possible to keep a routine for the children. They carried out their ordinary tasks, such as the cooking, cleaning and running the household, and also tried to find the time to spend with the children, playing hide-and-seek.

Leopold's aunt, Tante Emma, his mother's sister, was a spinster, who spent most of her time with the children, especially the baby, trying to fill the void their mother had left behind. A year later, Tante Emma became their step-mother.

The snow continued to fall, and the steam train continued on its way towards Altenbeken, a small village, twelve miles from Gut Holzhausen, the family home. Leopold tried to distract

*The Second Son*

himself from the thought of his father's wrath, and of what was to become of him, by focusing on Dostoyevsky's book.

The train's fireman half closed the small metal door which fed oxygen to the coals as they would be arriving at their destination in minutes, and Leopold would soon be at Gut Holzhausen, the Big House: the home he loved and the family he treasured.

# Two

Leopold had pulled the collar of his blue jacket up around his neck and rearranged the scarf that had come loose when he stepped off the train in Altenbeken. He had tried to pull his knitted hat down as far as he could so that none of the skin on the back of his neck would be cold.

He rubbed his gloved hands together vigorously to try and get the circulation back into his ice-cold fingers, then cupped them together in front of his mouth and huffed warm air onto them. In spite of it not being 'the done thing', he pushed his warmed hands into his coat pockets to keep them that way.

He had only stayed for a moment at the gravesite of his mother Ludmilla, for the cold had begun to seep into the very pores of his skin, and he was now so cold that he felt wet.

Even though it had been almost six months since his last visit home, somehow, he thought, things had changed more than he would have expected.

The five-hundred-year-old oak trees were the same, forming an alley, like a Gothic shaped arch above his head, as they led to the family estate of Gut Holzhausen not far from the cemetery; the branches drenched in snow were also the same; yet something felt different about this visit.

Every so often the wind would blow strongly enough to dislodge a clump of snow, which would fall to the ground, showering Leopold.

'Agh!' he cried aloud, 'It's so cold.'

On either side of the road grew bracken ferns, ivy, and other grasses and plants. To the left of him were open fields, with rich soil all partially hidden beneath the day's snow, and to his right, beech and pine forests as far as his eyes could see. As he walked, he heard the crunch of snow beneath his feet, and cows protesting in the distance.

Leopold looked across to the Big House and to its hip roof which looked somewhat like a pyramid. The hip roof was not only on the eaves side, but also on the gable end of the house, and had a sloping roof. It replaced the gable and helped to create the four roof surfaces, and was held together by the roof ridge. The sloping surfaces and the hip rafters made it a stronger structure when the strong winds blew.

Near the manor house were four permanent barns with gables that were partially plastered with rubble stone. Some rebuilding had been carried out in the seventeenth and eighteenth centuries, and he could see that there would always be some repairs to do.

On the west side of the estate, a pigeon tower had stood since the early eighteenth century between the barns and would soon need more repairs.

'After all,' he thought, 'it's been in the family since the fifteenth century … can't expect anything else.'

After ten minutes of walking he came to the heavy iron gates which marked the boundary of the property. He pushed on the gates and walked along the path toward the haunted wishing well to his right when he suddenly heard the laughter of his sisters. Leopold tried to hold himself back, but the laughter beckoned him to run. His stride became longer and faster, and he freed his hands from his pockets to be ready to hug his sisters as soon as he got there. The snow was slippery, and he lost his footing a couple of times, but it did not stop him from going as fast as he could.

Therese was outside on the doorstep talking to the staff about something she wanted them to do. When she realised someone was watching her, she looked up.

'Leopold? Leopold? Is that you?' she said hopefully. She walked down the steps and started to walk over the cobblestone path which led to the bridge over the moat.

'Yes, just me and the angel with gold wings: we flew here to see you as fast as we could,' he replied, thinking back to the time when she was about seven and had thought she had seen an angel by the moat. They both giggled.

'I saw Hans bring in suitcases, but I never dreamt they'd be yours,' she exclaimed.

Leopold started to run, his arms out to hug her. The laughter had made him forget about his troubles. He moved quickly over the wooden bridge and held onto the railings to steady himself. As he ran, snow was flung from the railings onto the ground.

'Leo. My dear Leopold,' she cried.

Therese took off his hat, and, with both hands, messed up his hair. 'I missed you.'

With his arm around his sister's shoulder, they walked through the front door, the blue woollen hat in Therese's hand.

'Have my bags been taken inside?' he asked.

'I think your ears must be frozen from the cold, dear Leo. I just finished saying that Hans had brought in suitcases … Yes, they're in your room,' she answered, still smiling.

'It's madness here, Leo. Everyone's preparing for father's birthday celebration and the evening events,' informed Therese.

Leopold stopped for a moment and listened. He could hear the sound of the pianist tapping out a few notes, and the sound of brass and winds.

'I'm home,' he said, and hugged his sister.

'Where's Mother?' Leopold asked. All the children had decided, when their father married their mother's sister, Emma, they would call her mother.

'Come. She's in the attic looking for something. You know Mother. She always likes to have something special to surprise Papa on his birthday,' Therese said, as she took Leopold by the hand and began to walk up the stairs.

'So much has happened since I saw you last,' said Leopold.

It was late afternoon, and the light coming through the windows had faded. A small beam of light shone in the middle of the well-worn stairs and made them look as though the edge of the steps were missing.

Leopold took off his boots and socks and walked up the stairs in bare feet. This had always been his favourite pastime, no matter what the weather. The wooden stairs were smooth, and moulded into the arch of his foot with every step. As children, they would sit on a thick woollen blanket and slide down on their bottoms, laughing all the way.

'You must be crazy, Leopold. You know what Mother will say,' said Therese, looking down at his bare feet.

'I know what she will do. She will give me the biggest hug and say, "Leopold you have come back to me."' Leopold's stepmother, Emma, was the most important woman in his life. After his mother had died, she would come around to have breakfast with the children every morning. She would supervise the staff, and make sure the table was set correctly. She would place the silver serviette rings, each with the baron's or baroness's crown and an initial of each child on the table, and she would make sure the cutlery with the family crests were used. Leopold's serviette ring had the baron's crown with its seven points and the Initial 'L'. Emma would make sure the staff knew what the children needed for the day, and then she would leave.

Leopold's father was kept busy with staff and the responsibilities of the estate. He had loved Ludmilla greatly, and they were a couple that everyone admired. When Ludmilla died, Carl was bereft. He was lost without her, and, with ten children under the age of thirteen, he was unsure of how to cope. He increased the number of personal staff to help him with the children, but it was impossible for him to read to them all at night. His heart was heavy, but he made sure he saw each child every day and spent time with them, and that he was there to give them a kiss goodnight. *'Schlaf gut,'* he would say, and then blow out the candle, close the door and leave. Carl had come to loathe the smell of the candles when they had been extinguished. It reminded him of his loss.

Finally, Therese and Leopold walked the two flights of stairs and opened the door to the attic.

'Leopold? Leopold Friedrich Carl Gotthard Hermann von der Borch. What are you doing here so soon?' Emma said. She had been expecting him to arrive after his father's birthday. Leopold was taken aback.

'I need a hug first from you, Mama. It's been so long …'

'Come. Give me a hug,' she said, holding out her hands to hold his. 'You must forgive my surprise; only your father must not see you until after his birthday. It must not be spoilt.'

He let go of her hands and was silent for a moment. 'Spoilt! Does he still not forgive me?' Leopold asked.

'I don't know that a day goes by when he doesn't think about that suit … he has become unwell by it all.' She patted the seat next to her and beckoned him to sit beside her.

'Here,' she said. 'You must not be too hard on your father. His reactions have been fuelled by those of others. Naturally he was upset with you, but he knows that it is expected of him to punish you in a harsh manner. He has spent many nights deliberating over your punishment.'

Emma paused for a moment thinking of how to word what she was about to say.

'Leopold, I want to ask you to do me a favour,' Emma said and kissed him on the cheek.

'Could you stay in your room tonight and not come down to the party … I don't think your father would cope seeing you there amongst all the other faces, and have people ask you, or him, awkward questions?'

It was the last thing she had wanted to ask of Leopold. She knew that he had not meant to create such a problem or cause his father embarrassment, but it had to be said. She preferred not to be the one to say it.

Therese looked at Leopold's sad eyes, 'Come on, Leo, I will

get the staff to make you a special dinner, and I'll bring it up to you. I'll tell the others that you're here, and we can take turns sneaking upstairs to see you. It'll be fun.' She, too, could not believe her mother's request.

Leopold looked at his mother. His stomach muscles were tight, and he could feel his heart beating fast.

'I'm sorry that I have caused so much pain for you ... I will do as you ask ... I do love all of you ... and if I'd known what those men were like, I never would have bought the suit. I'd like to have an opportunity to explain it all to you some time. Please don't believe all you've heard.'

Leopold stood up to go. 'I only wish Papa hadn't sent me to the army. I never did want to go.'

Emma stood up and looked up into his blue eyes. He was tall, had broad shoulders and a wonderful, generous smile. How could she be cross with him?

'We love you, too, Leopold, but you cannot blame your father for your misdeed. It is difficult having the responsibilities that we have as aristocrats. When my siblings and I were growing up it was even more difficult. My mother was a teenager when she inherited the title of Her Serene Highness Princess Therese Bentheim-Tecklenburg-Rheda, and with it came huge responsibilities. The Bentheims as you know were sovereign rulers of the Holy Roman Empire, and as her children we had to have impeccable manners. We had to be seen and not heard and only associated with our cousins. I have to admit it was a big family ... living as we do provides us with certain responsibilities to ourselves, our staff and our community, and it provides us with certain privileges. If we don't do the correct thing, then how can we expect others to do so?'

Leopold hugged his mother. He knew that what she said was correct.

'I'll go to my room and just wait to see Papa. Could you ask one of the staff to come up and make my bed, unpack my bags and prepare a meal for me, please, Mama?'

'Certainly! I'm busy right now, but Therese will do it for you, won't you, dear heart … I'll send Amalia up with your breakfast tomorrow morning … Catch up with your brothers and sisters first and see your father after lunch. One o'clock would be a good time, when the rest of us are doing something else.' Emma gave him a kiss. 'We do love you, Leopold Friedrich Car …,' she said laughing. Leopold knew that she did.

# Three

The night of the birthday celebrations, Leopold was tempted to go downstairs and watch the guests, most of them family. He knew that most of the members of his family would be there, and that one of them was probably the person his father mentioned in his letter. If only he could catch a glimpse of him, or maybe her, and see who his father was chatting with most of his night. Instead, Leopold had to be content to watch the parade of visitors from his upstairs window, hidden behind the velvet curtains of his room with his younger brothers laughing in the background. One of the boys, Siegfried, carried a toy sword and leapt about the room, sword pointed ahead of him yelling 'charge'. Every so often he would plunge the sword into the curtain and jab Leopold. Trying to restrain himself, Leopold gestured to him to be quiet. 'Stop doing that, Siegfried. Stop being so tedious.'

Leopold looked out to the blackened evening, but he could only see as far as the edge of the bridge that crossed over the moat: the same bridge he ran across earlier in the day to greet Therese.

At the very end of the drive, he could see a glimmer of light burning on the stone fence, showing the entrance to the estate. A large covered carriage with his Uncle Friedrich Wilhelm, along with some of the other members of his grandmother's family, was making its way toward the Big House. The von der Recke's had substantial properties and were Counts, which provided them with a certain power and prestige greater than that of his father's. As a child, Leopold wondered if his father ever felt at all intimidated by his mother's family. After all, he thought, his maternal grandmother was a Princess.

'Ouch! Siegfried,' said Leopold in a loud voice. 'Stop jabbing me.'

Siegfried laughed a muffled laugh as he put his hand over his mouth.

Another carriage came through the gates. The first carriage was that of his uncle and the first to alight was Friedrich Wilhelm, the most senior member in the carriage. He stood tall and proud in his dark tailored suit and waited for his wife to step out of the carriage. She wore a beautiful gown, typical of the fashions of the Eighteen sixties, with a square paisley shawl folded on the diagonal with a full skirt held out by crinolines. Friedrich Wilhelm's daughter, Agnes, was the next to step out of the carriage. She was wearing a dress with a tight bodice, a high neck and buttoned fronts. It had white lace on the collar and cuffs, with sloping shoulders that flared out into wide sleeves. The skirt was full and bell-shaped. The light by the carriage showed her hair, which she wore with a centre parting tied into low chignons at the nape of the neck, with loops covering the ears. How pretty she looked, thought Leopold.

More carriages arrived, each with men and women dressed much the same. The men in single-breasted coats and jackets semi-fitted, extending to the mid-thigh; collarless, single-breasted vests and trousers cut from a narrow check cloth; high, starched collars were worn with cravats and neck-ties. Their hair was parted from the centre and moderately waved, some of the men with a full beard and drooping moustache. The women were in bell-shaped dresses in various colours, or patterns with ostrich feathers, butterflies, or pomegranate flower patterns.

As Leopold watched the parade, he felt very much alone. His sense of belonging to this family felt frayed, his stomach tight and empty.

'Perhaps it was Uncle?' said Leopold aloud.

'Perhaps uncle what?' asked Siegfried.

'What … what are you talking about, Siegfried? First, you're jabbing me and yelling out "charge", and then you're asking me questions?' said Leopold, rather confused by Siegfried's actions. He had not realised that he had said anything out loud. 'Don't bother me for the moment. Just let me think.'

Siegfried happily took his sword and went off and started jabbing at the other curtains and the soft duvet cover.

Leopold looked out to the carriages and went on thinking. 'Who did Papa feel answerable to?' He had remembered his father and his uncle discussing an article that had been in the paper about putting young, undisciplined men into institutions … and it was his uncle who had actually offered to pick him up from Berlin and drop him off into one of those places after the 'suit' incident.

As far as he could remember, the idea was to teach the men strategies to make them think before they acted. His mother's family were well known in Prussia, not only for their position in life but also for setting up institutions for desolate and orphaned children after Napoleon's men had plundered Germany. The institutions had become the models for other institutions to follow, which included those for young, undisciplined men.

He tried to recall more of the article. 'That's right ... it had discussed how to prevent crimes without encroaching on the liberty of the young subjects,' which he had thought at the time was a good idea but certainly had nothing to do with his situation. The idea was for the offenders to be voluntarily employed in their own intellectual and moral elevation. The purpose was to separate the young men from bad influences, which he thought, might be behind his father's letter demanding he return to Holzhausen. He could not stop his mind from thinking about the suit and what might happen to him. Leopold could only hope that his next twelve months would not be spent in one of those places.

A suit! Of all things, it was a suit that had brought him to this moment. That, along with not handling his money very well, that had got him into so much trouble and caused such embarrassment to his father.

'A suit! Not stealing from anybody or killing anyone or committing adultery, but a suit.' The more he thought about it, the angrier he became.

'How could I have been so stupid? Why didn't anyone teach me about being conned or about spending money?'

Leopold, along with his siblings, had learnt English, French, Latin, German, Maths, History and Art, and had been taught how to ride a horse, and how to fire a gun, but not once had anyone ever thought to teach them how to spend money wisely. Indeed, they employed a man by the name of Hille for that very purpose: to manage their accounts for them.

'Herr Schneider … Schneider … good name for a tailor. Well, he certainly had my measure, cut me up and spat me out. And I was silly enough to fall into the trap! Should have been called Herr Traitor!'

With all the guests inside now, Leopold, his younger brothers and some of his other siblings crept out into the poorly lit passage near the stairwell to listen to the celebrations. His mother had organised a quartet to come and play, and the music filled the house and wafted up the stairwell much like the way perfume lingered in a room.

The children sat down on the top of the stairs and listened to the music and the laughter. How they longed to be downstairs with the rest of their family.

'Siegfried, why don't you go down and sneak into the kitchen and bring us up some food? I'm sure one of the staff, especially Hannah, will get something for us: she always spoils you,' said Fritz.

'No. Someone will see me,' replied Siegfried.

'Of course they will, but we can't let them see Leopold, and I can't go, so you'll have to go,' explained Fritz.

'What about one of the girls?' suggested Siegfried.

'The girls can't go: it's too late for them. If Mama or Papa saw them, they'd get cross, but you are little, and people expect little people to get hungry before they go to sleep,' said Leopold. 'Oh, and have a look who Papa's talking to for me, will you?'

While Siegfried edged his way down the stairwell, the others peered through the railings to watch the women dance and to hear the music.

'Isn't it wonderful, Leo,' remarked Therese. 'I'd love to be down there dancing in a magnificent gown and sweeping my way across the floor and into the arms of a handsome gentleman.'

'You're a hopeless romantic,' said Leopold.

Leopold strained to see who his father was talking to, but the enormous skirts on the women's gowns blocked his view.

'I'll never know,' said Leopold.

'What won't you ever know?' asked Fritz.

'Nothing,' replied Leopold.

'That's true. I don't think you know nothing already!' laughed Fritz.

'Fritz, it's, "I don't think you know anything," not "nothing,"' said Amalia, who loved grammar. Like Leopold, she was good with languages.

'Are you listening, Leo,' asked Therese.

'No. I'm concentrating.'

'Yes, leave him alone,' said Fritz. 'He's concentrating on "nothing", so we should let him.'

Leopold was too busy trying to concentrate on the task at hand to bother with his sibling's silly conversation.

Siegfried returned with some sweets, with Hannah carrying a jug of milk and glasses. 'Did you see who Papa was talking to?' asked Leopold excitedly.

Siegfried looked at the floor. 'I forgot.'

'He was busy helping me, Sir,' said Hannah.

'Thank you, Hannah,' Leopold said, and continued watching the activities downstairs. 'Don't worry, Siegfried. It doesn't matter.'

'Nothing matters,' said Fritz, and they all tried not to laugh.

# Four

The day had arrived when Leopold would confront his father. It was another cold October day. Only this day, Leopold felt particularly cold, and no matter how many layers of clothes he put on, it seemed he could not get warm.

Leopold went downstairs and stood by the stone fireplace in the dining room, trying to warm himself. On one side of the stone mantelpiece was the von der Borch family crest, featuring three jackdaws, and on the other side of the mantelpiece was the crest of the von Scheirstadt family. He traced his fingers over the von der Borch crest, following the shape of the birds' heads and around their bodies to their feet, and then looked at his sooty fingers before wiping them on his pants. The cavity where the wood was burning was large enough to fit five men standing side by side, and the mantelpiece was the height of his chest. Within minutes he felt warm.

After lunch and time spent with his siblings, Leopold went to his father's office.

Carl was waiting for him in his library, surrounded by leather bound books from floor to ceiling. His huge oak desk took pride of place near the double windows, which had been made by a local carpenter from one of the trees in the alley leading to Holzhausen that had fallen during a storm some years ago.

Carl turned the leather chair he was sitting in around, and looked out through the windows, across the moat, and cast his eyes along the driveway to the two pine trees that stood like sentries at the stone wall that surrounded his estate. His home, the estate of Gut Holzhausen, everything he could see related to his history and was the framework by which he lived his life.

Gut Holzhausen had been in his family for over four hundred years, given to them by Prince Bishop Simon the Third. It was a grand old home, where generations of von der Borchs had left their mark. To the right, about half way down the path, on the left-hand side as one walked through the front gate, stood the oldest house on the property, built in Fifteen seventy-two as the gatehouse. It was three stories high, with cladding on the first two floors, and wooden framework with cladding on the top floor. Some of the windows were tiny and had white wooden frames, and not even a child could squeeze through them. Leopold knew, because he had tried to do so. Once he got stuck and his younger brother Siegfried had to pull on his legs to free him.

Leopold had heard the story of *Hänsel und Gretel* by the Grimm brothers and he wondered if on one of their journeys through their forest, they might have come across the gatehouse and used it as the idea for the house of the witch. Leopold was not certain, but he did know that the Grimm brother's patron lived next door.

On the walls in the office and in the entrance hall hung the portraits of relatives dating back ten generations. The portrait of his father with its dark background hung next to that of his grandparents and great grandparents and various other paintings of family estates.

Leopold stood in the doorway of the office, watching his father. He studied his father's face, trying to read his expression. He could see that his father was lost in thought.

Leopold knocked on the door to get his father's attention. The thick doors and the empty passage way made the sound echo, startling his father.

'Leopold! I had no idea what that noise was at first. I was miles away. Good to see you, young man. It has been a while.'

'Good afternoon, Papa,' said Leopold as he came over to hug him.

His father's arm reached around him with equal strength to hug him. They stood there for a minute, neither one wanting to let go, for they knew that when they did they would have to discuss the situation as what to do with Leopold.

'How was your birthday party?' asked Leopold.

Carl sighed, knowing that Leopold had missed his birthday. 'It was just another day. We do things sometimes even if we don't really want to. It is expected of me, of us.'

Carl pointed to a chair for Leopold to sit in. 'My birthdays have never been the same since your mother died.'

Both men sat down. 'Emma is so good to me, and I love her dearly; however, it is not the same as with my Ludmilla.' Carl looked at his son. 'Don't say anything to Emma for I'd hate her to be upset and possibly judged by others.'

'Mother died almost eight years ago now, Papa,' Leopold responded. He paused before he shared his next thought. 'Do you think we'll ever get over losing her?'

'I don't believe we do ever forget the one we love; we just have to get on with things,' Carl replied.

'I wish I could believe that. I miss Mother, and I'm sad that I can no longer remember what she looked like,' Leopold said. 'I remember the things we did together, but I don't seem to remember her face much anymore, unless I look at her portrait.'

Carl looked at his son. It was a difficult time for him. His son looked like a man, and was tall and strong like a man, but he was still a boy. A somewhat immature boy, Carl thought.

Leopold was thoughtful. 'Nothing seemed to change when she died really ... somehow everything seemed the same ... the same routine,' he said.

Carl looked puzzled. 'I don't know what you mean, young man?'

'Well, it's meant to be different, isn't it ... a death? Death is meant to change things. When someone dies, your life is meant to change somehow ... but when Mother died, things seemed to go on much the same ... I felt sad and cried myself to sleep sometimes. I was only twelve. I would wait for her to come in and say goodnight, but she wasn't there ... when I'd wake up in the morning, it was as though I'd had a nightmare. Maybe I had only dreamt that my mother had died, and that she was still alive, and when I'd wake up, she'd be there ... because when I woke up, everything was the same as before, only I couldn't see her,' said Leopold with tears in his eyes. 'I think you tried your best for things to stay the same, but it made me feel as though you didn't care about her.'

'Oh, Leopold!' said Carl.

'Our lives went on without change. We got up at the same time, ate the same things, did all the same things. It was as though everyone wanted to forget her. Yet I knew she had died, because I remember her ice-cold face when I kissed her goodbye and the cold walk to the cemetery and all the sad faces.'

Carl thought his son sounded very much like the twelve-year-old Leopold, not the young man Leopold. He looked at his son, aware that he had said, 'do you think *we'll* get over losing mother. Not you, but we. Carl had often wondered if Leopold's loss of his mother and grandmother at a young age—two significant people in his life—had any bearing on the impulsive behaviour he had shown leading up to his misdeed.

Leopold had always been his favourite son. He had always been the son that was interested in going with him everywhere, and he had the gentleness of his mother. He was keen to go with him around the estate to check that everything had been done correctly, and, if not, he was prepared to hop in and help. If there was a sick cow or horse, he would tend to them—one night even sleeping in the barn with a beloved horse.

Carl and Leopold had spent a lot of time together, as father and son, so much so that sometimes Leopold wondered if Alhard felt left out. They spent a lot of time talking about Carl's childhood at Holzhausen, and of the Dutch van der Borchs, where his grandfather Jan Carel, or Johann Carl as the German's called him, was born. Leopold thought it was Jan Carel's son Adrian, his grandfather, who had come to Germany as the heir to Gut Holzhausen, due to the lack of male von der Borch heirs in Germany.

As a child, the most affection Carl showed Leopold when staff were around was to put his arm around Leopold's shoulder. He would never have hugged him, even for the saddest occasion. It was expected that the family would contain their emotions in public.

## The Second Son

Leopold was taught to shoot from a young age, as was the tradition for their class. Each of the male von der Borchs had their own guns, handmade from a dark wood with a gold family crest featuring the three jackdaws, somewhat like blackbirds, on the underneath side of the gun, just near the bolt. A silver plate with shooting scenes adorned the rifle on both sides.

All the family and friends would gather on their property, with some ten or so staff who would walk in front hitting the ground with sticks to encourage any grouse to fly, or walk beside the group and stomp on the ground to encourage the rabbits to run out into the open. The shooters would carry their guns in a safe position, with the barrel broken so as not to shoot anyone by mistake. Ducks, rabbits and an occasional deer were shot and then taken back to the house to be prepared for dinner the next day. They would only ever shoot what they could eat, and the 'catch' would be shared among both the family and the entire household staff of thirty.

After Leopold's mother died, Leopold no longer wanted to go out shooting with the others. He didn't want to see dead things. It was on a day returning from shooting that he had discovered his mother had died. It was so sudden; she had only been ill for a short time.

After Ludmilla's death, Carl noticed that Leopold had become more reckless. He remembered Leopold commenting that everyone had said, 'only the good die young,' and Leopold had responded by saying, 'then I'm never going to be good'.

Carl looked at his son. He loved his children, but he was lost when Leopold was so honest about his emotions. It was not the Prussian way. He looked away from Leopold and focused on a painting of Ludmilla on the opposite wall.

'I think a hot drink is in order,' said Carl as he pulled the tapestry cord on the wall, which signalled to the kitchen staff that he required something to eat or drink. One of the staff entered and awaited his orders. Carl requested hot chocolate drinks and home-made biscuits.

'Now, Leopold, we have to address this business of yours with regard to the suit you bought.'

Leopold sat up straight and leaned forward.

'I have come to the conclusion that you must stand on your own two feet a little more. I will be giving you a small wage, and you will go and live with your sister Minette and her husband at Westhusen. I've organised the staff to pack your bags, and Minette has organised one of the rooms for you to stay in.'

Leopold didn't speak. He was surprised that his father had got to the point so quickly.

'How long will I be there?' Leopold asked.

'Six months. I think that in that time, you will have learnt, or it is hoped that you will have learnt, to look after yourself a little more. I have given strict instruction that they are not to provide any personal staff for you as you have here. You really do need to be more organised. As I said, I will provide you with an allowance, out of which you must contribute to the food and pay for any clothes and any transport you need. Of course, you can come home to see the family every so often.'

Carl paused for a moment.

'After the six months is up, you will to go to Schönebeck for a further six months. If I can see that you've shown restraint, then I will provide some staff at Schönebeck. If you can't manage yourself, you certainly can't manage staff. Discipline comes first and foremost. I think that covers everything. Any questions?'

Before Leopold had a chance to respond, Carl continued, 'You may think this a harsh punishment, son, but I can assure you, Minette's husband, in his role as Prussian Cavalry Officer, is what you need. If this doesn't work, if you do not take heed of the discipline, then the consequences will be far-reaching. Remember, it is not just me making the decisions, even though I have the final say; I have to get advice from the more senior members of the families. And be aware that their form of punishment would be far more severe than mine.'

Leopold thought back to the newspaper article about institutions his father and uncle had been discussing, but he would never know for sure who was behind the decision to go to Minette's.

'Staying with your sister and brother-in-law will provide you with the opportunity to see what you're made of and it will be a good opportunity for you to stand on your own two feet. I truly hope that this next year will bring you to your senses.'

Leopold just nodded his head. He thought how exciting it would be to live with Minette and hoped he would do the right thing, something he was unsure of sometimes.

'I have found this whole exercise exhausting, and it hasn't been good for my health.'

'I'm sorry, Papa, if I have caused you any worry. It was not my intention,' said Leopold. 'There is, however, something I need to discuss with you, Papa, and I don't know how it will affect your health. But there is no-one else who knows about this.' He paused for a moment.

'If anyone comes looking for me,' he continued, 'don't tell them where I am. I fear for my life. Ever since I went to court, I have heard from friends that when the conmen get out of jail they will come after me. Going to Minette's might help me to hide from them for a while. Hopefully, they'll give up and get on with their lives for the better.' Leopold paused again and looked out the window.

'It's my fault. I should never have made you go to court,' said Carl.

Leopold did not respond. A part of him blamed his father for pushing him to go into the army.

'When am I to leave ... for Minette's?' asked Leopold.

'You will leave at the end of the week. Until then, you can help out here where they need you and then head off to Westhusen.

'The test for you, Leopold, will be to stay within your budget and not get tangled up with the wrong type of people. Just because we have a lot of money doesn't mean you can take advantage of it. One day, Alhard will have to manage the estate and look after all the family as I do now. I have not been well over the past few months, and the doctor has advised me to let Alhard start to take over the reins a bit more. If you spend more than is allowed, all the others, especially Alhard, will have difficulty.'

Leopold held his tongue. Alhard was not quite a year older than him, yet their lives were mapped out differently, simply because Alhard had been born first. He thought it a rather odd way to live a life. Not a life determined by skill and knowledge or good humour, but one of birth order. Certainly, he loved and enjoyed the prestige he was born into, and the opportunities it afforded; however, he thought it an unfair tradition, and it had come at a price.

Leopold was of two minds. He was saddened by his actions and his father's ill health, but was excited about going to his sister's to live for a while. He loved going to Minette's house for holidays. She was quite a bit older, by almost nineteen years, born from his father's first marriage to Countess Jenny von der Recke. He'd always thought it was sad that Minette had never known her mother, who had died shortly after giving birth to her. For the first time, Leopold wondered who had looked after Minette after her mother had died.

# Five

It was cold, and Leopold's sheets were crisp from the night air. He had trouble getting to sleep. He tugged at his covers, pulling the duvet up over his shoulders, and tried to think of the next few months at his sister's as being an opportunity for him to hide from the conmen, who had threatened to harm him.

Over and over in his head, he played out the events that had brought him to this consequence.

The day had started out like any other. He had decided to take a horse-drawn carriage to his shoemaker on Leipzigerstrasse in Berlin: Carl Nagel was the craftsman behind some of the best hand-made shoes in the area.

Leopold had stopped to post a letter to his father, just near the Spittelkolonnaden, a beautiful monument built in the late Baroque neoclassical style by Carl von Gontard in Seventeen seventy-six. He had crossed the road to Jerusalemerstrasse and walked its length to Mohrenstrasse until he reached the shoe shop.

The shop was usually bustling with people, but on that day it was quiet. 'I wonder where everyone is,' he had thought to himself, trying to understand what had made him do something so out of character.

Two young men had come into the shop, dressed rather smartly, and seemed friendly enough—perhaps 'familiar' would be a better word? They had made conversation with Leopold and seemed quite charming and well-spoken, and within a very short time had established that they had a friend in common, in the same regiment as Leopold.

Leopold fluffed up the pillows on his bed and sat up against them. He pulled the camel haired duvet up around his chest and stared out into the dark. The only light was from a half moon. 'Bit too coincidental,' he said aloud.

He closed his eyes to try and get a better picture of the events that day. 'They had come into the shop and said hello to me? Or was it to Herr Nagel? Then what did they do?'

He tried to picture it in his mind. 'What was it that they did … I must have noticed something? They came in and said hello and then asked me about the shoes … and I said I had ordered some but that they weren't ready, so I was going over the road to look at suits, because I was going with Amalia to an event … everything there seemed normal … but there was something.'

As Leopold looked back on the event, to the conversation he had with the tailor and the conmen, he realised just how much they had been working to encourage Leopold to buy the suit in his father's name.

'Think, Leopold. Think!' he said aloud.

His mind was starting to wander. 'How did they come to follow me to get a suit? I'm sure I didn't invite them? I said goodbye to Herr Nagel and continued to the tailors … I had to get a suit for the event, but I had no money because of the shoes and because I hadn't planned to get a suit,' he remembered and grew cross with himself.

'Papa was right. They were low lives. Stupid, stupid, man,' said Leopold, admonishing himself.

'I knew only too well that I had insufficient funds and that if I needed something I would have to discuss it with Papa. So why did I do it?' thought Leopold, as though he was having a conversation with someone else.

'"After all," the conmen had said, "you'll inherit everything, won't you? Or are you just the second son that has no say?" How did they know who I was?'

Their comments had infuriated Leopold to the extent that he bought the suit. Not in his name, but in his father's name.

The hours passed, and still Leopold tossed and turned in bed, until finally he decided to get something to eat. 'I've never been able to get to sleep when I'm hungry,' he said to himself.

He stood up out of bed and threw his dressing gown on, lit a candle and went downstairs. With each step he took, the flame flickered and reminded him of his childhood, of the scary stories the children told each other before they went to bed at night.

'I wonder how many people know about the suit? Or if they think I'm stupid or spoilt?'

It unnerved him to think that anyone would see him as anything but loyal and caring.

'No-one else knows what it's like to be me, or to have been in that situation, and to be accused of such things.'

The wind caught the flame of the candle and blew it out, splattering hot candle wax onto his hand. Alone, he stood in the dark, waiting for his eyes to adjust while trying to peel the hot wax off his hand.

Ahead of him, in a downstairs room, Leopold could see a shaft of light from under the door of his father's office.

'Surely Papa hasn't left the light on.' It was two o'clock in the morning.

Leopold walked tentatively toward the door, feeling his way along the walls with his outstretched arm. The house was quiet, except for the sound of his feet on the floor that changed as he stepped off the wooden floorboards and onto the flagstone pavers.

As usual he was barefooted, and the flagstones were ice cold. He remembered back to his childhood when he used to pretend to be blind. Just as he did back then, he now felt his way through the dark passageway.

A coughing sound came from behind the door where Carl was sitting at his desk. 'Come in, Leopold,' his father called out.

Leopold opened the door. 'How did you know it was me?'

'I'm your father … besides I can't sleep either … we're so much alike, you and I. Do you remember? As a boy, when you couldn't get to sleep, you'd always wander down to the kitchen to find something to eat. I'd hear you get up, and follow you down to see if you were alright. Then we'd both get something to eat, clean the dishes, so no-one knew we'd been up, and then I'd carry you upstairs on my shoulders back to bed.'

'And I'd have to duck, so I wouldn't hit my head when we went through the doorways.'

They both laughed. How good it felt that they could still laugh together.

'I wish you were still that little boy, and I could put you on my shoulders and carry you upstairs,' Carl replied. 'Perhaps if I had done things differently, life would have been easier for you. It was a difficult time for me, for all of us, and I know you took it very much to heart after both your mother and grandmother died within years of each other.'

They looked at each other. 'I wish I was still that little boy, too, Papa. However, what is done, is done.'

'That is very true,' replied Leopold's father. 'It's what we go on to do after the events that make us true to ourselves and to our values. I hope you won't let me down.'

'Hungry?' asked Leopold, ignoring his father's comment. His father smiled, then suddenly began to cough.

'Are you alright, Papa? Your health I mean … I feel like you're—,' but Leopold was interrupted by his father.

'I'm fine. I had a couple of little turns, but nothing to worry about …' He went on, 'These are uncertain times, Leopold, so I'm telling you these things because it's important. We'll be away from each other again for a while. None of us knows what will become of us.' Carl paused for a moment. 'I'm glad that you have left the army … it really wasn't suited to you, and I'm sure Germany is heading towards another war with the French.'

'From what I've read, the French don't seem to want Germany to be a unified country,' said Leopold.

'No, and von Bismarck keeps making comments that Germany needs to have a fight with France before it can be united. Spain has offered the Prince of Hohenzollern-Sigmaringen the throne and the French are not too pleased with this idea because he's Prussian.'

'Let's not worry about what Napoleon the Third and von Bismarck are doing, but I do agree with you, these are unsettled times. Another thing I'm pleased about is not being in the infantry any longer,' confirmed Leopold.

'I want you to do something for me, Leopold. Alhard would do it for me, but I want you to be the one that keeps the family together. I worry about the girls, and hope they will find suitable suitors to marry. And your younger brothers are still learning about life and what being a von der Borch is about … the responsibilities etcetera. I see Alhard as the one who will look after the estates and make sure we have food on our plates, taking care of all the monetary needs we have, but I see you as the one to keep the family together and to help the girls find suitable proposals of marriage.' Carl paused while he slowed his breathing.

'Your mother loved you all, and her sister, your mother now, loves you, too. I want you to stay in touch with her family. The von der Recke's are a good family and so, too, are your grandmother's family, the Bentheim-Tecklenburgs-Rheda. Honour your family and teach the younger ones to honour them, too … I've loved every moment of fatherhood. Remember that.'

'You sound sad, Papa. Are you sure you're alright?' Leopold studied his father's face, and noticed the dark rings under his eyes, as though his father had tended the fire and had charcoal on his hands and wiped his eyes.

'I think we should go to bed, Papa.'

Carl put his hand on Leopold's shoulder. 'Remember, I've loved every moment of being a father. Now let's do what we both intended to do and eat. There's plenty of time to sleep.'

Leopold looked at him, 'Every moment?'

'Yes. Every moment … I've loved being a father. The thing

I've detested was having to be the strict disciplinarian. It's not in my nature,' he said as they walked into the kitchen.

Leopold sliced the cold roast meat and placed it on thick slices of bread. He never was very good at slicing meat, bread, or indeed anything, evenly. He handed a sandwich to his father, who looked at the indelicate creation, and they both burst out laughing. 'Some things never change, do they? 'said Carl.

Nothing more was said between the men. They finished their sandwiches, washed and dried the dishes and walked upstairs to their bedrooms. Carl smiled at his son from his bedroom door and waved him goodnight. Leopold nodded to him. He wanted his father to know he respected him. Then he walked over to him and gave him a hug. 'You have to know I love you, Papa.'

Leopold closed the door and held onto the metal knob as though mesmerised. He was deep in thought. Then he walked to his bed, pulled back the duvet, jumped into his bed, nestled his head into the pillows, and looked out to the starry sky.

'To be a child again, innocent and trusting … just counting stars to get off to sleep,' he thought.

He closed his eyes.

A vision of walking across the road from Carl Nagel's shoe shop to Schneider's, the tailor, sprung to mind. He would have to try to forget what had happened or he felt it could drive him mad.

Leopold thought about his father, and pondered what he had said about his health.

He turned on his side and pulled the covers over his shoulders. 'Tomorrow will come only too soon, and I have lots to do before I leave for Westhusen. Go to sleep, Leopold,' he said to himself, and went off to sleep.

# Six

As the carriage entered the long driveway to his sister's house, Leopold could see Minette standing in front of the two-storey house, waving.

'I think she's pleased to see me,' Leopold said to Stefan, his friend and butler, who had brought him to Westhusen Manor.

'She was somewhat like another mother at times; after all, she was almost twenty when I was born … from Father's first marriage.'

'I suppose she would seem like that,' replied Stefan. 'I'll leave you here and come back to get you when it's time.'

'Let's hope that time comes soon,' replied Leopold.

The carriage stopped outside the main entrance, and Minette greeted Leopold with a big hug.

'Minette, this is Stefan. He's come to drop me off and leave me in your care. Let's hope he's done the right thing,' said Leopold.

Stefan nodded.

'Would you be so kind as to …,' started Leopold.

'To help you with your bags! Certainly,' said Stefan and made his way to the front door with the bags.

'Westhusen, with its gable rooves, was built from the local quarry stone. Look up there, Stefan, on the eastern side to the polygon tower. I spent many hours slaying dragons and enemies as they approached, with my wooden sword. I was quite convinced of the reality of it all, too,' Leopold told Stefan, not thinking that his family history was of no interest to Stefan.

Stefan smiled. 'Yes, I'd heard you had quite an imagination.'

'Some say I still do,' laughed Leopold.

'Did you know that the stairs in the towers were designed in a clockwise spiral? Knights wore their swords on the left-hand side and drew them at the last moment,' Leopold continued, not looking to see if Stefan was at all interested in his tale.

'Knights that came into other people's castles and ran up the stairs to attack them found it difficult to draw their swords, for the swords would hit the steps and often drop onto the ground by their feet. The nobility, usually nobility, or whoever the owners were, could easily draw their swords to defend themselves whilst coming down the stairs. It was all to do with the way the sword was drawn from their belts.'

Leopold seemed to be the only one excited by his rambling about the staircase.

'Glad I asked then,' said Stefan with a wink.

Minette looked at Stefan, surprised at his familiarity.

Leopold could see she was not happy with Stefan, so he explained: 'It's quite alright. You see, Stefan and I were in the army together, and he looked out for me, and I looked out for him. We still do, don't we, Stefan?'

The men both laughed. 'Well, he can but try,' said Leopold.

Stefan placed Leopold's bags on the slate step by the main door of the house and shook Leopold's hand, in readiness to leave. 'I expect you will do great things here, Leopold,' he said, and got back into the carriage.

'Thanks, Stefan. Well, you might as well go now, as from herein I'm on my own,' stated Leopold, determined to do well.

◈

Leopold was to sleep on the third floor of the manor house, and with every step he took after the second floor, he groaned. He was a fit and healthy young man; however, the stairs were narrow, and he found it difficult to manoeuvre his bags.

'So much for the spiral stairwell,' he said to his sister.

Minette and her husband, known as the Plettenbergs by everyone, had already planned a routine for Leopold, keeping him as busy as they could. He would awake at the same time every day, shower, and then come down for breakfast by nine-fifteen. Breakfast would consist of boiled eggs with brown toast, or honey and butter on rye, or a variety of cold meats on toast. Freshly squeezed orange juice was always popular with the family, finished off with a hot coffee with a touch of chocolate.

So the next morning Leopold sat to the table with his sister, brother-in-law and their son Karl, as staff placed their breakfast on the table. Leopold lifted up the corners of the cotton egg warmer and surveyed the boiled eggs hidden inside, and then glanced across the table to the honey and rye bread. He made eye contact with Ida, who was waiting on the table.

She met his glance and shifted the bread and honey, so it would be in easy reach for Leopold.

'Thank you, Ida,' said Leopold.

As he took his first mouthful of rye bread with honey, he looked across the table at his cousin Karl, who was smiling and chatting with his mother. Leopold watched the way Minette responded to him, and smiled.

'What is it, Leopold?' asked Minette.

'Watching you with Karl reminded me of Mama and me when I was about the same age as Karl … it brought back some lovely memories,' replied Leopold, 'and that twelve isn't very old. A lot has happened in the last eight years. I am a man now, and ready to meet the challenges life has for me.'

Minette smiled and reached out her hand across the table, to let Leopold know that she understood how much he still missed his mother. 'Sometimes, Leopold, men have the hearts of boys,' she said, as she continued with her breakfast.

After breakfast, they would go out on horseback, riding across the property, with its forested terrain and farming land. On occasion, Leopold would go out on his horse with the dog to look for truffles.

Mornings for the women were spent telling staff what was required of them for the day and who would be coming to dinner that night. Menus had to be organised and food bought. Once this was done, Minette would get one of the girls to go with her to shop for any food and supplies that were not grown on the property. The afternoons for the women would be spent reading or doing either tapestry or some form of needlework together.

The vegetable garden was large and set out as a parterre garden that the French seemed to have invented. It was a large circle divided by triangular beds and edged with box hedges. Here the Plettenbergs grew herbs such as oregano, basil, rosemary, coriander, thyme and chives, and smaller vegetables such as lettuces, cucumbers, onions, cabbages and broccoli. Other larger vegetables such as tomatoes grew alongside companion plants such as marigolds to help keep the pests away. In another section of the garden grew sweet corn, beans and peas along with various fruit trees. Empty, unwashed wine bottles were buried with the necks of the bottles just above the surface of the ground to attract insects that would otherwise eat the vegetables.

In spite of the fun he was having at Westhusen, Leopold missed his siblings and their adventures around Holzhausen. He particularly missed Therese, who he had always felt very close to over the years, and he missed the freedom.

Leopold had been at Minette's for less than two weeks and was familiar with their regular staff, so when on one particular day he spotted a stranger, a man, off in the far distance, he became suspicious. He had not noticed the man at first, and he had no idea how long he had been there, but the sun had shone on something the man was wearing and had caught Leopold's eye.

He was a slightly-built fellow, and with the little sun that shone, he was mostly hidden, but his willowy body cast a long skinny shadow across the ground.

Leopold shouted out to the fellow to invite him over, but the stranger dashed off, which Leopold thought rather peculiar.

Leopold got on with the task of polishing his saddle, cleaning his horse's hooves and generally mucking out the stable. He did not mind polishing the saddle and indeed took pride in its appearance; however, he did object to doing everything else. 'Rather a harsh punishment,' he thought, but one he knew he must do; after all, this exercise was meant to bring him back to earth and teach him humility, something his father thought had been missing.

When Leopold returned to the house, what looked like the same slightly-built fellow was drinking tea with his sister in the drawing room. As Leopold walked into the room, the fellow stood up to show his respect, shook Leopold's hand and bowed his head.

Mathilde, one of the kitchen staff, had placed handmade Fürstenberg porcelain cups and saucers, white with gold edging, on the coffee table, along with a matching teapot on a warming stand, a coffee pot and silver spoons. A plate of delicate shortbreads was also presented. She smiled courteously, and then left the room.

Minette remained seated.

'I'm afraid I have some rather disturbing news for you, Sir,' said the fellow.

'Have we met before?' Leopold asked as he looked the fellow over.

'No. However, I do know your father, and it is he I have come to discuss,' said the man.

'Well, what is it? Do tell,' said a worried Leopold.

'Your father ... I'm ... he's suffered a stroke. A rather bad one, I'm sorry to say, and they're not sure that he'll be able to speak again. The fact is, Sir, that he may not make it through the night.'

Minette sat quietly, trying to take in the information.

'Has the doctor been called?' asked Leopold.

'Of course, Sir ... he is responsible for my coming to you. I think you should come with me at once. I have a carriage outside the gates.'

'Come on, Minette. That means you, too. Perhaps leave Karl with his nanny. I don't think Papa will be feeling like noisy children around him,' Leopold commanded. 'We can't spend too much time fussing, as the journey will take us hours.'

'Tell me, was that you I saw standing by the gate about half an hour ago?' asked Leopold.

'No, Sir. I only just arrived,' he replied dutifully.

Minette's bags were packed by her personal servants, and Leopold grabbed a few pieces of clothing and threw them into his bag.

The driver closed the door of the carriage, and as they went through the gates, the horse kicked up the ground behind them. When they looked out through the window toward Westhusen, they could see Karl holding on to his nanny's hand and waving goodbye.

Leopold wondered about the man he had seen at the gate.

# Seven

When Leopold entered his father's bedroom, Carl was lying in bed asleep, a deep sleep that made Leopold wonder if he had arrived too late. He walked over to the bed and kissed his father's forehead. It was warm. His father's eyes flickered and then opened. There was no eye contact, but a reflex, some recognition of touch. Carl's eyes closed and a part of Leopold died.

Leopold looked around the room as tears rolled down his face. His eyes met with those of the doctor's. The doctor had been standing by the fireplace when Leopold entered the room, but Leopold was unaware of him, or indeed anyone else, until he heard the doctor speak.

'Your father has little strength on his left side, and his speech has been affected. He should be able to understand you; however, he won't be able to say anything to you. We're not sure if his condition will improve, but we need to do what we can, and hope for the best. He's able to have small sips of drinks, so that's a start … we must be patient.'

Leopold nodded his head, and then looked up to see his mother walk over to his sisters and hug them.

Silence filled the room as Leopold sat down on the bed next to his father, holding his hand. He looked down at his father's well-manicured fingernails, the shape of his fingers and the valley of wrinkles on the back of his hands. His father's hand was warm, but lifeless, and it was difficult to imagine that his father would never play the piano again.

Leopold thought back to the last night they had spent together, and the laughter and conversation they had when they sneaked down to the kitchen to get something to eat. He looked into his father's face, a handsome and strong face, which was now distorted from a stroke.

'Surely with the right care he will improve …,' asked a hopeful Leopold.

'It is far too soon to make such predictions; however, I fear for the worst. This is not the first stroke he has suffered.' Leopold had only recently been told of his father's minor afflictions.

As a child, Leopold and the other children would awaken, shower and dress, and then come down to have breakfast with the family at a quarter to nine every morning. As they walked downstairs, they would hear their father playing Bach or Chopin. It was such a beautiful and gentle way to start the day.

Leopold stood up from the bed and went over to his mother, put his arms around her, and held her until she was ready for him to let go.

Everyone looked at Alhard, who was standing alone next to the fireplace. He would have to take on the responsibility of the family and the estate now. His face was downcast, one hand in his pocket, and the other arm resting on the mantelpiece. He continued to stare at the floor as though looking for guidance. He was twenty-one years of age.

'Do you have any questions, Sir?' asked the doctor of Alhard. He paused for a moment, then rephrased his question, 'Is there anything more I can do here tonight for you, Sir?'

'Alhard! The doctor's talking to you,' said Leopold.

Alhard looked up with a start.

'What do you think, Alhard?' asked the doctor.

'I can't think of anything for the moment,' he replied.

'Perhaps the doctor could return first thing tomorrow morning,' suggested his mother.

'Yes, of course. Thank you for coming here to see Father so promptly. If you could return tomorrow morning to check on him, I would be most grateful,' replied Alhard.

'Before you go,' said Leopold, 'would you mind staying with us just a little longer. I know Father thought highly of you, and I know he'd like you to share this with us.'

'Of course. What would he want me to share with you?' asked the doctor.

'I think Father needs to hear some music,' Leopold said, as he looked around the now crowded bedroom at his sisters. 'Which of you can play Bach or Chopin?'

Amalia replied hesitantly, 'I can, but not very well.' She looked at her sisters—Therese, Elisabeth, and Agnes—but they all looked away. The younger children were growing restless.

'Then it must be you, Amalia. Do you think you can do this for Papa?' asked Leopold.

'But I want to stay in here, with him.'

Leopold understood how strong her feelings for their father were, but at this moment she needed to think of what their father would want.

'Give him a hug and a kiss. To hear his beautiful Amalia play for him … maybe for the last time? The others, I'm sure, will go with you,' said Leopold, beckoning to the other sisters with his eyes.

'I'll come with you, Amalia. I don't know that I'm strong enough to stay here any longer,' said Therese.

Amalia and Therese held hands as they went over to the bed and leant over to kiss their father. Therese stroked his face with her hand. 'I'll be back, Father. Wait for me … I won't be long.'

Amalia rested her face on his chest, then stretched her arm around him and gave him a hug. She stayed for a while, feeling the warmth of his body, hoping it would come to life. She tried to talk without him hearing her sadness. 'I'm going downstairs, Father, to play Chopin for you. Your favourite piece.' And their mother added, 'Nocturne, Opus. 9, No. 2.'

As Amalia and Therese went downstairs, the other children went over to their father's bed and gently kissed their father on the forehead, and then hugged their mother.

Emma had always felt that Carl was theirs first, their father, and that it was important for them to spend time with him. Emma and Carl's two children, Kurt and Jenny, were also there.

Emma looked at the pain in the children's faces. Minette, who looked like her mother, but never knew her. Minette was happily married with a son of her own, and Emma knew that Minette would be able to cope after Carl's death as Minette's husband was a strong, diligent man.

Carl had always admired the way Emma treated the children equally. She loved them and always looked for the best in them. It was one of the things Carl treasured about her.

Chopin's Nocturne was slow to start and faltered at first, then its presence and mood and fluidity filled the room, as Amalia's fingers glided across the piano keys. It was the first piece of music Carl had taught Amalia to play.

'It makes me feel better,' said Emma. 'I thought it might make me feel sad, but it's as though Carl is playing.' She stood up and went over to her husband's bed.

'Perhaps the music has helped?' said Leopold with a smile.

'Perhaps it has,' said the doctor. 'To be able to capture the music somehow, in some sort of device, and bring it up into this room would be marvellous. A Frenchman named Eduoard-Leon Scott de Martinville has developed such a thing; it's called a Phonautograph.'

Leopold frowned. What did that useless piece of information have to do with his father's present condition?

'To think that instead of the girls being downstairs on their own, away from their father, they could be here with him, watching how much it has relaxed him,' said the doctor.

'Let's listen to Amalia a moment, before she finishes,' said Emma.

Amalia finished the stanza, and she and Therese came back upstairs to be with their father.

'Your father needs his rest,' said Emma. Then she went over to Amalia with her outstretched arms and gave her a big hug. 'Your father heard you play, and it brought him some peace. The doctor said that he seems more relaxed now. Thank you, Amalia. You were very strong and selfless. I love you. I love you all. Now say goodnight to your father and off you all go.'

Emma knew there was little chance that Carl would make it through the night.

'I think I should go now,' said the doctor, 'let you say goodnight in private.'

# Eight

The bells rang out, as the funeral carriage made its way to the family cemetery.

Behind the glass wooden-framed carriage, the procession was led by Alhard and Leopold, with their mother walking between them, her arms threaded through theirs. Family and friends followed closely behind, walking in rhythm to the slow-paced sound of the horse's hooves on the wet, muddy ground. The clanking sound of the leather and chains that linked the horse to the carriage could be heard above the muffled voices, as stories and memories of Carl were shared.

'Death is so final,' thought Leopold, as he looked into the glass carriage, seeing his father's coffin draped in black, silken material, with flowers and greenery perched on top. Leopold's throat felt tight as he tried to keep from shedding tears. He looked at his mother and said, 'I'm pleased we were there when he died, that he didn't die alone, and that we were all together.'

Emma looked into Leopold's eyes. She rubbed his hand and smiled.

Leopold tried to quiet his thinking. 'Where will the essence of you go, Papa? Surely it is not lost? It can't be,' he thought, as he watched Bruno, the German short-hair pointer, trotting along next to the coffin. 'There must be something of you still here? Something that maybe only Bruno can sense.' Leopold looked over to Alhard for confirmation, as though Alhard had been privy to Leopold's thoughts.

They continued along Eichen Allee for a few more minutes, before leaving the huge oak trees behind as the road began to forge its way toward the beech forest. The incline was not very steep; however, the rain from the morning had left the road wet. The horse's hooves dug into the slippery road as the procession headed toward the cemetery, which was marked out by a large, square, dry-built wall, a task the workers had achieved over a hundred years ago. Native ferns and ivy grew freely, and made up most of the undergrowth, which in turn would die and rot into the soil, providing rich food for the beech trees.

The carriage stopped in front of ornate iron gates, and one of the men attending the funeral pulled at the small iron rod to open them. He pushed the gates forward, and they fell back against the two stone pillars with a clunk. In front of him, about forty steps away, stood a high wall, with a statue of Jesus on the cross, and below was the von der Borch coat of arms, with some words he could not read. On either side of him, the gravestones of generations of von der Borchs, most of them made from heavy stone, lay flat on the ground, ivy growing between them.

On the right-hand side of the statue, against the wall, were three upright stone crosses, which were the gravestones of family members, so old that any information about them had eroded.

As the coffin was taken from the carriage on the shoulders of the workers and brought inside the stone walls, Leopold ushered the rest of the family to take their places around the hole where

Carl's body would lay to rest, only a few feet from Leopold's beloved mother, Ludmilla.

The workers were strong men with broad shoulders and easy temperaments. Carl had looked after them well, and had enjoyed their company and the stories they shared, stories from generations of von der Borchs and farmers and shopkeepers.

Leopold looked at the faces of those who had come to pay their respects to his father. Their heads were cast downward, their hands clasped together behind their backs. Rain began to fall, and black umbrellas popped open with a whoosh.

'The baron was a strong man who cared so very deeply for his family,' began the priest. 'On one occasion after a church service, I remember him asking me to stay behind. He had something important to tell me.'

Leopold shuffled his feet. 'I hope it has nothing to do with me and my stupidity in Berlin,' he thought. 'Father probably did speak to the priest about me, but surely he won't mention it now … not here.'

'He spoke to me about losing his wife Ludmilla,' continued the priest, 'and he was very grateful to Emma for looking after his children so well for him … He said that he was developing deep feelings for her and wanted my permission to marry her.'

Emma looked a little embarrassed and took Elisabeth's hand, and Leopold sighed with relief.

'I said to him—and my very words were—you have my permission, son. She is a good woman, and she has given up her life of freedom to care for the young ones. She deserves to have your love, too.'

The priest looked at Emma. 'Those were my very words.'

Alhard tugged at his stiff white collar, and moved his toes around to free them up a little, for they felt cramped in his new black shoes.

'Your husband loved you, Emma, very much, and was always grateful for your care,' continued the priest. 'Before he had his stroke, Carl gave me a letter to read to you. I think he was aware that his time was close. I won't read it all to you now, but there are a few things that I feel are relevant for this moment.

'He wrote that he loved all of you. He loved his children, his brothers and sisters, and this home that has been a part of this family for over four hundred years. Alhard, he wanted you to carry on as he did, but for you to know that you must have your life, too. Leopold, he wanted you to know that he had to make some hard decisions, hoping you will grow strong from them. To the rest of you, he wants you all to stay loyal to one another, to be strong when change comes.' The priest paused, then folded the letter: he could see that everyone was feeling a little uncomfortable about its contents. 'Well, that's enough for now. Just know that he loved you all.'

'We should go back, I think, before heavier rain falls,' said Alhard, in his new role as head of the family. 'The last thing we want is for anyone to get sick.'

Emma, Alhard, and Leopold led the way out of the gate and along Eichen Allee back to the Big House.

'I wonder what he meant when he said, "when change comes?"' muttered Leopold to himself.

Bruno remained next to his master's grave. 'Come, Bruno,' said Rudolf, but the dog refused to move. 'Bruno.'

'Do you have his leash?' asked Emma.

'No. I didn't think to bring it.'

'Perhaps you could use your tie,' said Amalia.

Rudolf loosened his tie and placed it around Bruno's neck. 'Come, Bruno.'

'It's alright if he wants to stay, Rudi. He'll come to the house when he's ready,' said Emma.

'What is it you know, Bruno, that we don't?' said Leopold, patting the dog as he spoke to him.

'I don't want him to get too wet, Mama. He can't get sick and die,' said Rudi.

'Come, Bruno,' said Emma. She could see that Rudi was getting upset. 'There you are, Rudi,' she said as the dog started to follow them. 'Off you both go.'

Alhard had headed back to the house in readiness to act as host and the new heir to Gut Holzhausen. It was a big day for him. He had buried his much-loved father, and now, at a young age, he would be taking on immense responsibilities.

Leopold was the last to leave. He tried to balance holding the umbrella while threading the pointy iron bolt through the hole of the gate to lock it, unaware that the rain had begun falling more heavily. He pulled on the gate to make sure it was locked.

Leopold looked through the iron gate to the statue of Jesus, and then across to the gravestones of his mother and father. For that moment, he had no thoughts. He just stared at the ground where they were laid to rest, next to each other in death, as they were in life.

'"When change comes?" What were you expecting, Papa? What's the change that's coming?' Leopold said out loud.

# Nine

October was always that odd time of the year when no one knew what to wear. Today though, the day of the funeral, Frau Busch, the head housekeeper, knew that everyone would feel cold, not just from the weather, but the grief and loss of a loved one, so she had arranged for the fires in the Big House to be lit first thing in the morning. The wood crackled in the fireplaces and the warmth had slowly seeped into the thick stone walls.

The sound of the younger children echoed around the hall as the staff kept busy preparing for the gathering that would arrive after Carl's funeral. Long tables had been laid with crisp, white damask table clothes. In the centre of the tables were two large vases of flowers, mostly white lilies with greenery. White, matching cups, saucers, and plates, with blue edging and the family crest, had been placed on the table with white damask serviettes next to them. Shiny, silver spoons also with the family crest sat on a small tray to the left of the cups and saucers.

The chandeliers had been cleaned days before and were sparkling clean. Cream candles had been placed in stands on the mantel piece and on the sideboard. Decanters of red and white wine and glasses with gold rims stood out on the sideboard. Door knobs and light switches had been polished and any hints of cobwebs were nowhere to be seen.

Frau Busch looked around the room to make sure everything was in place and that staff were dressed appropriately. She smiled and walked toward the kitchen to prepare the plates of finger food to be served.

The walk from the family cemetery was an icy-cold twenty-minute stroll through the forest.

Leopold had caught up with the others as they walked down Eichen Allee. He pointed to a tree with a hollowed-out trunk.

'Remember how we used to hide in there from Papa when we were children, and we were sure he would never find us,' he recalled. 'And we would be so squished up together in the tree that I'm sure he would have heard our muffled giggles.'

'He did,' said Emma. 'At night when we were in bed, he used to chat about his day and about all of you … he used to laugh at the way you were so convinced that he had never seen you there … that was your father. He loved the magic that only you children could bring.'

Alhard and Leopold put their arms out to offer comfort to their mother. She looked up at the young men and smiled.

'We'll look after you, Mama,' said Alhard.

Emma placed her hand on his arm and looked into his brown eyes. 'I know you will.' She looked at Leopold and said, 'I know both of you will.'

They continued their walk, with Alhard, Emma, and Leopold at the front of the group and the rest of the family walking slowly behind them.

The Big House was well lit up. Large vases of flowers led from the hallway, down the passage, and into the *salle*. Alhard entered the room first, followed by Leopold and their mother, Emma.

They were all dressed in black and equally solemn. For Alhard, it was a difficult time. He was now head of the family, and knowing what was expected of him did not make the task ahead any easier. He and his father used to laugh about him being the apprentice and had given him the nickname of Baron Junior. Alhard could only hope to meet his responsibilities as well as his father had.

Therese, Kurt, Elisabeth, Jenny, and Rudolf entered next, followed by various friends and other family members. Some of the younger members of the family were supervised by their nannies, and within the hour they disappeared upstairs.

Carl had many friends, including singers and musicians and a dear friend of the family named Anna, who sat in the corner of the *salle* near the fireplace, playing violin.

Bruno lay down by the fire, as he always did. Rudolf went over and patted the dog, and gently stroked his neck. 'I miss Papa, too, Bruno,' he said, and sat down on the floor next to the dog. Bruno looked up at him and licked the salty tears from Rudolf's cheek.

'It's been difficult for Rudolf. He's still young,' Emma whispered to Leopold.

Leopold looked at Emma and said, 'The same age I was when Mother died ... it's not very old.' He kissed Emma on her cheek. 'We were, and are, so lucky to have you.'

For Rudolf, who was only twelve years old, the dog was the closest thing to his father that he had. Bruno had gone with Carl everywhere, and was rarely seen anywhere without him. The sight of the dog on his own made Rudolf miss his father even more.

'He is a sensitive boy, like you, Leopold,' said Emma. She went over to Rudolph and placed her arm around his shoulder.

'I think your father would want you to have Bruno,' she said.

Rudolf looked up at his mother and tried to hide the tears that were welling up in his eyes. He couldn't speak.

'He's yours now. Why don't you put your jacket on and take him for a short walk? I think he needs to know that you're his new master, just as much as you need to know he's your dog. Papa would be pleased to know you were looking after him,' said Emma.

'Don't forget your scarf and gloves. It's cold outside,' she added, as she leaned forward and enveloped him with one of her big hugs. 'Bruno's leash is hanging up behind the door in the cloak room. Off you go then.'

Rudolf smiled and wiped away his tears with the back of his hand and then gave his mother another hug. 'Come Bruno,' he said, and the dog bounded out of the room, nearly knocking over one of the guests.

Emma felt saddened that the children had lost another parent: first their mother only eight years earlier, then their grandmother, and now their father. She always felt she filled the space of their mother and that as a sister she was similar enough and loved them as much as their own mother could love them.

'Can I go with him? Please, Mama,' asked Kurt.

'Not this time, Kurt. I think Rudolf wants to be on his own,' replied Emma.

'But what am I going to do? I'm getting bored.'

'I think being bored is rather a boring way to express yourself, Kurt. Perhaps you mean that you are not sure what you can do? Where's Ella? Is she looking after you and your sister Jenny?' asked Emma.

She looked around the room for the children's nanny. 'There she is, Kurt. Ask Ella to take you and Jenny upstairs. You can both change your clothes and go off and play.'

Kurt thought that was a much better idea than sitting around listening to the grown-ups talking about his father dying and how sad it was.

'Jenny, Ella, let's go,' he yelled out.

Alhard, who was standing near Ella, walked over to Kurt and gently told him off for yelling across the room. 'Kurt, you must consider other people. Yelling is not the "done" thing for a young boy like you. It's like throwing a big ball around the room, and people don't know if they'll get hit by it. It makes them feel uncomfortable.'

'But I didn't throw a ball,' said Kurt.

Alhard looked down at Kurt's dear little face, angelic, some had said. Instead of pursuing the conversation about doing the right thing, Alhard picked him up and gave him a hug. After all, Kurt was only five years old and had no idea about what it meant to lose his father, about the permanency of death.

'Off you go,' said Alhard.

Jenny and Kurt ran off, with Ella close behind them looking embarrassed that 'her' children had drawn attention to themselves.

Emma went back to thinking about the heartache she felt for herself and the children and their loss. The stark realisation that she would now have full responsibility for the children weighed heavily on her.

Herr Schroeder, the butler, walked around the room and offered glasses of champagne to the family and guests in readiness for Alhard's speech, whilst Leopold walked over to his brother to offer him some support.

'Could we have your attention for the moment, please. Alhard would like to say a few words,' spluttered Leopold. 'Are you ready, Alhard?'

'Yes. As ready as I'll ever be.'

Alhard spoke in a gentle voice about his father and the love and respect they had for him, of the laughter he had brought to the family on cold dark wintry nights when they would sit around his chair by the crackling fire and listen to ghost stories, and of his marksmanship as a shooter. He also spoke of his father's gratitude to his workers.

'Let's raise our glasses to a much-loved father, husband, and friend. And to a man whose shoes I couldn't begin to fill. To our father, Carl.'

# Ten

It was decided by the family that Leopold would stay on at the Big House and help Alhard for the first few months. The enormity and the responsibility were starting to show. Alhard, who was normally an even-tempered young man, was beginning to get somewhat bad-tempered with his younger siblings, who, it would seem, had the luxury of being children. He was still such a young man doing his best to manage three different properties, forests, staff, and family. He was also expected to keep up with and arrange suitable social events, including those which would introduce his younger sisters into society.

Alhard and Leopold were quite different in the way they approached life, and as much as each one tried, they found it difficult to understand the other's point of view. Alhard always knew that one day he would be master and went about his new role with confidence. He was quite happy playing the baron and believed that the class system worked rather well. Alhard was direct, organised, and liked to make plans for the future. He thought that this way of life made it simple for everyone, as the staff knew their roles, got paid for their work by way of him supplying them with a small house in the village, a small plot of land on which to grow their vegetables and fruit trees, and a small wage. They were close by when he needed them and ready to carry out duties such as washing, cooking, cleaning, and farming. 'Quite a good arrangement,' he was known to tell everyone.

Leopold, on the other hand, was creative, a little messy, but nonetheless the problem solver. When Alhard's orders did not go as planned, it was Leopold who sorted things out for him, and if staff were hesitant to do certain chores, it was Leopold who coerced them into doing so. Leopold found it amusing that Alhard was seen as the organiser because, if the truth were known, it was Leopold who completed the tasks that Alhard set out to do. Nonetheless, Leopold was only too happy to help his brother.

Alhard had decided that it was time for Leopold to leave Holzhausen and travel to Vegasack near Bremen to live and manage Schönebeck. He had been contemplating it for a while and knew that it was his father who had suggested it long before he died. Alhard was standing with his manager near the old gate house when he noticed, in the distance, Leopold stepping outside. Alhard decided, now was the time to discuss his move and began waving his arm to get Leopold's attention.

'Leopold,' he called out, 'we need to talk.'

Leopold walked over to the old gate house where Alhard and his manager were finishing their discussion about the repairs needed to one of the barn roofs that had been damaged in a recent storm. The house was built in Fifteen seventy-two, and, although not very big compared to the main house, it was three stories high.

'Thank you,' said Alhard to his manager. 'I won't need to see you again today. There are some rather urgent things I need to discuss with my brother.'

'What exactly do we need to discuss?' Leopold asked, wondering if he had done something the family didn't approve of. 'It sounds serious. Is Mother alright?'

'Well, it's about you going to Schönebeck. I think you should leave next week,' replied Alhard in a rather clipped manner.

'Why so suddenly, Alhard?'

'Well … I don't think the men will ever take notice of me if they're looking to you to solve problems all the time,' said Alhard.

'I really don't understand, Alhard.'

'Last week, when I asked the men to make sure, by Thursday, that the barns were inspected and secured for the winter, they came and told me on Wednesday that they had finished,' said Alhard, looking crossly at Leopold.

Leopold looked puzzled. 'If the work was done, then why are you cross with me?'

'It's not that I'm cross with you. Not at all. Simply that I don't know if they're listening to me or whether it's you they listen to … they've never got things done before time, which makes me think they are listening to you rather than me,' explained Alhard. 'We have our roles to fulfil and we shouldn't blur them … it confuses everybody.'

'Isn't that a good thing, Alhard? I was asked to stay on and help, which I was indeed happy to do. You've been tired and very busy. All I did was go in and ask them to ensure the work was done on time, if not sooner, so that you could relax a little. Why would that make you cross?'

'I know I'm only one year older than you, not quite a year older, but in a way, our relationship has changed now. I have to make decisions and you need to go along with them, even if they don't make sense to you at times.' Alhard paused for a while, trying to choose the right words. 'Father, and indeed Mother, both told us at various times that we should never have to justify ourselves, and that we should never make other people uncomfortable by making them explain themselves ... I feel I shouldn't have to explain myself to you, Leopold. You know my situation, and you need to step back a bit.'

'That's the sort of thing that infuriates me. It's the same sort of thing those conmen in Berlin said to me. It's true: I'm merely a second son, and I have to take what comes,' said Leopold.

'I think it would probably be best for both of us if we start to get on with our own lives. You can go up to Schönebeck and get things organised, and I can get things done here. I'm sure the manager will be pleased to have one of the family there to give him directions,' said Alhard, trying to make Leopold feel better about the situation. 'You'll have to go sooner or later ...'

Leopold was completely taken aback.

'I was speaking with some of the older members of the family, and they think that as long as the men are looking to you for guidance etcetera, they will not take notice of me, nor treat me as their boss.' Alhard stood his ground. He was now head of the family, and Leopold would have to learn his position as the second son.

'Very well,' was all that Leopold said, before turning and walking toward the stables where he saddled Dina and rode off in the direction of the forest.

The manager came over to Alhard and looked at him, wondering what had been said to make Leopold take off so abruptly.

# Eleven

Leopold arrived at Schönebeck with Stefan, his friend and butler, on a sunny Tuesday afternoon. The manager of Schönebeck came out to greet them, bathed in mud.

'Hello Friedrich! What on earth have you been up to?' asked Leopold.

Friedrich looked down at his clothes and boots. 'Well … you see, Sir, I was … there was a large …'

'And it got away?' laughed Leopold.

The men laughed, and Leopold never did find out exactly why Friedrich was muddy. Perhaps it was better not to know, he thought.

'Friedrich, I'd like you to meet Stefan, my new butler.'

Friedrich put his right hand out to shake Stefan's hand. 'Welcome, Stefan. Good luck,' said Friedrich, with a laugh in his voice.

'Thank you. I have heard I might need it!' replied Stefan.

Leopold looked at Stefan. He was silent for a moment and then burst out laughing.

'Yes. Luck … I think you will need much of it. From what I've heard I take quite a bit of … quite a bit of looking after!'

The men walked along the path towards the front steps of Schönebeck castle. Leopold looked at the views that he loved so much. To his left, a lake that was fed by the river that ran through the property, ahead the castle and a few timber-framed outbuildings, and beyond that the beech forest. To his right, paddocks stretched out to the hills in the distance.

'I always feel so much at home here. I think it's more relaxing here. We're a bit more out of sight from the villagers, and I can be who I want to be. I don't even need to shave if I don't want to,' said Leopold.

Stefan looked at him.

'It's true, isn't it, Friedrich? If I didn't shave for a day or two at Holzhausen, people would think I was in trouble or depressed, or had run out of money. Or that I was dying!' Leopold exclaimed. 'It may seem that we have a wonderful life, but it comes at a price, Stefan. We are always on show, always have to behave impeccably and be seen to be doing the right thing—all very stifling at times.'

'I must admit I'd think, too, that there was something wrong with you if we were at Gut Holzhausen and you hadn't shaved,' said Stefan.

'Come, Friedrich, a little faster. I can't wait to be settled and then come with you to see how the farm is going,' said Leopold, excitedly. 'It's been months.'

'Did you know, Stefan, that Schönebeck has been in the family for hundreds of years? The castle was built in Sixteen fifty-five by a clever fellow named Franz von Schönebeck, who it is named after, of course, but it wasn't until about Sixteen eighty-two that the von der Borchs bought the castle. Schönebeck died without any heirs, and the city of Bremen and the Swedish council wanted to buy it. Eventually, the von der Borchs bought it, along with two hundred farms.

'Among other things, at one time it had a prison. The von der Borchs often spent their holidays and honeymoons here. Not in the prison of course, although some might say that to be married is to be condemned.' Leopold laughed.

'Go and clean up, Friedrich, and then come and have dinner with us. I believe Anna, our cook,' Leopold began, before turning to Stefan, 'will be making us a delicious meal. We usually start off with pumpkin soup, which has an orange and a little honey in it, and bread, followed by some form of meat with home grown vegetables, and sweets, which are always a delight.'

'Did you still want to look around the farm first, Sir?' asked Friedrich.

'I think we must eat. Don't you think so, Stefan?' Leopold looked at Stefan. 'Look, Friedrich, Stefan is very hungry. I can see it in his eyes. Come, we must feed him.'

Friedrich left Stefan to struggle with Leopold's bags alone, as there was little time to wash and dress for dinner. Friedrich walked off in the direction of the manager's house where he had lived for almost three years. It was a typical two-storey framework house, adorned with red geraniums on the window sills in long, rectangular pots.

'Really, Stefan. There are too many bags for you. Let me help you,' Leopold said.

'Sir, I can manage.' Stefan's idea of being a butler differed, he thought, to Leopold's views of his role.

'Please, let me help you. The rules are a bit more relaxed here, away from the eyes of those who think we should be austere and noble all the time. I think there is nothing wrong with my helping you. Surely you wouldn't disrespect me for that?'

Leopold suddenly felt a little uncertain about crossing the boundaries, once he had said it out loud.

'Perhaps you're right, Stefan. It is your role to look after me, and I mustn't interfere.' He had embarrassed both Stefan and himself, and he hadn't meant to do so.

Leopold recalled his father's words: 'If we can just hold onto good manners, Leopold, the world would be in a better position to look after its people. Everyone knows what's expected of them, and there is no embarrassment for anyone. We must never do anything that causes someone else to be embarrassed. Remember that, Leopold.' Carl had told the same thing to all his children.

'You see, Stefan. I sometimes find it difficult to maintain my role as a baron. I don't know what it is with me. Anyway, let's get on with it. Anna will have dinner ready, and we can't be late. We really can't be late!'

Leopold began to whisper, 'You see, she scares me a little—still scares me. When we used to come here for holidays as children, Anna would give us dinner while Mama and Papa were dining with friends. This was only sometimes, I must say. Anyway, on one particular evening, she decided to tell us a creepy story. A true story. It was a story about "The Angel of Bremen".

'According to Anna, the angel was a woman named Gesche Margarethe Gottfried. She had been born into a poor family and had a twin brother. Unfortunately, her twin brother died, and so did her mother and her father, as well as her daughters, her son, and her husbands. Gesche had looked after all of them, and had stayed up nights looking after their needs. But it was later discovered that she had murdered them all, and she was eventually caught. As a punishment, she was decapitated.'

Leopold spoke even quieter now. 'And there is a rumour that the wind that blows through the forests of Bremen on the night on the anniversary of her death brings with it her ghost.'

'How horrid. Why would she tell you a story like that, Sir? I mean, not quite the story to tell children, is it?' said Stefan, horrified.

'No. Not at all. My mother was furious when she found out, and my father sacked her. Instant dismissal,' said Leopold.

'Do they know why she did it, or how she did it?' asked Stefan. '"The Angel of Bremen", I mean.'

The men walked up the steps and through the double half-glass doors. On the glass was etched the family coat of arms.

'Put the bags down here, Stefan, and we'll organise them later.' They were standing in the doorway looking out at the meadows.

'She used arsenic, and they don't really know why she did it,' explained Leopold. 'Thought she might have had Munchausen by proxy.'

'Munchau … what was that, Sir?'

'It's … like a disease, I suppose one could say. She made people sick by sneaking arsenic into their food. The thing is, she wanted the attention of others. She would nurse them back to health and get a lot of attention for seemingly being a caring person. She had their lives in her hands. She did it over and over again: make them sick, and then nurse them back to health. In other words, poison them, and then look after them. This got her the title of "The Angel of Bremen". Only, she was slowly murdering them.'

'Could I ask, Sir? Why is she back cooking for you? Anna, I mean.' Stefan was feeling a bit out of place, but he was too curious not to ask, even if it wasn't his place to do so.

'My father felt bad about her not being able to provide for her family, so a couple of days later he hired her again. Besides, she's rather a good cook. She was instructed only to cook, and had to promise not to tell us stories again.'

'Dinner!' yelled Anna, who was suddenly standing right behind them. Both men jumped with fright.

# Twelve

The days turned into weeks, and the weeks turned into months. The seasons changed from warm summer days with blue skies and fun, swimming in the lake and eating outside in the fresh air, to the cold winds of autumn that whistled around their legs and drove them inside. Routines changed to accommodate the crops, and leisure time seemed to increase.

One morning, Leopold and Friedrich were riding their horses under the dappled light through the beech forest. In the distance, Leopold saw what looked like the outline of a man. Leopold called back to Friedrich.

'Friedrich, come closer please. I want to ask you something.' Not wanting to alert the stranger, Leopold tried not to point. 'Do you see a man, a slightly-built man to the left of the trees near the lake? Just down from where the path veers off to the left?'

'No. Where exactly are we looking?' asked Friedrich.

'Over there, Friedrich. Do you see him?' Leopold felt vulnerable. The figure looked enough like the shadowy, thin figure that he had seen lurking around the gate at his sister's house.

'Where?' Friedrich asked.

'Over there,' Leopold said, now having to point. 'Just to the left of the path … there.' Leopold had become determined to find out who it was. 'Come on man, let's go.' The two men galloped their horses in the direction of the figure, who almost instantly seemed to vanish into thin air.

'Where did he go?' asked the insistent Leopold as they reached the river.

'Sir, you go around to your left and ride alongside the river. He can't have gone through it or we would've heard him splash. I'll go around here, to the right.'

Within minutes Friedrich heard Leopold yell out for him to come. Then a shot was heard. The next thing Friedrich saw was Leopold falling from his horse and landing with a thud.

Friedrich pulled on the reins and galloped his chestnut mare to where Leopold had managed to sit himself up against the trunk of one of the beech trees.

'Leopold … Sir, are you alright,' asked Friedrich, alarmed. Leopold was supporting his injured arm. 'Sir … Are you alright? They shot you!'

Leopold grimaced and squeezed his arm to try and numb the pain. 'Careful, he may still be out there,' he said, his eyes searching for the intruder.

'Who? Who's out there and why did they shoot you?'

'Let's not bother about who it is now, get on your horse and see if you can find him. I'll explain what I can to you later,' replied Leopold. 'Before you mount, can you reload my rifle and bring it over to me. I fear for my life, Friedrich. You must go and find him.'

'Fear for your life?'

'Yes. There's no time to explain now. It's more important that you capture him,' said Leopold.

'Are you sure you'll be alright here?' asked Friedrich.

'Yes. Go!' ordered Leopold. 'I'm sure it looks worse than it is.' He looked at the blood trickling from his wound. 'Mind you, it does rather hurt.'

Friedrich loaded his rifle and helped Leopold to hold it the best way he could, so that if the intruder returned, he would have a clear shot. That is, if he was directly in front of him or off to his left.

Friedrich mounted his horse and galloped off in the direction of the lake, where there was thick undergrowth and plenty of bushes for the intruder to hide.

Leopold sat still and listened. He could hear Friedrich's horse as it galloped, as it expelled its breath, as it picked up speed. In the distance, the sound of cows bellowing as they came in for the night to be milked. Then, no longer were there sounds of Friedrich's horse, nor other horses, nor men walking.

Leopold began to feel anxious, the sound of his own heart beating in his ears. 'Where is he?' he asked himself. He loosened the grip on his rifle and wiped his sweaty hand on his jodhpurs. 'Where are you, Friedrich?'

Suddenly, behind Leopold, there stood Friedrich.

'I nearly shot you, you fool! Surely you know better than to sneak up on someone!' shouted an infuriated, anxious Leopold.

'Apologies, Sir. I can't find him anywhere, whoever he is, and I was beginning to get concerned for you out here on your own, and—'

Leopold interrupted him. 'Very well, let's go back to the house.'

'I'll fetch the horses,' said Friedrich.

'I think I'd just as soon walk … getting upon the horse may prove difficult.' Leopold stood up and felt a bit light-headed.

Friedrich tore at his shirt and tied a piece of it around the top of Leopold's arm to help control the bleeding. After he had slowed the bleeding, he retrieved the horses, put the reins in his hand and then looped his arm under Leopold's to help him back to the house.

'Thank you, Friedrich,' said Leopold, slightly calmer now.

'Let's keep walking, Sir, and once we're home I'll go for the doctor.'

The two men walked slowly along the gravel path, then across the wooden bridge, which went over the river and up to the front door of Schönebeck, about a mile from where Leopold had fallen from his horse. Friedrich could see Stefan inside the main entrance.

'Stefan! Stefan!' he called out.

Stefan came over, ill-prepared for what was to greet him.

'Take him into the kitchen, the downstairs kitchen where the staff prepares the meals. Give him something to drink … and I'll go for the doctor,' ordered Friedrich.

Anna had come out to see what was going on. 'Anna, will you help Stefan.'

'Let me have a look, Sir,' said Stefan, who helped to remove the blood-soaked cloth from Leopold's arm.

Leopold trusted Stefan's opinion as Stefan had seen quite a bit of action during the Austro-Prussian war, and on occasion had helped the wounded soldiers.

'It looks quite clean … you were lucky, Sir,' said Stefan. 'The bullet has only grazed your arm. Who shot you?'

'It was probably one of the local lads. They come here, you know, even in the day, to shoot a few rabbits for dinner,' suggested Anna.

Leopold looked down at the wound. 'Make sure you clean it out with alcohol, will you, Stefan. I find it difficult to believe that someone actually shot me,' he remarked.

Leopold was horrified at what had happened. 'I fought in the war of sixty-six in Austria, and had men dying all around me, and not a shot or a wound ... and yet here, in my own grounds, and somebody shoots me!'

Stefan tried to comfort him. 'Anna's probably right: local boys thinking it rather brave of them to shoot rabbits in broad daylight.'

'Nonsense, man! It was me they were after,' Leopold snapped, still in shock.

Anna and Stefan looked at each other. It was unlike Leopold to be so abrupt with anyone.

Stefan was very thorough when he cleaned the wound, before neatly wrapping it with a bandage that Anna had brought from the upstairs kitchen.

'This will do until the doctor comes. At least it will slow the bleeding,' said Stefan, rather pleased with himself.

'You know what I need, Anna?' said Leopold.

'A stiff brandy, Sir?' asked Anna.

'I hadn't quite thought of a brandy, although that does seem tempting. No, I was thinking more after the lines of a sweet cup of tea. Good for shock, they say,' said Leopold.

'Yes, Sir. And you, I suppose you'll want one, too?' Anna asked Stefan.

'Thank you. Please,' he answered.

Before Anna left, she and Stefan helped Leopold into a large armchair in the library.

'I'll get you a blanket, Sir, you look a bit pale,' said Anna, leaving the men behind to talk.

Leopold and Stefan chatted about what had happened and of Friedrich not being able to catch the intruder. Talking helped, and with the shock slowly subsiding, Leopold began to feel his normal self again.

Anna returned with a blanket. 'Here you are, Sir,' she said, handing it to Leopold, who put it on his lap. She headed back to the kitchen, and a few minutes later brought in a silver tray with a pot of hot black tea, milk, sugar, and biscuits. She poured a cup for each of the men, letting them help themselves to the milk and sugar.

'Who's that?' asked Anna suddenly, as she heard fast steps approaching. Talk of someone out in the forest trying to shoot Leopold had made her nervous. She was relieved to see that it was Doctor Heilen, approaching from the stairs.

'At last, dear Doctor,' said Leopold.

'Let me see that arm of yours, Leopold,' said Doctor Heilen. As he unwrapped the make-shift bandage, he turned towards Stefan, 'Has he lost much blood?'

'I wouldn't think so. It is more of a gouge than a bullet hole,' said Stefan.

As the last of the bandages came off, the doctor picked up a bottle and handed it to Anna. 'Could you be so kind as to take the cork out of the bottle of carbolic acid and pour a little into a saucer and mix it with water for me? Thank you.'

'Is it safe for Baron Leopold to use?' asked Anna. 'I've never heard of it before.'

'Of course it's safe to use, Anna. They're using this in England, and they believe it is much better for preventing infections than anything else we've been using. Even though we don't have a bullet, we must still be careful about preventing Leopold from getting an infection,' said Doctor Heilen, as he watched Anna mix the water and carbolic acid into a paste.

'Good. That's fine, thank you, Anna,' he said.

Doctor Heilen then picked up a wooden spatula and pushed it into the paste. 'I don't want to touch anything with my hands if I can help it. Reduces the chance of infection,' he said, re-emphasising the point. 'It's infections that tend to kill people more than the wounds.'

'Who is this bright spark of yours in England that seems to know what there is to know about infection?' asked Leopold.

'A young fellow … haven't met him myself … reads French and German,' replied Doctor Heilen, rather distracted from what he was doing. 'Quite impressive, from what I've read about him.'

'But his name, Doctor? What's the fellow's name?' asked Leopold.

'Lister … Joseph Lister … As long as it works, that's what I think … as long as it works.'

After Doctor Heilen had left, and Leopold had finished his dinner, he excused himself and went upstairs to his desk. He was still feeling unsettled by the morning's events, and wondered how this saga and the dread that came with someone wanting to get rid of him would conclude.

That night, Leopold wrote to his brother Alhard, pleased that it was his left arm that was wounded.

*Dear Alhard,*

*I write to you for a favour. Please keep the contents of this letter secret. If you do not wish to, then I urge you to read no further and destroy it.*

*Today, a stranger shot and wounded me. It was just a graze, but I fear for my life. I no longer have my duelling pistols as I had to sell them to pay off my debts. They were not, of course, percussion-lock duelling pistols like yours; however, if I could borrow them when I'm next at Holzhausen, I would be most grateful.*

*As I said, I fear for my life, so it seems I am not safe here. And I don't think it would be wise for me to come back to live at Holzhausen, as it could encourage whoever is after me to put our family in danger.*

*We will have to sort out what is to happen to me.*
*Your loving brother,*
*Leopold*

He folded the letter, with some difficulty, and placed it in an envelope. He then heated some wax and dropped some of it over the join of the envelope, before placing the von der Borch seal on it. After the wax had cooled, he went downstairs, and placed the letter on the hall table where the postman would pick it up first thing in the morning.

Leopold decided that he would leave for Holzhausen within two weeks, to pay Alhard a brief visit and discuss the matter with him.

# Thirteen

Leopold took his gloved hand and wiped away the fern leaves and pine needles from his father's headstone. He traced around the coat of arms and the three jackdaws, then around his father's name. A sprinkle of rain fell gently, and an autumn wind blew up.

Leopold felt solace in his visits to the cemetery. At a time like this he found 'talking' to his parents soothing.

'Dearest Father and Mother, forgive me for any wrongs I have done. I had no intention to bring embarrassment to the family. I fear that I will have to leave here soon, and perhaps even leave Schönebeck. This may be the last time I am here for some time. Look after them, Lord, and look after my little brothers and sisters.'

He stood up and bowed his head. Tears rolled down his cheeks.

'These are for you, Mother. It's the wrong time of year for your favourites; all I could find were these.'

Leopold reached forward, and onto the grave he placed a wreath he had made from the young branches of pine trees, with small pine cones in the centre.

'This letter is for you, Papa. I can't say all the things I want to now. Maybe Alhard will read it to you some time. I'll leave it here under some small rocks, for him to find … or maybe my words will just be blown away, like me, not attached to anything or anyone. Leaving my home and my family is the last thing I want.

I think you know, Papa, just how hard it is for me to leave you all. I only wish you had told me who it was that wanted me to go. Who it was that thought I should stand on my own two feet, and made you have to make such harsh decisions concerning me. I feel I shall be haunted by this lack of knowledge for the rest of my life.'

'Leopold, dinner will be ready soon,' called Rudolf as he approached. 'Alhard has been worried about you, and no-one knew where you were, so he sent me to come looking for you.'

Leopold looked over to his brother and said to himself, 'I don't know how I'm supposed to do this.'

The two young men rode off together on their horses, through the forest, each trying to be the first to get home. The horses jumped over fallen branches, kicked up chunks of mud on the path and then galloped down Eichen Allee where the young men laughed at how eager they both were to win. Within five minutes they were at the stables and handing the horses over to the stable hands to remove the bridles and saddles and brush the horses down.

'It's been a while, young Rudolf. You've developed a good seat,' said a rather proud brother.

'Thank you, Leopold. I take that compliment with pride.'

Leopold patted Rudolf on the back and said, 'Beat you,' before running off down the gravel drive, over the moat, and in through the double front doors to the hallway, where they collapsed in laughter in-between gasping for air.

'I'm out of condition, Rudolf, otherwise you would never have won,' said Leopold jokingly.

'You're an old man now, Leopold,' said Rudolf.

After they had recovered, they went into the dining room and sat down to eat beside the other members of the family, who had already started.

'Excuse us for being late, Mama. It was my fault,' said Leopold. And after a pause, 'Oh, I was meaning to tell you, I'm going to Schönebeck again next week. I don't think Alhard needs me here any longer. He's very capable, you know.'

Leopold had decided to be the one to tell his family. If he had to go and not have a choice about it, at least he could have some control as to who told them and when.

Alhard looked at him. 'Yes, thank you for your help, Leopold … and, yes, I think I will do well.'

'How long will you be gone?' asked Amalia.

'Well, that's yet to be decided, but a while. Alhard can't be expected to manage everything from here at Holzhausen, so I'm going to Schönebeck to help him out,' he replied.

'Won't you be so very lonely?' asked Therese.

'I know I'll miss you. I'll miss all of you, but I won't be lonely. I have Friedrich and Anna to look after me … and, of course, Stefan. I'll be busy, but when I get spare time, I'll come and visit … and you can always come and visit me at Schönebeck. That is, if it's alright with Mama and Alhard,' said Leopold, trying to make Therese feel better about his departure.

'I don't want you to go,' said Elisabeth.

'Nor I,' said his little brother Kurt.

'Like I said, you can come and stay with me. In fact, Mama could bring you all up, and we could have a picnic by the lake under the beech trees. Couldn't you, Mama?' said Leopold, rather excited at the prospect.

The children yelled with delight. 'Did you hear, Alhard, we can go!' said Kurt, who had only been to Schönebeck twice, as it took hours to reach by train, and he was still not very old, even though at six years of age, he thought of himself as a young man.

Leopold excused himself from the table, but before he had a chance to go upstairs, Alhard reminded him, 'We have to talk in the morning ... about the letter.'

Upstairs in his bedroom, Leopold reached into his desk draw and pulled out his pocket knife. Carefully and deliberately he etched his name, Leopold von der Borch, into the window pane. 'At least there'll be something of me left behind, so they don't forget me,' he thought. 'For now, though, the family can think I'm going back to Schönebeck.'

# Fourteen

It was one o'clock, and the household was quiet; the perfect time for Alhard and Leopold to discuss Leopold's situation.

One o'clock was that time of the day when each member of the family took an hour for themselves to read, catch up on correspondence, or simply sleep. Today, though, these young men had more important things to do. They would have to decide on Leopold's future.

'Sit,' said Alhard to his brother. Alhard had taken over his father's office and had changed very little about it. The only thing that caught Leopold's eye was a painting by one of the new impressionist group; which of the artists it was, he was unsure about, but it did add a soft tone to the room.

'By the way, I got the letter you sent me from Schönebeck, but as for not reading it, that's preposterous. And why should anyone want to take a shot at you? Surely they were shooting game?' questioned Alhard.

'I didn't want to drag you into this. It's bad enough that I got caught up with these rogues,' replied Leopold. 'It's not necessary to drag anyone else into it. Whatever it is.'

'Do you seriously believe that you are being threatened by this man, or these men, whatever the case is?'

'Not only do I think so, but I have proof,' said Leopold, and he unbuttoned the first few buttons of his shirt and pulled it across his shoulder to show him the wound. 'And then, of course, there was the time I saw a man at Westhusen, standing outside the gate, but running off when I yelled out to him. The men threatened me, Alhard, when I went to court over that wretched suit.'

Leopold buttoned his shirt, and the brothers decided to continue their conversation outside, away from any possibility of being overheard.

Before leaving, Alhard said, 'Just a minute, I have a book for you, which I will explain outside,' and he took a book from the desk and carried it with him.

'Did Father know everything about the incident at the time?' asked Alhard.

'Certainly. I chatted with him on the day, but I think at that stage, Papa didn't believe me. He certainly didn't believe what I had to say about the suit, and he was the one who convinced me to go to court! He told me that those conmen were well known to the police, and I honestly think he thought it was for the best,' Leopold said breathlessly. He paused for a minute to try and calm himself. 'Why didn't he believe me, Alhard? I told him my life could be in danger.' It was the first time Leopold looked to Alhard for support of any kind.

Alhard put his hand on Leopold's shoulder. 'There's only so much I can do for you,' he said. 'With regard to the gun, I don't know that it's a wise decision. After all, what would it accomplish?'

'I'd be alive for one thing,' said Leopold.

'I've never known shooting someone to accomplish anything. Say, for example, you do have a duel, and you shoot him, don't you think, knowing his type, that those other rogues would come after you? Really Leopold, this isn't one of your games; we're no longer children,' said Alhard, quite cross with his brother's short-term thinking. 'The only thing I can see is for you to go somewhere for a while. I've spoken with some of the family—'

Before Alhard could finish his sentence, Leopold interjected, rather abruptly, 'Who exactly do you talk to, and is it the same person Papa spoke to? I don't know that they've made terribly smart decisions about my life. If it hadn't been for them, I would never have gone into the army, nor been in Berlin in the first place, and maybe none of this would have happened.'

'You can't blame others for your shortcomings, Leopold. It is your responsibility, not only to yourself, but to the family. I have often wondered if you understood that,' said Alhard, feeling better for airing his opinion at last.

'When one of us does the wrong thing,' he continued, 'it impacts on all of us. It's not just you. I don't think you know how worrying it was for Father. It really took its toll on him … It was fine for you, but I had to pick up the pieces. Anyway, enough of all that for the time being; it won't solve the problems we have, that you have.'

Alhard never said who it was that was advising Alhard, and Leopold suspected that he never would.

'Do you remember Ernst? He lived in Detmold,' continued Alhard.

Leopold nodded. 'Go on,' he said impatiently.

'Ernst decided to go to Australia—,' but before Alhard was able to finish his sentence, he was interrupted by Leopold, 'AUSTRALIA!'

'Hear me out. You have to get away from here, that's obvious. Where better to go? Australia is relatively unexplored. Anyway, as I was saying, Ernst went out to Australia, about Eighteen-forty-two, and after a few years he returned. He had some fascinating stories to tell.'

Alhard continued, quite excitedly, 'You wouldn't have to stay more than about five or six years, earn enough to come back, and by then I'm sure they would've given up.'

'What would I do out there?' asked Leopold, thinking that Alhard had gone rather mad.

'It's all organised.'

'WHAT?' said Leopold.

'Ernst went back to Australia as Consul to Hanover. He's also the president of the German Club in Adelaide,' Alhard explained. 'The plan is for you to stay here at Holzhausen for a couple of months and enjoy life before your adventure to the colonies. We can have an early Christmas on December sixth for Saint Nicholas' Day. Then you can go back to Schönebeck, and take Stefan with you to help prepare for the trip. It will mean going to England to arrange insurance and your passage out,' said Alhard.

'Seems you've spent quite some time thinking about this,' Leopold said. 'Besides, what do you know of Australia?' He felt rather like a commodity than a brother.

Alhard could see it all working out well; after all he had been pondering Leopold's dilemma for some time, and he had discussed alternatives with his father before he died. He handed Leopold the book he had taken with him, entitled *Wanderungen in Australien*.

'The papers advertising South Australia have been plastered all over the stations, advertising for farmers, bakers, blacksmiths, cabinet makers, boot and harness makers, saddlers, tailors, and every other type of trade to come. It seems the incentive is for people of all trades to get free passage and the chance to own a piece of their own land. Some of those going are wanting to own land, which they couldn't afford here, but have been promised land in Australia if they get married and go to live there.' Alhard paused to catch his breath. 'Read the book and you might get a better idea of things over there.

'For years, Germans have been going over there teaching the people how to farm. They have named cities and villages after German towns and people. They have started exploring the inner part of the country. You know you would probably enjoy yourself if you only gave it a chance. You know how much you love to travel, and enjoy being around diverse cultures. Look at it as an opportunity to be an adventurer,' said Alhard.

'How am I meant to make a living? I'm hardly a tradesperson. We have people working for us. How do I make money when I don't have those skills?' Leopold was still thinking that the likelihood of him going so far away from home was ridiculous.

'I'm good with a gun, and have a good eye for shooting prey, not sure though what I am meant to shoot over there,' said Leopold, rather sarcastically. 'Unless, of course, there's an opportunity going for a young baron?'

'Ernst might be able to get you a job with a surveyor he knows, or you could join the police force. They like to have young men with a military background.'

'And money?' asked Leopold.

'I've arranged with a fellow called Meyer, from Bremen, who is also living in Adelaide, who, along with Ernst, will help you get started. They know something about money, so they may be able to help you save. I will send over a thousand pounds and they can deposit it into the bank, which should be safe. Then I'll organise with Friedrich to send your money from Schönebeck to you monthly. That should give you a good start.' Alhard looked at his brother. 'It'll be alright. You like a challenge.' And he put his firm hand on Leopold's shoulder. 'You should be able to buy a house, and from what I've read about Australia, it is quite like England, with lush green lawns and gardens. The advertisements refer to Australia as a "delightfully fertile and salubrious country".'

'How long am I meant to keep up this charade, for want of a better name?' asked Leopold.

'Hardly a charade! The thing is, you'll be safe. We've spoken about the length of time you should spend there, and we thought five years or so, as I said earlier. By then these wretched conmen would have lost interest in you. When you think of it, you would have spent about the same length of time in the army.'

Alhard thought he had done quite a good job of outlining the plan to Leopold. He had kept a level head, explaining things as they needed to be explained, without revealing the people he had discussed the issues with.

'Very well. Maybe it will give me that something I've been looking for,' said Leopold, 'that thing that's missing from my life, a challenge that I can master.'

'I'm not planning on saying anything to anyone yet. Let's wait until we know all the answers. That way it'll be easier for everyone,' said Alhard.

'If you're done now, big brother, I think I'll go up to my room. I've got some serious planning to do.'

As Leopold walked back to the Big House he thought about what Alhard had said, that if he went away, far enough away for a few years, things might be better for him; be safer for him. 'Unless, thought Leopold, that mysterious chap that keeps appearing and disappearing, disappeared altogether?' Leopold continued to walk towards the house, then up the stairs and past Alhard's bedroom to his own room. He went over to the window that looked out over the main entrance, and pulled the curtain open to see if Alhard was still down at the gatehouse. Alhard was deep in conversation with the manager.

Quickly and quietly he went into Alhard's bedroom, opened the drawer of his desk and pulled out Alhard's hand gun. He felt the cold metal of the gun pressed into his hand, and admired the craftsmanship of it. But could he shoot to kill?

'I don't know that it's a wise decision,' Alhard had said.

'Certainly, if it meant my life, I would have every right to defend myself,' thought Leopold.

Leopold could hear someone coming up the stairs. He hurriedly replaced the gun, and in doing so, shut the drawer with too much force, knocking papers from the desk onto the floor.

The housemaid walked in, not expecting to find Leopold on his hands and knees picking up papers.

'Can I help you, Sir?' she asked.

'No, thank you,' said a polite, but embarrassed Leopold. 'Anything I need is within arm's reach.'

# Fifteen

Saint Nicholas' Day arrived on the sixth of December, and the family would celebrate Christmas together. It would be Leopold's last Christmas before he left to go and live in Australia. It was the year Eighteen sixty-eight.

A fresh pine tree from their forest had been cut down the day before to decorate for Christmas, and the children had spent the night decorating it with cream candles, red and multi-coloured glass ornaments, wooden sleighs, and a few home-made stockings that Jenny and her older sisters had made. It took centre stage in the front hallway, and beneath it lay colourful boxes and treats for the farm hands and their children. The family would receive their presents from one of the local villagers, who was rather rotund and would dress up as Saint Nicholas for the occasion.

Staff were busy in the kitchen preparing legs of pork, to roast with potatoes, carrots, and turnips. The roasted pork and vegetables would be served with sauerkraut made with a hint of chilli to give it bite, along with a teaspoon full of sugar, some speck and onion, as well as boiled peas and sweetcorn, and a delicious home-made gravy made from the juices left behind from the pork and roasted vegetables. Apple sauce, made with a dab of butter, a squeeze of lemon juice, and a little sugar, was Emma's favourite, especially with pork, and it had become a family tradition.

Sweets were the children's favourite. And none were better than quark, beaten with a little sugar, until it was silky-smooth, and then served with rhubarb sauce made from home-grown rhubarb, which had been preserved when they were in season.

Outside, the snow had fallen steadily, and Alhard and Leopold would soon be inside to join the festivities. The water in the moat had iced over, and earlier that day the children were heard laughing as they skated on it.

'Alhard, dear boy,' said Prince Adolf Ludwig as he put his hand on Alhard's shoulder. 'And you, Leopold. How are you boys?'

'Uncle,' they said, almost at the same time, to Prince Adolf Ludwig, who was actually their great uncle because he was a sister to their grandmother Therese.

'We didn't expect to see you here,' said Alhard. 'I'll get the girls to set another place at the table. You will join us, won't you? We're having ... an early Christmas this year.'

'I am not at all surprised young men ... I heard a rumour that Leopold was leaving us?' said Prince Adolf Ludwig.

Leopold felt rather confused by his uncle's comments. He had thought it was more of a plan than a rumour. Why would his uncle suggest it was a rumour? If it wasn't his uncle, who had written to Papa about Leopold standing on his own two feet and sending him away from his family and home, then who was it?

He looked at Alhard, and then to his uncle. 'A rumour?' reiterated Leopold.

'Yes, young man, a rumour,' replied his uncle. 'I had no idea you were going, and I must say I was rather offended that you hadn't come to me, to discuss the matter. Perhaps I could have helped you, but the wheels are now in motion, and my hands are tied.'

'I'm truly sorry, Uncle. I'd thought—'

'That's it, young man. You thought … but you didn't think it through. You have always been a little naïve, Leopold, and have not thought enough about things that should have been important to you and to the family. Your actions in Berlin demonstrated that.'

'I was only eighteen years old at the time, Uncle,' said Leopold, trying to defend himself. 'And I still don't feel very old at times.'

Prince Adolf Ludwig wrapped his arms around Leopold and hugged him.

'Eighteen isn't very old, and, no, you're still not very old now, but as men, particularly as aristocratic men, we must honour our punishments, no matter how difficult they may be,' said Prince Adolf Ludwig, trying to comfort Leopold. 'You are a man now, and your maturity and your actions from now on will define who you are.'

Leopold took a few deep breaths. 'It's been difficult. So many things have changed for me … and I miss Papa, and I've tried to be strong for Mama.'

'You've had a great many losses, Leopold,' confirmed Prince Adolf Ludwig. He placed his gloved hands on Leopold's shoulders. 'Don't let this one incident define you as a man. You have so many good qualities. Go forward from here, and learn from it. I don't know if I'll still be alive when you return, but know that there won't be a day that goes by when I won't think of you, and all the good things about you.'

'Don't say that, Uncle. I need to know you'll still be around,' replied Leopold. 'How did you actually find out about my going to Australia?'

'A friend of mine, who works at Lloyd's of London, wrote to me, saying he saw the von der Borch name come up on the list of those leaving for Australia, and he asked me if you were related. I must say it was rather a shock, but then again there have been a few of those lately,' said Prince Adolf Ludwig.

'Have you told Mama?' Alhard asked his uncle.

'No, of course not. It is not my place or anyone else's to tell your mother, but I would suggest that you do it sooner than later.' He continued in a paternalistic, authoritarian manner. 'What were you boys thinking? Not saying anything to your mother. What if she had heard about it from somebody else like I did? It would certainly have broken her heart. If I know about such things, then surely others do, too. It's your duty to let your mother know before she hears it from someone else.'

'We planned to get through dinner first and then chat with her, when the younger ones had gone to bed,' replied Leopold.

'Australia? What on earth has possessed you to want to go to Australia?' asked Prince Adolf Ludwig. 'I know there seems to be quite a bit of advertising lately trying to attract tradespeople and farmers, but you, dear Leopold?'

'It would seem, because of my stupidity with money and getting caught up with the wrong people, that I am to be punished this way,' Leopold answered. 'Papa said to me once that the best punishment for me would be to be without my family and my home. I didn't think he meant *this* though!'

'Maybe he didn't. Did this come from you, Alhard? One of your decisions?' asked Prince Adolf Ludwig. 'I can't quite understand it myself, Leopold. You have been quite a decent fellow, haven't you?' he said to Leopold. 'Aside from this last wretched thing about the suit, of course.'

The rest of the family came to join them in the hall.

'Mama, give me your arm and let's go into dinner,' said Alhard, rather pleased that he did not have to explain himself. 'Doesn't it smell absolutely delicious!'

Emma and Alhard sat down at the table, with Emma at one end and Alhard at the other. Prince Adolf Ludwig sat to the right of his niece, Leopold to her left, with the rest of the children sitting in their usual places.

'The table looks so pretty, doesn't it, Mama,' said Amalia, looking at the wreath in the middle of the table. 'We have blue candles this year, instead of purple.'

'Yes, Leopold asked if we could. In fact, having Christmas early was his idea too. I'm not sure what he has planned, but I've learnt not to ask questions. Apparently, Alhard and Leopold will explain later. The blue candles represent hope, by the way,' answered Emma.

And then she whispered to Amalia, 'I think we'll have Christmas a second time this year, on Christmas Eve, as usual, and then we'll have completed advent, continuing to add a candle each week, so that at Christmas, we'll add the fifth candle and light it to show God's light into our house.'

Meanwhile, Kurt, who thought no-one was looking, plucked a small piece of pine needle from the wreath and held it over the flame of the candle.

'Kurt,' scolded his mother.

Therese, who had overheard parts of the conversation

between Alhard, Leopold, and Uncle Adolf Ludwig, had been waiting for an opportunity to say something. 'Where are you going, Leopold? Not too far I hope, or I shall miss you very much.'

'I think he's going to Minette's again,' said Rudolf.

'Maybe he's going to live with Uncle Adolf Ludwig?' said Elisabeth.

'No, you are all wrong. I'll discuss it further with Mama after dinner, as I had planned with Alhard, and let the rest of you know tomorrow,' said Leopold, trying not to be angry at Alhard for deciding when his mother would learn the truth.

As the family placed white damask serviettes on their laps and popped bon-bons to retrieve the paper hats to put on their heads, the staff brought in the dinner on silver platters. The vegetables were each in their own containers with individual silver serving-spoons, so the family could help themselves.

Christmas was a time when they liked to be free of staff, a time to chat in private. The sweets were placed on the sideboard along with anything else that may be required for the evening.

The staff said their farewells, and Emma reminded them that, although their gifts were already under the tree, they would have to wait until Christmas Eve to receive them.

'This is so delicious, Mama,' said Jenny, who was named after her aunt, Carl's first wife.

'Can I have some more sauerkraut?' asked Therese.

'Good manners to finish what you have on your plate first,' Alhard reminded his sister.

'And isn't it good manners not to comment, Mama?' exclaimed Therese. 'Don't think you have any jurisdiction here today, dear brother. Today is for all of us. Now, if you could pass me some sauerkraut, please?'

Leopold smiled to himself.

Alhard passed the sauerkraut to Therese and also offered her some of the other bowls of vegetables.

The evening was filled with laughter and chatter, especially amongst the girls, and the hours passed by very quickly.

At some point, Leopold stood up from the table and yelled out, 'Presents everyone!'

There was much excitement as the children leapt from their seats and rushed to get their presents. Wrapping paper and empty boxes were strewn around the room.

Leopold sat back and watched everyone, just as he would if he were watching his favourite theatrical performance on stage.

'It's time for bed, children. Take your presents with you, and I'll come up to tuck you in later,' said Emma to the youngest of the children. 'You, too, Amalia, Therese. I have to say, I'm quite curious about what Leopold has to tell me.'

'Night. *Schlaft gut,*' Emma sang out to the children as they made their way from the table and headed upstairs to their bedrooms. '*Gute Nacht, Mama,*' yelled the children, racing each other up the stairs.

The night had been special for Leopold. He closed his eyes, trying to record every moment of it, unaware it would be his very last Christmas in Germany.

# Sixteen

Alhard and Leopold were in their father's office trying to decide who would tell their mother that Leopold would be leaving shortly for Australia to live there for five years or so. Leopold thought that just the idea of him being at sea for four months would unsettle his mother.

'Don't you think you should tell her,' said Leopold, having thought more about the consequences of telling her himself. 'After all, it is your idea?' He looked out to the gatehouse.

'Not exactly my idea, but it could be said that I am responsible for telling you to go, I suppose,' answered Alhard. 'Don't you think, though, it would be easier for Mama to believe it was something you wanted to do, rather than being sent away?'

'I think it should be you, the first-born son,' said Leopold. 'To be honest, I have no idea how to tell her ... it was bad enough dealing with Papa about the suit ... I know she's going to be upset.'

'That's what I mean. If she thinks it's your idea, she may be upset, but upset in a different way. And we know she'll worry about you, anyway; she always has, more than me or any of the other children,' said Alhard, trying to make Leopold see reason.

'What do I say? I have never even talked about Australia, and now suddenly I'm off to the other side of the world. It has to make sense to her, Alhard. I certainly can't tell her that those conmen, or someone they know, has taken a shot at me, and that I'm leaving for my own safety.'

'Is that why you think you are leaving? Because of the conmen?'

Just as they were chatting, Emma walked into the room. 'What were you saying about a shot?' she asked.

The young men turned around to see their mother standing by the door. They had no idea she had entered the room, and they wondered how long she had been standing there or what she might have heard.

'The manager ...,' said Leopold. 'Taken a shot at a rabbit, I think he said.'

Alhard looked relieved that Leopold had come up with an answer so quickly.

'Sit down, Mama,' said Leopold. 'Would you like a pot of tea? Alhard will make it for you, won't you, dear brother,' he said, smiling to himself.

'I know I could well do with one,' continued Leopold, referring to something much stronger than tea. Alhard gave Leopold a stern look.

'Something I'm not expecting is going on, isn't it? It's not like you two to worry about whether or not I have a pot of tea,' Emma stated. 'With that said, I think I should respond with a resounding yes.'

'I'll pop out to the kitchen and get the tea while Leopold tells you his news,' said Alhard, as he quickly headed out of the door.

'So, what is it you're up to this time, Leo? I imagine it's rather interesting, as you never were one to sit around being bored. Even as a young boy, you were always looking for challenges.'

'I'm not sure how to start?' said Leopold, hesitating.

'Just start, *Liebling*,' said his mother.

'I'm going to Australia to—,' he started.

'Austria?' said his mother. 'Why on earth are you going to Austria?'

'No, Mama, I'm going to Australia.'

'Australia … LEOPOLD? What do you mean by Australia? What for? I don't understand!'

'I leave on the fifteenth of December, Mama. It's been decided …' Leopold tried to explain, but was interrupted by Alhard coming in with the tray of tea and biscuits.

'Alhard, did you know about this?' asked his mother.

Alhard looked up at Leopold, not knowing what had already been said. 'We've discussed it for a while, but we've come to the conclusion that it's the best thing for Leopold.'

'What if I don't agree with you?' exclaimed Emma.

'She might as well know, Alhard, otherwise it won't make sense to her,' said Leopold.

'What won't make sense to me? Leopold, tell me what's going on. You're making me feel unsettled,' said Emma, holding onto her pearl necklace.

'That's the last thing I wanted to do. Alhard, tell her,' demanded Leopold.

'I don't like this, Alhard. Not at all,' said Emma.

Leopold poured her a hot cup of English tea, the milk poured in first, and a spoon of sugar. 'It will be fine, Mama.'

Emma looked at Alhard.' I'd like you to explain what's going on, Alhard, and I'd like you to do it now.'

'Very well, Mama.' Alhard looked to Leopold. 'Remember the suit incident and the court case?'

'How could I forget,' Emma replied.

'I don't know if Papa told you or not, but those men who conned Leopold were well known to the police. One of father's friends told him that if Leopold stood up for his case and told the truth about them conning him to use Papa's name, it would be enough for the courts to put them away for a long time. Unfortunately, they threatened Leopold, they said that if he did take them to court they would come after him,' said Alhard, almost relieved that the truth was out.

Emma looked to Leopold, worried for his safety. 'Leopold, is that true?'

'I'm afraid it is,' said Leopold, who knelt by his mother as he took her hand.

'But it was such a long time ago. Why would they suddenly do something to you now?' she asked.

The boys looked at each other. Emma saw the look in their faces.

'Oh my God, they've already done something, haven't they? I want you to tell me the truth, Alhard.'

Leopold undid his shirt and pulled the shoulder of it across for her to see the scar. 'I'm afraid they've had a go at me already, a couple of weeks ago,' he said.

Emma sat back in her chair and gasped for air.

'Are you alright, Mama?' asked Alhard. 'Maybe we should finish this later?'

'No. If it is going to be told, do it now. I wouldn't be able to settle to anything with unanswered questions in my mind. Certainly not sleep, and I doubt I'll sleep anyway after this news.'

The boys looked at their mother with admiration. She rubbed

her finger over the scar and looked into Leopold's eyes. 'Did it hurt very much?'

'It was more of a surprise than anything else and … so annoying,' Leopold answered. 'You see, Mama, part of my going to stay with Minette was to be away from Holzhausen where they knew I lived … Papa wanted me to learn how to stand on my own two feet, so that's what he told everyone. There has been someone following me around everywhere I go, and every so often I see a figure in the distance, never close enough for me to identify him, but they're waiting for me. I don't know who it is or if it's one of the conmen, but after this …' He looked at the scar. 'Papa wasn't sure how they found me or how they got hold of the court records, but they did. I saw the same fellow at Minette's the day that man came to let us know about Papa's stroke …'

Emma sat, listening intently to what Leopold had to say.

'So, then I went with Stefan to Schönebeck. Stefan had been in the army with me and was there as a friend more than a butler, and as someone to look after me.'

'Doesn't seem he did a very good job, does it,' said Emma, still in disbelief at the story she was hearing.

'After that attempt, Leopold is not safe here or at Schönebeck, Mama,' said Alhard. 'I think the best thing to do is for him to disappear to Australia for a few years. It makes quite good sense. He can start over. Stand on his own two feet, as Papa and the older family members have been wanting him to do.'

Leopold looked puzzled at Alhard's comment. 'It won't really be starting over … it will just be for a few years, I thought you said, so why is that starting over? I'll learn to stand on my own two feet, just as Papa and the others wanted me to do, but then

I'll save and come back home, in about five years. By then this fuss should have died down.'

'What will you do for money, and how will you live?' Emma asked.

'Ernst Pustkuchen, who lives there, in a city called Adelaide, is the president of the German Club and Consul for Hanover,' explained Alhard. 'I've arranged for him to look after Leopold when he first gets there, and for he and Meyer to be his administrators. You remember Pustkuchen, don't you? And Meyer is from the Bremen Meyers.'

'Yes, they are a lovely family from Detmold ... the Pustkuchens, I mean,' Emma replied.

'Yes,' agreed Alhard.

'Friedrich will be managing Schönebeck during the time I'm away, and I'll be sent a monthly wage,' said Leopold, sounding a little more enthusiastic about his new life. 'The thing I least look forward to is the four months at sea.'

Emma looked from one son to the other. 'I still don't like this. Surely there must be some other way.'

'There isn't. You have to believe us on that,' said Alhard. 'If there was another way, we wouldn't hesitate.'

'I will miss you so much, Leopold.'

Leopold put his arms around his mother and gave her a long hug. 'I'll miss you, too, more than you can imagine,' he said, trying to hold back the tears.

'It's like losing your father and my sister all over again. Oh, Leopold ... my dear Leopold,' said Emma, not daring to look him in the eyes. She could feel her heart sinking.

The door opened suddenly, and their uncle entered. 'I see

you've told her then?' He turned to Emma. 'The young man will be fine, dear Emma. You shouldn't worry so. He went to the war, remember, and came back.'

'And things have never been the same, Uncle Adolf Ludwig,' she stated.

'Prince Alfred's been over there, in New Zealand and Australia, and he loves the place … First English Royal to go to Australia, and planning to go back again, I hear. Possibly when you are there, Leopold. You could meet with him, if at all possible,' said Adolf Ludwig.

'Prince Alfred and these boys are from the same stock,' said Adolf Ludwig, looking from Alhard to Leopold. 'Good breeding—strong, ambitious, courageous. You shouldn't worry, my dear niece. I have great faith in this young man.'

He continued. 'I heard about a young English writer, Adam Lindsay Gordon, who also belongs to an aristocratic family, who went out to Australia and joined the police force. He worked as a groom to the Commissioner of Police at one time. Rumour had it that Gordon had been heir to his mother's estate in Scotland, and that he had a lot of financial difficulties in Australia. The news of his inheritance cheered Gordon up but for a brief time, only to find out later that the entail of the estate had been abolished, and he would receive nothing. Shot himself apparently. He was sent out to Australia to start over again, too, and about the same age.' Adolf Ludwig had got carried away with his story and became rather thoughtless. 'Hear the place is full of convicts.'

Alhard could see that his mother was worried. 'There are no convicts in South Australia, Uncle, and there never will be. Apart from that, the English are talking about stopping all of that by the end of this year. And Leopold's hardly going to shoot himself ... Anyway, enough talk for tonight.'

'Please don't worry, Mama. I shall be fine. For a start, those men wouldn't have the money to follow me, and, secondly, as I'm paying my own way to Australia, there is very little paperwork they can follow to find me. It's only people who have been contracted to go to Australia that leave paperwork around that can be traced.'

# Seventeen

Elisabeth grabbed at the knife and fork and fumbled to untie the string with her gloved hands. She had always found the game of 'Shooting the Eagle' difficult, and could never throw a six for ages, no matter how hard she tried.

'My turn, I threw a six,' yelled Kurt, as he pulled the knitted hat off Elisabeth's head, spilling her hair over her face. Then he grabbed at the chocolate, put on the gloves and furiously started to cut at the wrapping with the knife and fork.

'Quick, throw a six,' said Elisabeth to Leopold.

As the game progressed, and the urgency to break open the chocolate from its paper grew stronger, more laughter could be heard echoing around the downstairs rooms. Emma sat watching her children and longed to hold them close to her and never let them go. She focused on Leopold, as he sat with Kurt on his lap, and she wondered how he would cope without his family.

Emma thought back to a time when she was visiting her sister. Emma had been unaware that within a few weeks her sister would die, and that she would marry her brother-in-law, and the children would become *her* children. She pictured them, on that particular day. They had all gone to the forest to play hide and seek. Alhard was twelve and trying to act grown up, pretending that he was no longer interested in playing hide and seek. Leopold was eleven, and the twins, Therese and Amalia, were ten. The younger siblings were searching with Emma, trying to find where the older siblings had hidden. The twins had quickly got bored with the game, and, as usual, they had come out from their hiding spot to get caught. Alhard and Leopold were competing with each other, both wanting to be the last to be found. Alhard was eventually spotted, but Leopold was nowhere to be seen.

Leopold eventually turned up with a small, injured bird tucked under his jacket, keeping it warm. He was a gentle soul; she had always thought so—the one that would be there for you if something went wrong. He was a lovely, fun brother to the younger children, listening to their chatter, chasing them around the moat or giving them piggy-back rides.

Emma had never wanted to believe the story about the suit, and that Leopold had forgotten everything he had ever been taught. The von der Borchs were expected to live by the values they had been taught over generations, and to value and respect the family. She knew he had been careless with money, but to think it would lead to him living so far away from them was too much for her to bear. And yet, to put her in such an embarrassing position, she had to admit, annoyed her.

Sudden laughter from Amalia distracted her from her thoughts.

'Time for supper everyone. We're going to have it a bit early tonight. I have something to share with you,' said Emma. 'Come and sit with me, Leopold.'

Leopold's siblings, including Minette and her husband, who had called in to see everyone for Christmas, sat on the soft lounge seats, with the smaller ones sitting on laps.

'This is boring, Mama. Can't we go back and eat more chocolate?' asked Kurt.

'Don't be so rude, Kurt,' said Emma firmly. 'This isn't the time. In fact, there is never an appropriate time for boredom or rudeness.'

'Mama,' said Amalia, wondering why her mother had reacted so abruptly.

'I'm sorry, Kurt. There is no excuse for me to speak to you so. I'm just feeling a bit—'

'Grumpy,' said Elisabeth, not giving her mother time to finish the sentence.

Leopold took the lead, 'I'm going away for a while ... to Australia, and I'll be living there for a few years,' he began, trying not to mention the length of time he would likely be gone. 'It takes a long time to get there, and Mama is worried about it and how I'll get on ... You'll all have to look after her, and understand that if she's a bit grumpy, it might be because she's worried about something ...'

'You can't go, Leopold. Alhard won't let you,' said Therese. 'You're the second son, and if something happens to Alhard, you need to be here to look after Holzhausen and us.'

'Fritz will take my place for the time being,' answered Leopold.

'But he's so much younger than you. He wouldn't even know what to do,' argued Therese.

Fritz looked at his brothers. 'What do you mean by saying I'll take your place?' asked Fritz.

'It means this: Leopold is the second son, and always will be, no matter where he is—here in Germany or over in Australia. If something happens to Alhard, he is next in line, and you, Fritz, will fill in while he's away,' explained Emma.

'It means that you, Fritz, will have to grow up, too,' said Leopold.

Jenny and Kurt had already lost interest in the conversation and were sitting by the fire with Bruno, playing with the ball. They had no real understanding of how Leopold's life was changing. To the younger children, Australia was only as far away as Schönebeck.

'When do you go?' asked a rather quiet Elisabeth.

'I will be leaving tomorrow afternoon to return to Schönebeck, and then, shortly after that, I'll go to London and sail from there to Australia. Stefan has packed my woollen things; I've had shoes and bags made by the saddler, and I'm taking my favourite bronze.'

Leopold paused to think what else Stefan had packed into his trunk. 'Alhard has provided me with a rifle to protect myself. What from? God only knows,' he thought. 'And, of course, the book, *Wanderungen in Australien*. I'm hoping Alhard has remembered to give Stefan some ammunition to fire!'

'Of course!' Emma suddenly realised, 'Stefan will be going with you. That makes me feel a lot better.'

'No, Mama, I'll be going by myself,' said Leopold.

'But—,' Emma started to say.

'If I'm to stand on my own two feet, Mama, I need to go alone.'

'Then at least take something familiar from home. Choose a book from the library, or take paper and your watercolours and brushes. You'll need something to occupy your time, otherwise I can see you getting bored,' said Emma.

'How big is the ship?' asked Fritz, interrupting Emma's train of thought. He was sounding excited about the adventure his big brother was going on.

'It's a barque of—'

Leopold was interrupted by his brother Kurt. 'What's a barque? Are you going by dog?' Kurt was rather pleased with his effort at being funny, and started to laugh.

'Not a bark, but Bach, the musician,' said Jenny, who had been learning the piano.

'A barque is just a type of sailing vessel. I don't remember what I was trying to say. Mama, you never let us interrupt like that!' Leopold was starting to feel tense, and having second thoughts, not that it would change anything.

'The ship leaves before the end of December and takes four months to get to Australia. I have a man at Lloyds of London preparing what's needed for my departure. If the Suez Canal had been finished when expected, it would take less time to travel to Australia, but as it is, the canal won't be finished until later next year. I'm dreading being at sea for so long,' admitted Leopold.

'What does "dreading it" mean? Does it mean he's going to be dead?' asked Kurt.

'No, Kurt. It means that he's not looking forward to spending so much time at sea,' Emma explained.

Amalia came over to Leopold and gave him a big hug. 'Leopold. I'm so sad that you're going. I'll miss you so much.'

'Me, too,' said Therese, who joined them for a hug.

Kurt looked up to see everyone coming together for a hug. 'What's going on?' he asked.

'Leopold's running away from home,' said Elisabeth.

'I'm doing nothing of the sort, Kurt. I'm going on a big ship to live in Australia, and I'll be away for a few years.' Leopold looked at his little brother and thought about him growing up without him there. He could not imagine not teaching his brother to shoot, nor tasting Elisabeth's cooking and watching her gain confidence. He would miss seeing who the twins courted, and if he would approve. The seriousness and permanency of what was about to happen, suddenly dawned on him. He wanted to yell at the top of his voice and say, 'I can't do this. I don't want to do this,' but instead he tried to be strong for his mother. He knew if he faltered, his mother would find it difficult to be strong for his siblings.

'Couldn't you stay just a little longer, Leopold? So we can do something special together?' asked Amalia.

'Every day, since being back from Schönebeck, has been special. It has helped me realise just how much we take everything for granted—walking in the forest together, riding the horses, playing silly chocolate games …'

'They're not silly games,' said Kurt.

'Of course, they're not, Kurt … What I'm trying to say is that I want to remember my life as it was when I was younger and Papa was still alive, and we'd wake up in the morning to the sound of him playing the piano.'

'But Papa is dead,' said Kurt.

'Really, Mama! Alhard, you need to keep him in check,' said Leopold, growing short-tempered.

'I will be able to remember him like that, Kurt, that's all,' continued Leopold. 'What was I saying? Oh, yes, I will imagine Mama in the garden, and all of you doing your daily things. It'll be so important that I can remember. I'll take some photos with me, of you all. At least I'll have a bit of you with me then. All of it has been special. The privilege of living in such a beautiful home and such peaceful surroundings, and of sharing our lives together.'

'How will you remember me?' Kurt asked Leopold.

'I shall remember you asking questions all the time,' said Leopold. He went over to Kurt, picked him up and put him on his shoulders.

Amalia and Therese started to cry. 'Does he have to go, Mama?'

'It seems that this is something I have to do,' answered Leopold, watching his mother closely.

Alhard remained in the background. There was nothing he could say, and he hoped the family would understand that it was his duty as the heir to carry this out.

'I'm going to write to you every day,' said Elisabeth.

'Me, too,' chorused the rest of his siblings.

'I'll certainly be sending letters home. I imagine I'll be quite busy, so I'll probably write to Mama, and she will be able to read the letters out to you,' said Leopold, trying to reassure everyone that he would not forget them.

They all gave him a heart-felt hug.

# Eighteen

The passenger manifest had been completed, and the non-paying guests of the government were directed to their cramped quarters below deck, herded together like sheep. They had been encouraged to go to South Australia to make a new life. They weren't convicts, but the close proximity to one another made them wonder what the journey would have been like for the many convicts that had been transported from Britain to various parts of Australia.

Leopold and the four other paying guests were shown to the quarters they would share for the next four months. They weren't large, but had enough room to sleep and dress, and had a couple of windows, framed by dark red velvet curtains.

The crew made their final checks to ensure that the much-needed cargo for the vastly unexplored country of Australia was secured and that the mail bags were on board. Their voices could be heard echoing around the barque to let the captain know that all was well, and they could set sail.

When the George Shotten pulled away from the port at Rhyde, England, Leopold had less than five pounds in his pocket. The ship's discoloured sails—tethered at the corners, somewhat like a kite tethered by a string—stretched out to embrace the strong winds. The sails looked frail, and even Captain Bailey hoped they would hold together for the journey. This was his third and last trip to Australia for the year, navigating around Africa.

'Pity that damn canal from the Red Sea to the Mediterranean isn't finished … tens of thousands of poor beggars slaving away when they started, so they could get it done, and still it isn't finished,' Captain Bailey yelled out to the crew above the noise of the ship's daily routine.

'At least some bright spark gave it some thought a couple of years ago and brought in those custom-made steam-powered bucket-dredgers to help widen and deepen the canal,' continued the captain. 'Powerful machines were needed to help lift the soil from a great depth. They had three hundred men, but they couldn't manage. The soil kept sliding back into the canal. Twenty thousand men they used, every ten months, and then another twenty thousand men, using their hands with picks and shovels.'

The crew looked at Captain Bailey, and then looked behind him, trying to alert him to the fact that there were passengers on deck. 'Captain, Sir,' said one of the crew men, lifting his eyebrows and nodding his head for the captain to turn around. 'You'll have to excuse me, but on deck I can't be held responsible for anything you might hear,' said the captain, making no apology for his conduct.

Six weeks into their journey, they were heading for a storm. Captain Bailey ordered the crew and passengers to batten down any loose objects and prepare themselves for what lay ahead. They helped tie down any loose objects which might become projectiles, securing them behind hand-made mesh screens. Tins of meat were wedged in between blankets, as were other sharp objects.

'Might be best to stay below and settle yourselves,' the captain said to the passengers.

The storm began to blow up and the waves on the horizon became choppy.

Within hours, the grey sky completely darkened and released a heavy downpour.

'Batten down!' yelled Captain Bailey. 'Waves are crashing over the sides, some twelve to fourteen feet high!'

The jingling sounds of the rings that secured the ropes and pulled at the sails were deafening. Leopold and the other four paying passengers sat beneath the wooden deck, desperately wanting to come up for fresh air, but the captain reminded them to stay below as he had no intention of losing anyone overboard. Leopold wondered how the non-paying passengers in their cramped quarters were faring.

Clothes fell from the hooks they had been hanging on. Water gushed down the steps like a water fall. A trap door beneath one of the beds burst open, and an enamel basin slid out and floated across the cedar floor.

The masts stood tall and straight, but the sails, which were linked together with rope, began to tangle as the crew lowered them to help stabilise the ship. Looking up at the two half-furled sails against the darkened sky made it look like the masts were going to hit one another. The wind blew in under the sails and lifted them up, the sails flapping against one another, the rings shaking from the strength of the wind.

The passengers were unsettled and started to feel the effects of nausea creeping in. Leopold had his back to the side of the ship, leaning slightly forward with a hay-filled pillow supporting him against the hard-curved wood. The others, two couples from England, sat huddled together. With the exception of the whimpering from one of the women, no-one talked.

Leopold cast his eye over the others and wondered why they wanted to go to the other side of the world, probably never to return.

Because he couldn't swim, Leopold wanted to talk about anything but the storm, but he was too afraid to open his mouth to speak as the nausea he was feeling increased with every bounce of the ship on the waves. To make matters worse, the fumes from the mixture of vinegar and chloride that was used to wash the decks, and the pure vinegar used liberally to prevent the spread of disease, was wafting up into his nostrils.

The ship slid up and forward over the waves and then thumped down. There was no measure, no way to predict which way the ship would roll or when it would lurch forward.

Leopold closed his eyes. He wanted to shut out the world. He did not want to think of this trip or the challenges that lay ahead.

He tried to be brave, and tried not to think about drowning at sea, and, that if he did drown, that no-one would know for sure what had become of him. He thought back to the window in his bedroom and how he scratched his name on the pane of glass.

His thoughts rolled around his head at sickening speed, and he could hear his heart thumping faster.

'Think of something, Leopold ... Just one thing ... Something, anything ... Concentrate ... Just one thing ... Just one thing.'

He heard his father saying, *'If you can't stand on your own two feet at Schönebeck, there will be harsh consequences.'*

'Not that ... Therese and the angel at Christmas ... Concentrate Leopold. Think of something happy.'

Memories of the Prussian War were foremost in his mind. The rocking of the ship reminded him of the rocking motion of his horse as he went into battle against the Austrian soldiers. The sound of the wind rushing against the sails and the metal holdings hitting against the poles were like bullets that he had fired while serving in the 45th Infantry of the Prussian army. He recalled the Dreyse needle-guns they had been issued. The Dreyse was a breech loading rifle much more capable of rapid fire than the muzzle loading Lorenz rifles the Austrians used. The metal rings from the sails kept tapping and banging against the wood.

The Eighteen sixty-six campaign had been carefully planned in the unification of Germany under Prussia's Hohenzollern dynasty under Bismarck. The railway system in Prussia had allowed for large numbers of troops to enter Austria. Austria only had one railway line, and it took them forty-five days to transport the two-hundred-and-fifty-thousand soldiers they needed to fight. Prussia defeated the Austrians, and Leopold, along with the other soldiers, received a medal made from melted-down cannons captured from the Austrians. However, Leopold preferred to forget his time in Berlin, forget that his father thought it would be good for him to go into the army.

The ship suddenly lurched forward, and Leopold's eyes opened wide as he looked around the wooden space. One of the women had fallen onto the floor and broken her arm. The bone was poking out through her skin, and she was bleeding and in shock. Her husband clambered to the stairs, holding the sides to keep him from falling. He yelled out to the sailors for help, but they were too busy trying to keep the ship afloat, and the noise of the waves crashing on deck made it impossible for Captain Bailey to hear.

'Quick, pick her up off the floor … we don't want her drowning,' said Leopold, as the other men helped him pick the woman up and carefully placed her on the table.

'Can you put one of those blankets on her … and we'll need a sheet!' Leopold insisted.

The woman's husband reached towards the nearest sheets and blankets that had been stuffed amongst the tins to keep them from being flung across the room. He kept one arm hooked around a pole to provide him with some stability while he stretched the other as far as possible. Leopold took the sheet and ripped at the edges with his hands to make thin strips of bandages. The other couple helped by hanging onto him and guided him to the table. The water on the floor swirled around their feet.

'Do you know what you're doing?' said the woman's husband.

Leopold looked at the husband's face. It was a strong face, weathered by the sun, with a wiry beard of some months' growth, large brown eyes and a friendly smile. His teeth were stained with tobacco. 'Probably a farmer,' thought Leopold. It was not unusual for farmers to smoke. 'I saw my father tend to a cow that had its leg caught in a fence,' he said, 'and it had panicked. The cow pulled and jumped to get free and had broken its leg.'

The pain was too intense, and the woman, he later came to know as Nan, fainted.

'Quick,' said Leopold, 'if we work fast, she won't feel as much pain.'

'I think the ship's not lurching as much now,' said the husband.

'Someone pass me the whisky,' said Leopold. He poured the alcohol over his hands and over the gaping wound to sterilise them.

'What's your name?' Leopold asked, looking at the youngest of one of the women standing beside her husband.

'Elizabeth,' she replied.

'I want you to keep an eye on her. If she starts to look white, you must lift her legs up. Get something to put under them. I want them up,' he said. Elizabeth nodded her head in agreement.

Leopold looked at the husband of the now unconscious woman on the table and asked his name.

'Norman,' the man replied.

'Can you help me, Norman? I need you to focus and to be strong … I want you to hold your wife's wrist and gently pull. If you don't think you can do it, then get out of my way, and I'll get someone else.' Leopold was quite stern, but he knew that he needed to get the bone in place as quickly as possible. Any delay might cause nerve damage and further bleeding. 'Norman! We must do it now.'

'I think I can do it,' said Norman.

'Norman, I want you to hold her wrist with both hands, but I want you to hold it gently, but firmly,' instructed Leopold.

Norman took hold of his wife's wrist.

'Are you ready?' asked Leopold. 'I'm going to pull her from behind, under the arms near the shoulder. You hold the wrist, and as I slowly pull her arm, I'll try and guide the bone into position. You,' he said to Elizabeth, 'you watch to see what colour she is. Let me know if anything changes … Right. Let's do this together.'

Leopold gently grabbed the woman and began to pull. 'I want to get the bone inside the opening and then I can work on it from there.' Gently they both pulled and stretched her arm. The bone jutting out was difficult to get into position, and as the ship rocked, the broken piece of bone kept jagging the skin around the wound.

Leopold looked at the other man. 'I need you to wash your hands in alcohol like we did, and then, when I pull, I want you to guide the bone into the opening. We'll never get it in otherwise. When it's there, I'll ease off ... got it?' Elizabeth was looking pale.

'Give her a mouthful of whisky, Norman, will you. She needs to keep an eye on your wife. We don't want her fainting, too,' said Leopold, and with that, Elizabeth gasped from the strength and taste of the alcohol. Once again, she was attentive.

They worked well together as a team, and within a few minutes the bone was inside the open wound. The flesh of her arm felt soft and pudgy, with nothing holding it together.

'Feels a bit like an undercooked piece of meat,' said one of the men.

Leopold removed two pieces of thin wood from the side of a crate and strapped them to the woman's arm using the torn pieces of sheet. 'I'll get the doctor to check it when we're finally able to get him to come down,' he said. 'As long as the bone's inside the flesh.'

'How's her colour?' he asked Elizabeth.

'She looks okay.'

'When she wakes up, she'll need a strong, sweet cup of tea. Three spoons of sugar ... but don't let her eat for a while,' he said. 'And only let her take sips of the tea. Don't let her drink it, just let her have sips.'

Leopold wasn't usually bossy, but he had to make sure they all worked together.

It took a few more hours, but eventually the stormy seas began to calm, and Captain Bailey came below deck to see the damage.

'What have we here?' he asked, unprepared for what he saw.

Elizabeth explained in great detail, forgetting to mention she nearly passed out at the sight of the bone sticking out through the flesh of the woman's arm.

'We could do with some fresh water,' she said.

Algae had started to form in the water in the wooden barrels onboard ship, and one of the crew men had found a dead rat in one. Although the water was being boiled, it still tasted bitter to them.

None of the passengers ate for a few hours, their stomachs unsettled by the sea and the woman's broken arm. They all sipped warm milk with nutmeg and sugar, and a little whisky, and looked at the mess around their feet.

Leopold climbed on deck and looked up at the stars. They always made him feel more settled. When he was small, his mother would often take the children outside at night, especially in summer, and they would lie on their backs on the grass and look up at the sky. Wispy clouds often floated by, and they would imagine what the shapes of the clouds looked like. But it was the stars that made Leopold's face light up. He believed they connected him to everyone he knew. His mother used to say to him that when someone died, they would go up to heaven and become a star. He knew that it wasn't the case, yet it made him feel better to think she may be looking down on him.

Leopold was twenty-two years old, on a ship in the middle of the ocean, making its journey to the other side of the world.

It would provide him with company of sorts, and food and a warm place to sleep. A mistake with his name had occurred when he registered to come on board, and he had decided that for the time being he would keep it: he was now Leopold van den Brock, and he could be himself—not the son of Carl, or the grandson of Princess Therese—just Leopold, a young, sensitive man interested in writing, painting, languages, and having philosophical discussions. He toyed with the idea of changing his name for good; after all, he would be changing his entire life.

Here on the ship it did not matter at all if he had not shaved for a day or if his boots were not highly polished. He could be Leopold, and the people he met along the way, he hoped, and in Australia, would get to know him as an individual. He relished the idea that people would like him for who he was, and not for his family connections or for any money and influence they would think he might have.

It had been a tiring day, bailing water out from below deck, looking after the woman with her broken arm, and trying to keep food down, all of which had taken its toll.

Everyone settled down for the night, almost as soon as they had eaten dinner, except Leopold, who had decided to sleep on the deck of the George Shotten. The day had made him feel claustrophobic, and he desperately wanted to breathe in fresh air and have more time to himself.

He listened to the ocean, to its now much quieter rhythm, and to the waves lapping against the ship. The gentle rocking calmed him, and the sound of soft, muffled voices below deck faded as he nodded off to sleep.

# Nineteen

Perhaps it was due to the hardship of the journey, but when the George Shotten entered the waters of South Australia, Captain Bailey mistook Mount Schanck for Mount Lofty and the ship ran aground. After months of sailing, of endless bouts of sea sickness and injuries, they had now arrived, wrecked on a reef, some two-hundred nautical miles south of their destination.

The seas had been rough, making a rescue impossible, so for three days they remained wrecked on the reef. They were hungry and tired, forced to live off what little rations remained.

For every passenger on board, the ship was required to have fifty ounces of biscuits, six ounces of beef, eighteen ounces of pork, twenty-four ounces of preserved meat, forty-two ounces of flour, twenty-one ounces of oatmeal, eight ounces of raisins, six ounces of suet, three quarters of an ounce of peas, eight ounces of rice and eight ounces of potatoes.

Most of the substantial supplies were gone, and passengers were grateful to the cook for making delicious meals out of almost nothing, but now they just wanted to feel the dry land beneath their feet and to eat a proper meal and to sleep in a proper bed.

Finally, the boats came to rescue the passengers. As they headed off towards the Port River that would take them into Port

Adelaide, Leopold and those with him looked back to farewell the George Shotten and the remaining crew. They cast their eyes over the broken masts lying across the deck and the tangled sails flapping in the wind.

After days at sea, they could see the harbour ahead of them, marked by floating, wooden barrels anchored to their spot. Seagulls flapped above, squealing with delight at the fish swimming below. The mouth of the river was wide, but not deep enough for the steam boat to enter. It would be here, where to the left and right there were miles of swampy land and mangroves, that they would be transferred to smaller boats.

'If the tide is out, we'll have to tread through this muck and get in best ya can,' said the boatman.

The edge of the river was a boggy, sludge—sticky, and coloured brown with cloudy-blue water lapping over the top of it. Small crab holes and bubbles came up from out of the water, and unfamiliar water birds stood over the bubbles, waiting for a crustacean to appear, their long necks drooped in readiness to eat.

They made their way slowly down the river, with the oars smacking at the smooth waters, hoping to gain some leverage to push them along. In the distance, swallows skimmed the surface in search of insects.

The sun shone across the ripples, the light dancing across its surface and out to sea. On either side of the river, stood tall mangrove bushes, higher than the jetty that Leopold and the others were soon to walk along. The colour of the leaves reminded him of the camellia leaves he had seen in England, shiny and green. Even their almond-shaped leaves looked similar. The earth below was brown and slimy.

## The Second Son

Leopold studied the ground, trying to work out what type of birds had left their footprints behind in the moist clay. Small arrow shapes led to nearby bushes, and he wondered if their feet were designed like that, to leave signs for the other birds to follow. Larger, flat, wedged-shaped marks were scattered closer to the edge of the water, and he thought they belonged to the brown ducks swimming nearby.

Ahead of him, to the left, sat a pod of seagulls. Leopold watched as they huddled together, their feathers soft and fluffy against their bodies, the strong wind at times nearly rolling them into one another.

He cast his eyes further afield, to see if anything was familiar to him. Ahead and on either side were vast amounts of blue-green water disappearing into mangroves. Where he could see the sand, it was yellowish-brown in colour, and at the very edge, it had the same, sticky brown appearance.

Beyond the mangroves, he saw endless paddocks of grasses, about three feet high, in shades of soft creamy yellows. It reminded him of the colour of pampas grass. The plains were dotted with small green bushes, and there was an occasional tree in the distance.

The day was beautiful, with a temperature he thought of as similar to autumn in Germany. White clouds, hanging over the hills in the far distance, seemed to grow in size and height. He could hear unfamiliar bird-sounds coming from the mangroves, and he studied the bushes and the movement of the branches, hoping to get a glimpse of the birds hidden within. He followed the ripples of water made by the boats as they passed, causing the lower branches to move up and down and the fallen leaves to float gently into one another. It was all mysterious and intriguing for Leopold.

They continued in their small boats along the Port River, past various rusted-out ship wrecks, until they reached the wooden jetty at Dock One in Port Adelaide.

A doctor from Port Adelaide met the first boat from the George Shorten, greeting the passengers and assessing if any of them were ill. As both doctor and harbour pilot, it was his duty to quarantine anyone who might risk the lives of others with sicknesses, such as small pox or tuberculosis. If so, he would need to have them quarantined on Torrens Island.

'Since Eighteen fifty-five, when small pox was brought into the port on the Taymouth Castle, passengers have been under strict scrutiny,' said the doctor. 'But as no-one here on the George Shotten appears ill, you can all go ashore.'

Leopold noticed the man's accent was a little different to the English he had heard in England.

As the goods were unloaded, the doctor pointed out to sea and remarked, 'A huge gust of wind brought a king tide into the port and swept away two hundred feet of embankment a few years ago … we've had lots of problems down here … they used to call it Port Misery a few years back.'

None of the five passengers wanted to hear that. They tried to ignore his chatter and looked down the pier to their futures.

'Did you see that lighthouse you passed on the way in? Well, that was brought out from England, and it was only placed here at the beginning of this year. January the first, think it was.' The doctor pointed to the bulbous base of the lighthouse. 'Anyway, they had planned for a family to be able to live in the base of it, but they had no idea how hot it gets out here ... Stupid if you ask me. So no-one could ever live in it ... more likely to be boiled to death in the thing!'

Leopold thought the doctor was a very chatty historian, but a bit too friendly for his liking. The four months it took to get from Germany to Adelaide had made him grumpy, and all he was really interested in doing was finding Ernst, the family friend, and to lie down in a nice warm, comfortable bed that did not move.

Waiting at the end of the pier to greet them were men who had carted barrel-loads of fresh water from the River Torrens in Adelaide, seven or so miles from Port Adelaide. Fresh water was scarce at Port Adelaide, and the men knew they could make a profit from selling it to thirsty passengers who had been at sea for months. Once the men had unloaded the barrels, they offered their services to the passengers who were encouraged to put their luggage onto the cart and take the ride into Adelaide. However, Leopold and the other passengers from the George Shotten decided to take the train. The station was only a short walk along Divett Street to the Customs House on the corner of Commercial Road and St Vincent Street.

The docks were bustling with activity. Ships being loaded and unloaded, animals running loose, and people greeting their friends from the ships. Beyond the docks, the roads were quite empty, with a few buildings they assumed were either hotels or shops.

They continued to walk along the road, crossed over Commercial Road and then turned and walked towards the customs house. They soon discovered that the customs house also incorporated the police station, and the court house, which had only been completed some eight years earlier. 'Looks rather Italian looking,' thought Leopold.

They went inside, and once all the necessary paper work was completed, they made their way towards the railway station, walking past carts and across a wide, dirt road, then over red and black pavers to reach the waiting room. The building itself was made of hard stone with brick quoins, and had two verandas for shade from the sun.

'The first steam train of its kind in Adelaide was built by a London firm and sent to Adelaide by ship, in Eighteen fifty-six,' said the man behind the counter, filling in time while the passengers made up their minds how much they wanted to spend on their tickets.

'First class tickets will cost you two pence per mile; second class, one and a half pence a mile; and third class, one penny per mile,' he told them.

'Second class is a compromise. I think I'll take that, thank you,' said Leopold, who was too tired, and still trying to get his land-legs, to bother about making a decision. The other passengers did the same.

Leopold looked out through the station window to the steam train.

'The train's recently been fitted with larger tenders to increase the amount of coal and water capacity,' he heard the man behind the counter say. The train stood tall and shiny, with its green boiler barrel, black smoke box and chimney, and copper flare. It had a brass dome and safety valve, and a red plate. 'Quite a colourful train,' Leopold thought.

## The Second Son

They were helped onto the train; their trunks were stored in a separate carriage. The passengers were impressed to hear that the engine could pull up to twelve carriages at a time.

'They had to have new train tracks ya know. Yep. They had to put in wooden sleepers. Some idiot put 'em wrong way 'round when they first laid the tracks. They should have put 'em like a ladder. You know! Long one's going down and the shorter one's going across … like a ladder. Would ya believe they only put the long ones down? Didn't bother to put the short ones across the long pieces of track to keep it together, just laid the long tracks down almost side by side … just wide enough for the train to fit on. Huh! What a joke … Instead of looking like a ladder with steps going up, it just looked like two long lines, with nuthin' in the middle. The steam trains almost got bogged 'cause they were too heavy and pushed the tracks into the mud. What a laugh we had. Tried to tell 'em, but of course those know-it-alls wouldn't listen. Think we know nothing,' said the local.

'You probably *don't* know nothing, Jack,' said his mate, who was laughing out loud.

Once in the steam train, they travelled alongside Commercial Road to the centre of Adelaide. Leopold looked out at a more primitive world than the one he had left behind in Germany. 'It's certainly going to be both challenging and compelling,' he thought to himself. 'Wide open spaces, with buildings dotted here and there; the earth a different shade of brown, and lots of it.' He thought back to his trip from Berlin to Holzhausen, and the snow that had been falling onto the trees.

He put his hand against the glass as if to connect himself to this new place. It was warm.

# Twenty

Ernst had arranged to meet Leopold outside Government House on North Terrace. It was an easy landmark to find and not far from where the train would arrive when it came into Adelaide.

Ernst lived with his uncle Otto in Kent Town on the east side of the city. The middle to upper class Germans lived around the Walkerville and Kent Town areas; the lower-middle class and those with a trade lived in Chichester Gardens just north of Adelaide, where the first vines in South Australia were grown; and the poorer and more destitute Germans lived near Angas Street, south of the city.

It had been years since the two young men had seen each other; the last time was in Detmold, Germany.

Dressed in a smart suit with a matching vest and crisp white shirt, Ernst stood waiting for Leopold, anxious to see him again. He felt responsible for Leopold and hoped he had not met with any mishaps along the way or been held up passing through customs and sorting out his immigration papers. Ernst had been given a very brief outline as to why Leopold was coming to Adelaide to live, and had been asked if he could help to set him up initially, and to assist with his money matters.

Within minutes, Leopold's train arrived, and he stepped off the train with a big case and a coat over his shoulder. He was busy chatting to the others that had sailed on the George Shotten when he noticed Ernst waving to him.

'Ernst, over here!' he yelled. 'I have a heavy trunk over here ... any chance you could help?'

Ernst was pleased to see Leopold, but surprised that he had come second class. He walked quickly over to the train and embraced Leopold. 'Hello Leo.'

'Ernst ... Hello,' replied Leopold. He looked around to introduce the people that had travelled with him, only to see them rushing off to meet friends.

The porters handed down Leopold's trunk, and with Ernst's assistance the two young men lifted it and carried it in the direction of Ernst's small carriage. The driver, with a box seat at the front of his four-wheeled waggonette, flicked the reins, to encourage the horses to 'walk on'.

'I can't wait to step foot in a house and sleep in a soft bed that doesn't sway,' remarked Leopold. 'In fact, I still feel like I'm moving.'

'Yes, I know precisely what you mean. It's quite a journey.'

Within a few minutes, Ernst and Leopold were seated in the carriage and heading to Kent Town with their luggage tucked away in the back.

'Uncle Otto is at work and will be home shortly. He might not recognise you. It's been a very long time,' said Ernst.

'And I think I have only ever met him two or three times back in Germany,' said Leopold.

The young men arrived home to Kent Town, and Ernst showed Leopold to his upstairs room, which had a bathroom adjacent to it. A fresh white towel and matching face cloth were on the foot of the bed, along with a cake of home-made soap.

A book written in German sat on the polished, wooden table beside the bed, with a jug of water and a glass.

'Settle yourself, and come down when you're ready. Sophie has prepared *Schweinefleisch mit Kartoffeln, Erbsen und Karotten* for dinner,' said Ernst, who smiled at the look on Leopold's face. 'Sophie helps us with the house and cooking. Her family came out here a few years ago.'

When Ernst's uncle came home, the men sat around the table, ate, and drank wine that Leopold had brought from Germany. Leopold enjoyed the conversations, particularly reminiscing about home and family. As the evening went on, the laughter became louder. Leopold could not remember when he last felt so happy. They discussed the trust-fund set up by Ernst and another fellow named Meyer, and how much and how often Leopold could access the money that would come from his estate in Bremen.

'There is meant to be a thousand pounds here to start me off,' said Leopold. 'Couldn't imagine managing without it. I have only five pounds with me, and I had to spend some of that to buy a train ticket.'

Ernst and his uncle looked at each other. 'I'm afraid the money hasn't come through yet, and it might take some time before it does … we can help you out of course if you need it?' said Otto.

'I have travelled for four months, and endured wild storms at sea, and have left my family and friends and my home behind, to come to this! Surely Alhard had time to send me the money?' said a disappointed Leopold. 'I am starting to wonder who I can take at their word anymore.'

Otto put his hand on Leopold's shoulder. 'It's been a long journey for you, Leopold. Get a good night's sleep. Things often look different in the morning. Besides, you wouldn't be the first, nor the last to have a setback like this, Leopold.'

'Uncle Otto and I can help you any way we can,' said Ernst, trying to re-assure his friend. 'I'm sure Alhard has tried his best to make sure you have something here when you arrive.'

'Thank you, I appreciate the offer, but the only reason I have come this distance is to learn to stand on my own two feet, and I want to prove to my brother Alhard that I can,' said Leopold. 'You probably know already that they tried other ways for me to sort myself out. Even back when my father was alive. He tried to get me on the council in Austria, but I wasn't a citizen, so that was no good; and then to be with relatives in Holland, I think something to do with the army, but they didn't need anyone, and finally the Belgium army,' explained Leopold. 'You see, they exhausted every avenue, and I think it has exhausted me.'

'Go upstairs. Get a good night's sleep,' commanded Otto. 'We can chat in the morning.'

'I will need help to find work,' said Leopold.

'Let's talk more in the morning, Leopold,' said Ernst.

'I need some idea of what my possibilities are for work, or I'll toss and turn all night. It's in my nature to do so. Can you give me some idea?' Leopold asked. 'I work much better when I know what I need to do. As much as I hate to admit it, Papa was right. I need some direction in my life.'

'Well, to be honest with you, there aren't many jobs around the city at present, but there is work further out if you want to work in the copper mines or the country,' said Otto. 'But it's hard work! Pays between four to six shillings a day. Otherwise I know a surveyor who may need someone. Perhaps you could work with him as an assistant if you're interested. That can take some time to organise, though, because the paperwork has to be done in London through the Colonial Commission. But let's not talk about work at this stage. Let's wait and let you settle into your new life first.'

The men finished their meals, finished off the bottle of wine, before they finally said goodnight. 'I don't know if it is the wine or if I still have my sea legs, but I feel a little unstable,' commented Leopold as he continued up the stairs to bed.

*

The following week, Ernst introduced Leopold to his friends, and took him to the German Club, which was the place for the middle to upper class to meet and listen to music, dance and be entertained. It had a Liedertafel, which Leopold decided he would join at some point. He had always loved to sing, and he loved being around other Germans and listening to his mother tongue.

Leopold spoke further with Ernst and Otto about going up north to the mines, but he did not want to let others know of his intention.

'Is it true that there is a class distinction here?' asked Leopold. 'Among the Germans, I mean? From what I heard, before I left England, there certainly is amongst the English.'

'Unfortunately, or fortunately, whatever way you look at it, class distinction has come out here on the journey with everyone,' answered Ernst. 'Your education, the way you dress, and your formality, will be an indicator to people about your class, Leopold.'

'You might be best done by being proud of who you are and your family's history,' said Otto.

'I don't mean to be disrespectful, Otto, but I am a very long way from home … to be going off to a copper mine up north is certainly not what I expected to do. Nor, I imagine, what the family would expect of me,' said Leopold. 'Perhaps we could keep this as our secret?'

'Go up north, and when you get back we'll see what we can do to get you into the police force. They look for healthy young specimens like you with a military background,' said Otto.

Leopold found it interesting that, as a German, before he could buy a home or work for the government in Adelaide, he would have to prove his loyalty to Australia, which meant living in the same place for a year, as the Germans were largely untrusted by the British. Until the Germans had proven themselves, life would be more difficult than it would be for the British. At this stage in his life, it would be impossible for Leopold to buy a home, even if the thousand pounds had been in the bank when he arrived.

Ernst introduced Leopold to quite a number of influential people in Adelaide, who were also his friends. Leopold met the Austro-Hungarian Consul, Adolf von Treuer; the Barr-Smiths and the Elders, who as brother-in-law's had gone into business together; the Governor, Right Honourable Sir James Fergusson; the von Bertouchs and von Doussas; George Strickland Kingston, Colonel William Light's deputy; and a number of others who would become his friends, too.

Leopold could see that his life would always be a contradiction to the life he should be living. Here he was in Adelaide, an aristocrat from royalty, with very little money, no home of his own, and no family to support him.

Leopold found the city of Adelaide easy to get around and quite appealing, with its symmetrical layout. Roads were parallel to each other and criss-crossed at regular intervals. He loved to walk along the River Torrens, which was originally a series of smaller waterways specifically engineered to form the shape of the River Torrens. On the western side of the river stood the government buildings, consisting of the Land and Survey Department Leopold had heard George Kingston talk about.

Ernst had told Leopold that the farmers had been keen to have a market built in the city, next to Victoria Square, and the council had promised them it would be finished by the end of the year. For the time being, the growers set up their own market place, alongside the government buildings under the gum and willow trees next to the River Torrens.

Leopold liked to follow the river to Andrew Street, which ran off Morphett Road, and gaze at the first two portable wooden homes that had been brought out on the first ship to Adelaide. He was amazed at the fortitude of the people that set off to explore this new country of Australia. From there he would walk along North Terrace and past Government House toward the museum, the police station, and the public hospital, hoping he would never get sick, as he hated being ill. He prided himself on being strong and healthy. His Prussian military training had taught him to value strength above pride.

On cooler days, he enjoyed walking to the Botanic Gardens, situated on a hundred and twenty-five hectares of land just outside the city. He would bring a sandwich with him, and have a cool drink from a fountain there. When he had finished eating, he would lie down on the lawn and look up at the sky, just as he did as a child. He would watch the white clouds float by, imagining how he would paint them at a later date, when he could afford brushes and paints. When he painted, he preferred water-colours, as they were easy to use and dried quickly.

Chichester Gardens was a little further on from the Botanic Gardens, and he would often walk there to chat with the German farmers about their grapes and their vegetable gardens. It was there that the first vineyard in South Australia was planted.

Leopold loved the little cottages of North Adelaide, and the walk along Melbourne Street to Hackney Road where the council had planted hundreds of olive trees. Ernst had told him that olive trees had been grown in the Adelaide parklands since Eighteen thirty-seven, and that the first six olive trees were brought on the HMS Buffalo in Eighteen thirty-six by Governor John Hindmarsh. Hindmarsh had planted them in his garden. And not long before Leopold came to Adelaide, more olive trees were planted around the Old Adelaide Goal to provide employment for the 'light-sentenced' prisoners, and to generate some income.

By the time Leopold had to travel north by train to work on the copper mines, he was beginning to feel comfortable with his new surroundings. On the day, Ernst helped him with his bag and his few provisions, and dropped him off at the train station ready for his next adventure.

'Bye Ernst. See you in a few months. And when I get back, I'm sure you'll have something organised for me.' Leopold waved goodbye.

# Twenty-One

Leopold was waiting to catch the train to the Kapunda copper mines, and the sting of the sun on his unprotected skin was a new sensation. It burned, and felt just as hot as when he had boiled the kettle for a cup of tea and the water had bubbled up and splattered onto the back of his hand.

He stepped into the train, sat back and listened to the clickety-clack as the train headed north towards Kapunda via Gawler, an hour or so from Adelaide.

'Is it ya first time up here?' asked the middle-aged Irishman sitting next to Leopold.

'Yes, and hopefully my last,' answered Leopold, who was looking out to the nothingness of the countryside.

'And why would a youngen like yourself be coming up here, just to want to be going back?' the Irishman asked. 'If ya don't mind an old fella asking ya dat.'

Leopold looked at the Irishman and studied his face. He had small features, with flat, blue, beady eyes, high cheekbones, and cheeks that looked like the man had sucked them in. His lips were thin but were ever smiling, and his face was framed with raven, black hair. 'A pleasant, friendly face,' thought Leopold, 'and easy to talk to. I like that.'

Before Leopold had much of a chance to answer, the Irishman

continued speaking.

'I know … I've been told a tousand times, I ask too many questions … but If ya don't mind, I'd like ta know.'

Leopold was amused by both his questions and his accent.

'Well, I was supposed to have some money here when I arrived, but it hasn't shown up in the bank yet, so I have to look for work straight away, and this was the best thing going. Friends offered to help, but that would defeat the whole purpose of my spending four months at sea only to have someone else look after me … so I'm going to Kapunda,' answered Leopold. 'What's it like up there?'

'Well, now, what can I be telling ya … let me see. Well, did ya know dat de copper was discovered in de Eighteen forties, and dat dey built dis very railway line specially for it. First of its kind, da copper mining … Open cut now … Not much ta see. Olive and pepper trees and da usual wildlife … used da be a lot more of da trees but dey cut em down for firewood,' said the Irishman.

'Me name is Mick … and what'd be ya name lad?' asked Mick.

'Leopold.'

'And what'd be ya age? I'm tinking about twenty-five,' said Mick.

'Twenty-two. No … I had another birthday on the ship. So, twenty-three. I had my first Christmas and my first birthday at sea aboard that ship coming here,' said Leopold, who was surprised that he had forgotten to tell anyone on board the George Shotten about his birthday.

'One of the men dat found de copper is a fella called Dutton, and he has dis big place called "Anlaby",' said Mick.

'Beautiful it is … built demselves an English garden … acres of it. Ya can imagine, here, where noting grows, and der da are, with dis beautiful garden. Home to the oldest Merino sheep farming in the country.'

'Must be beautiful, out here,' replied Leopold.

'Dat it is. Da fella Dutton sold his share. Got tirty tousand pounds, or was it more dan dat? Sold it he did, not four years in.'

'Have ya heard about da ghosts?' continued Mick, looking to see Leopold's reaction. 'I tink dat's a reasonable question to ask ya.'

Leopold shook his head.

'Well now … where to begin. Der's a few stories, all about da dead … mostly little'uns. Before da open-cut mines, dey used da children. Not dat many went down da mines. Dey did da picking. Sometimes, if da mine shaft was too tin, not wide enough for da men, da send da children down. Twas notting for da Cornish. Deyd be doing mining for generations. If dey lived long enough of course.

'One o da little mites, fell down a shaft, a deep shaft and dey couldn't get him out, and he died down dere. Dey has tossed him down some candles and matches to light it, but da draft kept blowing it out. Dey sang to him dey did, just ta keep his spirits up. All by himself, he was. Da men reckon dey can still hear him crying out, 'specially at night, or when it's cold and dark from the weather dat dey get up here sometimes … bit like a dog howling,' explained Mick.

Leopold listened intently. 'The Irish are such good story tellers, but I wonder how much is truth and how much is tale,' he thought. 'If it's true, what a horrible ending for a young boy.'

'Another little'un drowned in the pump house, and men have lost der lives. Da miners will tell ya, dat dey have felt someone slap der face, and seen stones flung about … and picks moving wit no-one der. Poor little'uns trapped in Purgatory.'

Mick paused for a moment. 'I don't tink ya believe me?' said Mick. 'Oh well, we Irish are used to dat ... but I'm a God-fearing catholic, make no mistake bout dat, so I aint in the habit of lying. Ya can read about the little'uns in da old newspapers if ya like.'

'I'm more fascinated than disbelieving,' answered Leopold.

'Some kind of "spectral illusion"!' thought Leopold. 'Fascinating how people are so strong in their beliefs about ghosts ... don't say anything, Leopold. It doesn't matter what he thinks ... you don't know him well enough to discuss it.'

'Makes ya wonder dough? What happens to ya when ya die?'

The train continued through the dry countryside to Kapunda.

Leopold wanted to ignore the conversation about whether or not people went to hell or heaven and talk a little bit more about the mines. 'Do you know much about the history of the mines?' asked Leopold, trying not to seem too rude that he had no intention in pursuing the conversation about ghosts.

The Irishman was keen to chat, whether it was about ghosts or mines.

'Da mines were discovered in Eighteen forty-two, but when da gold rush was on, most of da men left in da hope of makin' demselves a fortune ... so da mines closed down and didn't open 'til Eighteen fifty-five ... few years after dat, da rains came, and ... well, not just rain but serious kinda rain dat collapsed da very foundations of da draft engine and dey had to put it somewhere else, so it wouldn't happen again,' said Mick.

'Was anyone killed?' asked Leopold, having second thoughts about what to expect when he got there to mine the green stone.

'Don't tink so ... not den anyways. I tink it was a Scotty company dat changed it a bit ... put in someting called a

Henderson someting ... someting ta do with cooking da copper ... or was it roasting it? Yes ... dat's it ... dey roasted da copper ting wid da salt to make someting else?' said Mick, trying to explain.

'Sounds complicated,' said Leopold.

'It's *me* dat's complicated! Let me tink ... dey roasted da low-grade copper sulphur wid salt to make .... copper chloride ... I tink I need a drink after dat ... a good strong Guinness,' said Mick, pleased with himself.

The men chatted and laughed about coming to a new land and learning to understand the English accent, and settling into Adelaide. When the train lurched to a stop at Kapunda Station, the men hoped off, with their bags in hand.

The land was flatter than Leopold expected it to be, and from the train station he could see the smokestack and a few other buildings.

'Ya can see what I mean, not a lot for da eye ta see. Got rid a so many of da trees for firewood ... dat's how cold it can get here,' said Mick.

Off to the east and west of the mine, Leopold could see the open cut mines, like big scars, scratched out of the earth. 'It looks so ugly and desolate, but I suppose people will do anything to make money,' thought Leopold.

'Can ya see in da distance? Dat's da Engine House, and opposite dat, is da Henderson Plant ... up der on da hilltop,' said Mick. 'We sleep in miner's cottages ... on Morton Street, I tink it is? Just over der. Don't know if you'll be der wit us or put over at da Mugg Street cottages. A big tall fella like yaself might have ta bend over a bit, so ya don't go hitting ya noggin.'

'Ma noggin?' questioned Leopold.

'Yes,' said Mick and tapped his head with a closed fist gently, 'yes, ya noggin ... ya head.'

Leopold smiled and followed him to the cottages.

'And can ya see up der, da double storey house, dat would be the engineers' house.'

'What do you do entertain yourselves on the weekend or after work at night?' asked an innocent Leopold.

'Entertain yaself ... entertain yaself? What did ya do before ya came to dis country, lad?' asked Mick.

Leopold realised he had asked a ridiculously embarrassing question, which showed he had no idea of working hard.

'I worked on a farm, with my father and brother,' Leopold replied.

'Bit of a fancy kinda farm was it? Up here, ya work before da sun comes up, and ya got ta bed after it's gone done ... and den ya do it again on da weekend, and if ya lucky, ya get a day off,' replied Mick. 'Let's have a look at ya hands.'

Leopold showed him his beautifully manicured nails and clean, unscarred hands.

'Just wat I tort. Ya would'na known a hard day's work ...'

'At least I'm prepared to find out and do my bit to make some money for myself, and not get hand-outs. That has to be a good thing in your mind?' said Leopold, looking for support.

'I, dat ya do ... I admire a man, a gentleman I tink, dat's prepared ta give it a go. It won't be easy for ya, so I'll do wat I can ta help, but ya got a do ya own digging,' said Mick.

'Thank you,' said Leopold.

'As long as ya not expecting it ta be easy. You'll have blisters on ya, blisters when ya start, and ya'll get callouses for sure, but it'll earn money, and dat's what ya come for,' prompted Mick.

# Twenty-Two

The following morning, Leopold woke to a cold autumn day, and, for a moment, he thought he was back home at Holzhausen. He had dreamt he and his brother Siegfried were out riding their horses in the forest, up to the tower that borders the next village of Nieheim. The rest of his family were already there, having a picnic, and Rudolf and his father were playing with Bruno.

'Leopold,' he heard someone shout. He got off his horse, and went over to his mother and gave her a hug. He could hear his brothers and sisters laughing, but he could not see them.

'Leopold!' He could hear someone calling out his name again. The shouting disturbed him. He tossed and turned in bed.

The door of the Mugg Street miners' cottages where Leopold was sleeping, made a scraping sound on the cement floor as it opened, and a chink of light came in to the room and flashed across Leopold's face. As a reflex, Leopold's eyes closed tightly.

'Leopold!' the stranger shouted again.

Leopold opened his eyes, not sure where he was. The voice he had heard calling out his name in his dream seemed to be the same voice he could hear calling him now, only he could not work out what direction it was coming from. In front of him was an unfamiliar, half-opened wooden door, and walls covered in plaster, and a small window that looked out over a barren landscape. He got out of bed and walked towards the door to check where he was. 'Agh!' he exclaimed as he bashed his head on the low door frame. He rubbed his forehead with his hand and then looked at it, expecting to see blood.

As he stepped outside, he heard the stranger's voice again, 'Leopold, I've been banging on your door for ages. We need to get down to the mines soon.'

Leopold was feeling confused.

'Are you alright, young fella?' asked the stranger.

'I heard a banging noise in my dreams, but it must have been you. Just for a moment I thought I was back home,' Leopold answered, fully aware now of the reality of his current location.

'Well. None of us are home, but you'll learn to make the best of it. They call me Jack,' said the stranger, holding out his hand for Leopold to shake. 'And it's my job to show you around today.' His was a firm grip that squeezed Leopold's fingers just a little tighter than Leopold would have liked.

Leopold looked down at Jack's small, square, stained hand, which had callouses across the palm just below the fingers. Along the side of the hand, the skin was cracked and dirty.

'Grab yourself some breakfast. Here's some milk from the miner's shop. My wife put some of the basics in the cupboard for you; porridge, some bread and a pat of butter. Utensils are probably in the drawer,' instructed Jack.

Leopold took the milk bottle.

'Did you find your mining clothes, shoes and socks on the table?' asked Jack, without waiting for an answer. 'Make sure you wear thick socks. Even if you get hot, it's important you look after your feet, or you won't have any work. Up here, you need good feet. If they get wet, crumble some of the white stone, and rub it on your feet to dry them out.' Jack pointed to the endless supply of chalk stone.

'I'll wait out here for you,' continued Jack. 'I can show you where you can walk so you don't go falling down any mine shafts.' He smiled, enjoying seeing the fear on the new miners' faces when he told them that. 'We don't have to walk far,' he said pointing to the tall mine chimney. 'Bit over a hundred yards away I reckon. Can't miss it. That'll be your landmark and the meeting place if anything goes wrong, or if you need to know what you're doing.'

Less than twenty minutes later Leopold and Jack were walking along the dirt path and past the peppercorn trees to the chimney. Approximately two hundred miners and pickers gathered around.

'What are these young boys doing here?' asked Leopold, surprised.

'Here to make money just like the rest of us,' answered Jack.

'But they're only children. Surely they should be at school!' said Leopold, horrified that they were having to work like men. Everything Mick had told him on the train on the way to Kapunda suddenly seemed to resonate with him.

'Been easier for the boys now it's open cut,' said Jack. 'Their families can do with extra money and they can earn between threepence and sixpence a day, but they have to go to school for four hours a day, or they can't work here. They're keen, and that's what you want. Most of them are twelve, so plenty old enough to pull their weight. The eight, nine, ten, eleven-year-olds can't keep up with school work and mining, so mostly the older boys work.

'If they're earning up to sixpence a day, what do *we* earn then? Someone in Adelaide said the job paid five to six shillings a day.'

Leopold was dismayed at the thought that he had travelled this far north to earn a pittance.

'We get a percentage of how much copper we find. So, you don't want to waste your time. And don't forget to weigh it before it goes to the boys, or you won't get paid. You can work between eight and twelve hours a day, six days a week, so make it count for something,' said Jack. 'When they hand the tools out, see if you can get a Jack ass or a poll-pick. A strong, tall, young man like you can probably pick out quite a bit of copper with one of those tools.'

'What's the difference between them?' asked Leopold.

Jack laughed at him. 'Not much, just got different shaped ends on them. They're heavy tools for breaking the rocks with force, or you can dig into the stope real well, I reckon.'

'What's the stope?' asked Leopold.

'It's the wall where they've already dug it out. Given you a head start, they have,' answered Jack. 'We get to dig out the copper and rocks, and then we put it on the kibble.' Jack could see by Leopold's frown, that he was understanding very little of what he was saying. 'Over there. That big, iron bucket. That's a kibble. We dig out the rock and copper, and put it on the kibble, and from there it goes off to be crushed. And before that can get done, the pickers, the boys we saw before, well, they got to break the rocks in smaller pieces before it gets crushed.'

'Sounds like a long and hard process,' remarked Leopold.

'Ours is the easy job, if you don't mind getting blisters and ending up with hands like mine,' said Jack.

'Then the fellas have got to do the jigging,' said Jack. 'I know, you don't know what I'm telling you, do you, young fella?' He paused for a breath.

Leopold shook his head, as if to say, no, I have no idea.

'Jigging is where they separate the muck from the copper. The broken pieces are put in a big, sieve in a wooden box, and then that wooden box gets dipped down into water, which is in another box underneath. There's a couple of fellas that put the broken bits in, and then they use a lever attached to the box so they can jiggle the sieve, and then every so often they lower it into the water. Finally, the copper's the only thing left in the sieve.'

'Not sure that I'm taking all of this in, and what order it's in?' said Leopold.

'Don't worry. You'll be here long enough to know it off the top of your head,' said Jack.

'Off the top of your head?' asked Leopold, confused.

'It's a saying we have here. After about a week doing the same thing, you'll know it so well, you'll know it without thinking about it. So, you'll know it off the top of your head,' explained Jack.

'I understand, I think,' said Leopold. 'And what happens next?'

'Most of the Germans up here are the ones cutting the trees down, to burn, so they can get charcoal for the smelters.'

'So that's what happens next? It goes to the smelters?' asked Leopold.

'Yeh. You know that odd, pungent smell in the air at times?' said Jack.

'Hadn't noticed it,' answered Leopold.

'You will. It's sulphuric acid. They use it to leech out the copper. Anyway, whatever they do to it, and it changes at times, once all the smelting's done, and they're just left with copper, they melt it down into ingots to make it easier to transport. That's when the Italians, well, usually the Italians, pack it onto the carts and get their bullocks to cart it to Port Adelaide. Takes them six days in all to get there and back again.'

Leopold looked down from the mine chimney to see where he would be working. It was a scarred landscape that he saw, eroded by all the digging and the weather. A lot of the open-cut areas had cracks that had opened up, and had grown wider as the men dug into it, and the colours, soft green from the copper, and pink, seemed to seep out of the cracks, and run down the sides of the cracks, a bit like a suppurating wound. There were pock marks in the ground, dark holes where the mine shafts had been dug, anything up to hundreds of feet deep.

The ground where the men walked to get to the stope was sticky, and in some places around the edges of the lake, where it had dried up from not enough rain, the clay was cracked and peeling up from the edges. In the middle of the cracks, there seemed to be a greenish, white lake. 'Such a beautiful colour amongst the white, barren landscape,' Leopold thought. The water in the lakes had been made when the miners dug to eighty feet and hit the water table, and now it seeped out.

'Here's your helmet,' said Jack, laughing at Leopold's surprised look when he saw the papier-maché hat. 'Won't do much to protect you from falling rocks, but we got to wear them.'

Leopold plonked it on his head and then tapped it with his knuckles. 'Glad it's open-cut mines, and not underground,' he said.

'Only thing they were good for was to hold the candles, when the miners were deep down in the mines. They'd put a bit of wet clay on the front of the helmet, and then stick a candle in it,' said Jack. 'And if you were lucky, they'd light it for you.'

'Let's go over and get the pick, and I'll get a gad sedge to help break the rocks. Come on, let's go,' said Jack, as they walked past Bagot open-cut mine where the Italians worked, and down to the main open-cut mine.

'I can see you've never done much with your hands before. I've never seen such hands. Looks like the hands of a fancy man,' said Jack.

Leopold had no idea what he meant by a fancy man, but he knew enough to know that if someone had to point something out to you, and you had no idea what it meant, you needed to attend to it. He put his hands in his pockets to try and hide them.

'Don't be ashamed of them. Besides, they won't look like that for much longer. Here you'd better take this.' Jack handed Leopold a Cornish pasty.

'I'm starting to think I haven't ever really done any hard work before,' Leopold replied.

'Tuck this pasty under your shirt. Helps to keep it warm for longer, and the ants and other creatures can't get to it. We get a break about half past ten, and believe me you'll be hungry. See the bits at the end?' said Jack. 'That's to hold it while you eat it. Then you toss it into the shafts for the knockers. The cousin Jacks brought the Cornish pasties with them when they came here. Well, the recipe they brought with them.'

'Cousin Jacks? Are you referring to yourself?' asked Leopold.

'Some call me Cousin Jack, even though I'm not Cornish,' replied Jack.

Leopold was still unsure what Jack was talking about, and frowned.

'The Cornish came out here to Australia to use their mining

skills. They were running out of work back home, so ended up going to places like Canada, America, and out here, and once they'd been working here awhile, they kept asking for jobs for their cousins. Most of them were called Jack. So most of the Cornish are called Cousin Jacks or Jennys.'

Leopold nodded his head to let Jack know he understood, and then asked. 'Did they bring their children out here to work the mines as well?'

'They did. Generations of miners have worked alongside their children, so it was nothing new.'

'But they don't work down the shafts now, do they?' asked Leopold.

'You're right, young fella. They don't. Quick off the mark, aren't you? I'm going to enjoy working alongside you, Leopold,' said Jack, sarcastically. 'Now, back to the knockers I started telling you about. The knockers are the spirits that live in the shafts; they're not boys. Sometimes, when you're working, you can hear them. Sounds just like someone's knocking.'

'I think that bump on the head earlier has rendered me silly,' said Leopold. 'I'm not able to follow what you're saying.'

Leopold listened intently. 'When the Cornish miners were digging away in the mine shafts, and they heard a knocking sound, they'd come up from underground real fast. Saved their lives. They reckon the knockers know when the shaft is about to collapse,' explained Jack. 'In exchange for their safety, they believed that if they threw the ends of the pasties in to them, the knockers would keep them safe.'

'What are the pasties made of? I haven't tasted one before,' asked Leopold.

'You haven't heard a thing I said, have you, young fella?' said Jack. 'You better pay attention. If you don't, it might cost you your life one day. Then you won't be too happy, will ya?'

'I've been told before that I don't listen. Not necessarily that I don't listen, but that I listen to the wrong people,' said Leopold.

'That's your business, young fella. Probably best to keep it to yourself. Now, you were asking me about the pasties. Potatoes, turnips mostly with a bit of meat. Sometimes, just whatever you have in the kitchen. Sometimes the women who sell them put cooked apple at one end with a little piece of pastry between the vegetables and the meat, so it doesn't get mixed together.'

Leopold popped the Cornish pasty inside his shirt.

'Here, take this. I always keep strips of old shirts of mine in my back pocket. Wrap some of them around your hands, otherwise your hands will have blisters on your blisters,' said Jack. 'And break a bit of this off,' he continued, as he gave Leopold a piece of Aloe Vera plant, 'and wipe it on your hands first, so the pieces of ripped sheet stick to it. When you've done that, I'll knot the strips on the back of your hands. If you don't do that, you'll have a terrible lot of pain. Not tomorrow or even the day after, but for weeks.'

'I'm sure I will,' said Leopold.

'Still, better than being stuck down one of those mine shafts, like poor old Sam Rule a few years back.

'Yep. Poor old Sam Rule met his end down one of the shafts. I'd only been working here a bit, when it happened,' said Jack.

'What!' said Leopold.

'The shaft collapsed, and Sam was down there for eight hours. Williams forced himself under a large rock to try and get to him.

He went head first, so he could see where Sam was, but the hole wasn't wide enough to get Sam out, so Williams had to squeeze himself out, scrambling backwards like a crab. Sam was in a terrible condition, bleeding from his mouth and his nose, and everyone thought he'd die before they dug the shaft out wider. They eventually dragged him out by the hair. It was all they could get a hold of,' said Jack. 'Doctor Blood came out to check him out, but the poor fella died a few hours later.'

'I don't think I could go down in the shafts. I'd feel like I couldn't get out. I think I'd struggle with that,' said Leopold.

'It depends on how much you need money, and how many mouths you got to feed. We don't always get a choice,' said Jack. 'Let's get digging, and make a bit of money. We can't all afford boots like you, young fella. Not that I'm asking. None of me business. You just got to muck in and do your share. Don't let anyone down, or you won't have many friends,' said Jack in a more serious tone of voice.

'You're expected to be like everyone else here. Work hard, six days a week, at least eight hours a day. Help each other out, get your food from the miners' store, buy your vegies from the wives of the miners that cart their goods in every week, go to church on Sundays, and if you're lucky, watch an Australian football game.'

'When I came up on the train, I met an Irishman by the name of Mick. Do you know him?' asked Leopold.

'You get to know everyone up here, once you been here awhile,' answered Jack. 'There are a few fellas named Mick.'

'We talked about working together up here.'

'Well, they have us working in different parts of the mine. There's about five open cuts. The Italians like to work together, so they're in the Bagot open cut. They chatter in their language all the time, and like their own food. Just how it is. Most of the miners are Cornish so they're all over the mines. The Welsh work mostly up at the smelters.'

'Got a good humour, that Mick,' said Leopold. 'Made me laugh a few times.'

'When you start, you get to work with the Cornish mostly, to get to know how it's done,' said Jack. 'No doubt you'll see Mick around the miners' store or the miners' square … mostly where the miners go. We're not quite the intellectuals they want in the town.' Jack laughed. 'Heard one of the women wants trees leading up the main road, and an institute for reading. Don't think they'd even know our names. Or what we do. We look the same to them. Dirty and covered in muck. We're not important to them. You better get used to it.'

# Twenty-Three

On the way in to meet George Strickland Kingston, architect and deputy surveyor to Colonel William Light, Leopold thought back to his time spent in the mines at Kapunda. He had stayed a little longer than planned, so he was pleased to be back in Adelaide.

He looked down at his rough, scratchy hands, and thought about what Jack had said to him about people not always being able to have choices, like the miners who were desperate for money, and the story of Sam Rule being buried underground for eight hours.

Something about his experience in the mines changed him. He had no idea what it was about him that was different, but he could sense that his life would never be the same again. He knew one thing for certain: in Australia, he was alone, and whatever happened to him, he would have to look after himself.

When he had first arrived in Adelaide, Leopold had met Kingston through friends. Kingston, an Irishman from County Cork, had come out to Australia quite early on and had been engaged with surveying the new colony. He was also a member of the Volunteer Rifle Corps and shared an interest with Leopold in rifle shooting. Now, Leopold was to meet up with Kingston at Kingston's family home, named Marino.

When Kingston answered the front door, he saw Leopold standing on the front verandah looking out to the ocean.

'Such a beautiful view,' said Leopold. 'Standing up here, looking out to sea … It could make you forget any problems you had.'

Kingston put his hand on Leopold's shoulder in a fatherly manner. It was a firm pat, that got Leopold's attention. 'I decided to act as your advocate, Leopold, to get you into the Police Department here … What with your military history in the Prussian War, and your keen shooting ability and reputation as a good horseman. It seemed a perfect marriage of interests and skills.'

Leopold was just about to thank Kingston, when Kingston continued, 'Sent it off I have, to England … the documents of course, for verification and approval, and they've come back, without a hitch, as they say.'

'Thank you,' replied Leopold, pleased that he had begun discussions with Kingston before he had left for the copper mines.

'What happens now?' he asked.

'Well, let's see. From what I've been told … for the first month or so, you'll wear a suit and attend the courts for an hour each morning, so that you can learn to present to the courts and learn procedures … and in the afternoons, you and the other recruits will be instructed on the duties of a constable. Once that month or so is up, the inspector of Metropolitan Police will discuss your suitability to enter the force.'

'I should be able to manage that,' said Leopold, smiling to himself.

'You'll be on probation, don't forget, and sent to live in the barracks on North Terrace,' explained Kingston.

※

Leopold's first day and all the other days that were to come for that first month or so, started early in the morning, on most occasions even before the sun came up. He and the other police officers would line up at six, on the dot, with the exception of winter when they could sleep in an hour longer.

Parade started at ten o'clock, when the recruits would hone their skills in riding and marching, and by one o'clock, if the sergeant thought the men had worked hard enough, they could go and eat their main meal for the day.

'Right then, recruits, after you've mucked out those stables and mucked them out properly, you'll be given half an hour to tidy your rooms for inspections,' said the sergeant.

If the young men, including Leopold, intended being considered for the police force, they would need to clean their rooms and clean them well. 'A tidy room shows a tidy, disciplined mind and a disciplined officer,' they had heard the sergeant say on more than one occasion.

'As of this year, police hats will now have a silver number attached to them, to identify each of you. You will be known by that number, and if there are any reports by the public that a police officer has been out of line, they will be able to identify you by your number. So remember that!' shouted the sergeant.

'Police weapons of choice are Smith and Weston revolver-carbines, so make sure you are armed. As recruits, you will be expected to take turns to go out into the suburbs to check on the local larrikins, attend to any family disputes, and, occasionally, that might mean that you do not return to the barracks until the following morning. So remember your weapons. Some of the folk here have no respect for the police.'

Mid-way through his training, Leopold wrote to his brother,

*Dear Alhard,*

*It has occurred to me that the Government of Australia may be interested to purchase the German Mauser rifles to use as their weapons, and wondered if you and I might go into business together to fill the orders?*

*The new Calvary carbine Mauser they are working on now may be perfect. What do you think, Alhard? Let me know.*

However, no answer from his brother was forthcoming.

At the end of each day, after being physically and mentally present of mind, Leopold looked forward to spending time on his own in his room, reading a book of poetry, *Bush Ballads and Galloping Rhymes* by Adam Lindsay Gordon, in particular, the first stanza of DE TE.

*A burning glass of burnished brass,*
*The calm sea caught the noontide rays,*
*And sunny slopes of golden grass*
*And wastes of weed-flower seem to blaze.*
*Beyond the shining silver-greys,*
*Beyond the shades of denser bloom,*
*The sky-line girt with glowing haze*

*The farthest, faintest forest gloom,*
*And the everlasting hills that loom.*

It was more than a poem to Leopold: it was a connection to the story, and to the writer his uncle, Adolf Ludwig, had told him about; it spoke of his home, and the crops, and of the forest. It helped him to bring to mind the pictures in his head of walking through the beech forest at Holzhausen, and of the light at the end of the day that shone over the hill through the trees from Erwitzen.

*Beyond the shades of denser bloom,*
*The sky-line girt with glowing haze*
*The farthest, faintest forest gloom,*
*And the everlasting hills that loom.*

Leopold repeated this to himself before he went off to sleep.

# Twenty-Four

Leopold was unsure if the past two and a half years in the police force had prepared him sufficiently for the work he and the other officers—John Davis, George Tasker, Charles Muller, Herbert Ring and Henry Dann—were to embark on in the Northern Territory.

Like his fellow police officers, Leopold had signed a government contract to serve a two-year period, with the expectation that each officer would bring two of his own horses, their bridles and saddles, and leather soap to prevent the leather from cracking, keeping the saddles up to police standard. The officers would be responsible for the health of their horses and were to pay for the horses' food, which would be reimbursed to them monthly.

According to Leopold's superiors, the police troopers Fitzgerald, Keppler, and Jones, who formed part of the original contingency of eight police officers to be sent to Palmerston in the Northern Territory with Inspector Paul Foelsche, had resigned their positions in order to turn their attention to gold pursuits.

Gold fever was taking hold of everyone's imagination, and the Adelaide train station had been ill-prepared to manage such an excited crowd, all hoping to buy a ticket to Port Adelaide and then tickets to go up north by steam boat to find gold.

The unexpected crowds made Leopold grateful that the police department had secured tickets for him and his fellow police officers in advance.

'I can't remember seeing so many people here before,' said Leopold. 'Not even on public holidays.'

'We'll have to edge our way through the crowd, if we're to catch the train at two o'clock,' said Tasker.

Finally, they managed to squeeze into the train, where they could take a seat for the journey to Port Adelaide docks. The train was crowded and hot, and when they arrived at the docks, they were pleased to get off the train and be out in the fresh air again.

The Gothenburg steamship was bustling with activity. There were people everywhere, watching the preparations and activities involved with getting the Gothenburg ready to leave port.

Leopold watched as his two horses were the first to be loaded onto the steamship by means of a big leather belt that went under each horse's girth and was attached with ropes and a pulley system to lift and pull them on deck. The deck engine strained a little when one of the horses started to thrash around, flaring its nostrils and snorting. The noise of the machine, combined with being lifted into the air, had made the horse panic and struggle to get free.

One by one the police officers' horses were lifted into the standing stalls, which the deck hands hoped would stand up to the journey.

'Poor things. Most of 'em probably won't make it,' said a voice from behind Leopold. 'Up to thirteen of 'em fell overboard last trip we did, and got drowned.'

Leopold looked around to see one of the crew, standing with his hands in his pockets, watching the horses being loaded onto the ship. The man never looked at Leopold, but continued his chatter.

'Yep. The weather was very rough it were ... horses lost their footing ... knocked down them petitions, broke 'em something shockin' and over they went ... fell overboard. Yep ... thirteen of 'em, dead before they even had a chance.'

Leopold was worried about his horses and hoped that they would make the journey to Port Darwin without any problems.

He continued listening to the man, not sure if he wanted an answer.

'Still, probably better off dead anyway. Don't much matter. Up there in the heat! Crocodiles like 'em as food and then 'o course, there's the quicksand ... might as well drown along the way ... Poor beggars,' he said, and wandered off towards Levi Wharf, which lay opposite McLaren Wharf.

Levi Wharf had been built in the old style, with its main piles and sheet piles to the front, filled with stones, sand, clay and silt to make them more stable. Leopold had heard from one of the other police officers that at low tide the ships at the wharf lay on the mud and could not be loaded until high tide.

The South Australian Company Basin where the Gothenburg was berthed was just to the right of Levi Wharf, and a little beyond was McLaren Wharf. Two other ships, the Pekina and the Coonatto, were also berthed near the Gothenburg.

Leopold looked at his surroundings, noticing the minor advances that had been made since he first saw it when he arrived in South Australia. To his extreme left, he could see Hall Store, and Sawtell's standing next to Charles Cowner, the druggist, and then Ford's Hotel above Peake's corner shop on Nelson Street. In the middle, there was George Scarfe's store, and further on he could see Swing Bridge at the entrance to the basin.

Leopold still found it difficult to come to terms with how open the Australian countryside was, particularly at Port Adelaide. It felt as though he could see to the other side of the world, without interruption. 'If only I could,' he thought.

The dust from little pieces of hay blew into his eyes and made his eyes water.

'Nothin' to cry 'bout. Them horses wouldana felt a thing,' said the crew man.

'Pardon?' asked Leopold.

'Them horses goin' overboard. Not worth upsettin yaself,' the crew man replied.

Leopold decided not to explain himself.

'Been mighty wet this year,' said the crew man, stepping closer to Leopold.

'Yes,' replied Leopold.

'Wettest year was a few years back ... Eighteen fifty-one, and Eighteen sixty-nine was the driest,' said the crew man, hoping that Leopold would chat with him.

'The very year I arrived in Australia ... Eighteen sixty-nine. I had no idea it could be this hot and dry here. Not like Germany, where it rains a lot of the time, and where it snows,' said Leopold, remembering his first year in Adelaide.

'Wondered what part 'o the world you were from ... you speak good enough English. Quick learner are ya?'

'I seem to have a gift with languages. However, I did learn English before I came out here. Started when I was quite young.' Leopold noticed the man looking a bit bored, but continued trying to make conversation with him anyway. 'Had a tutor at home, and made a couple of trips to England, too.'

'Well,' said the crew man as he started to walk off to board the ship.

'There you go then.' Leopold smiled to himself.

As it neared the time to board, Leopold took one last look at his surroundings. He knew that mail would be scarce, with the Gothenburg making only four trips a year.

Captain Pearce was standing by the gangway and welcomed the passengers as they boarded. As Leopold walked past him, he asked, 'How long will the trip take from Port Adelaide to Port Darwin?'

'Depending, Sir. Anywhere from twenty-four to thirty-three days ... depending what the weather's like, depending if the ship hits a reef, depending ... I've found it rough from Melbourne through to Newcastle at times, and then of course going through the Inner Passage, the Great Barrier Reef, we can get snagged there, and then have to wait for the tides.'

'Thank you,' said Leopold, looking forward to his new adventure. As he walked towards his home for the next few weeks, he wondered what the next two years in the Northern Territory would bring.

Above him the woolly, white clouds seemed motionless, as a pair of pelicans rode the air thermals flying upwards in ever increasing circles. Seagulls joined them, and dotted the skies and squawked until they were out of sight.

'Nothing like an Australian blue sky, is there?' said Officer Davis.

'Took me a while to get used to it being so bright ... and to get used to how much of the sky I can see at any one time,' replied

Leopold, as people on the densely-populated dock cheered and yelled good luck to those on board. 'Port River seems so wide here, and it's so flat that the views never cease to amaze me.'

'Wide?' asked Officer Tasker.

'Yes. Maybe it seems wide because of the landscape? It's as though it blends into its surroundings and has no defined edges,' replied Leopold. He could imagine setting up an easel and painting the view.

'Let's hope the rain holds off. Don't know how we'd get on with all the animals, machinery and everything we've got on board? Imagine if it rained, we'd sink,' said Officer Dann.

'Doesn't look much like rain here, but someone told me that the weather going into Melbourne isn't good,' said Tasker.

'Don't think we'll have to worry about that. This captain sounds like he's done this trip for years and knows the seas well. Besides, we haven't much of a choice, have we?' said Leopold, with a smile on his face.

'Suppose not,' said Officer Muller. 'Heard that along the coast we might see flying fish and yellow snakes, some with stripes … and that around Queensland, it's dotted with beautiful little islands … Well, I'm going down under to settle myself in. See you down there.'

'I'll be there soon. I just want to watch as we leave the port. There are a few rusted-out shipwrecks a bit further along the mangroves. Chat to you later,' said Leopold, walking to the port side of the Gothenburg.

The crew seemed to take a long time to prepare for departure. Eventually, Leopold grew tired of waiting and decided to go below deck to join his fellow police officers.

By the time the steamship was loaded, the hordes of well-wishers had long disappeared. The dark had begun to close in, making it extremely difficult for the captain to navigate through the narrow waters. Finally, the steamship reached the gulf and was cleared by the emigration officer to proceed.

The Gothenburg slowly dropped away to swing into the stream.

# Twenty-Five

Two days out from Palmerston, the captain noticed a canoe of Melville Islanders coming towards the Gothenburg. They offered the captain a turtle in exchange for tobacco. They had been described by other sea faring sailors as ferocious, so it was a hesitant captain that received the men and their offering.

The captain made a quick exchange, before continuing towards Palmerston. 'Throw the turtle back into the water, men, as soon as they're out of sight,' demanded the captain. 'Looks like an old man turtle ... probably as tough as leather, and he's survived out there for this long, let's give him the respect he deserves and put him back.'

As soon as the islanders were out of sight, a small splash was heard as the turtle hit the water and swam off.

Finally, after twenty-four days at sea, navigating around the ragged east coast of Australia, from Adelaide to Port Darwin, the Gothenburg arrived and dropped anchor in five fathoms, about a mile from the beach near the other ships, Coorong, Loelia, Atlanta, and the Linn Fern. They, too, had brought with them a large number of passengers and livestock.

The passengers of the Gothenburg looked toward the land to see men starting to construct a much-needed jetty, but in the meantime the passengers would have to wait for the tide to come in. The currents were treacherous, with a rise and fall of eighteen to twenty feet every six hours.

The waters around Palmerston were home to schools of fish, sharks and crocodiles. Any boats in the area had to be wary of the varied and numerous reefs which could damage their hull and possibly sink the boats, drown people and lose baggage.

Leopold had asked around about Palmerston before he came, and he felt confident that he had prepared himself well for the two years that lay ahead of him. He knew that Palmerston had been settled by white men for four years now, and that it was the main town of the Northern Territory, and he knew of its commanding position high on a cliff. Fort Hill formed the eastern headland of the entrance to Port Darwin, whereas the western headland was some four miles away, and known as Talc Head.

As Leopold cast his eyes afield he saw boxes and boxes of goods on the beach. He was surprised to see that no machines were used to transport the heavy baggage to shore, and that it was the sheer strength of the men that were responsible for their safe arrival.

The beaches were far too stony on one side for the horses and drays to come in, or for the goods, and on the other side, the beach was muddy and boggy. Leopold knew the stories of the wild seas, and of times when the horses had been unloaded off the boats into the sea, and were expected to swim to shore. So many of the horses were drowned at sea, with some being caught in the tide and turning up thirteen miles from Port Darwin stuck in mud.

There were currently five hundred people living in Palmerston and not very many buildings. Among them were the British

Australia Telegraph, the South Australian Telegraph, two hotels built very roughly of poles and bark but well ventilated. There were also two restaurants and forty houses built mostly of bark.

Beyond the well-grassed line of sandhills, Leopold could see a thick belt of shrubs. The land looked harsh and wretched. He thought to himself, 'all this untamed land with its dry soil and rocks and dust that seeps into every crevice. How on earth are we expected to live here or grow vegetables for ourselves to eat?'

The boats were now able to reach the ship, and as the crew handed down the bags, Leopold chatted to one of the men.

'What do you do for food here? Doesn't look like you'd have much luck growing anything at all,' he remarked.

'Plenty of fish, only don't try using a fishing line, they won't take the bait. You'd have more luck with a net. Then of course we have dehydrated meat,' replied the crew man, who continued loading the boat with goods. 'Some of the men live off hawks. Not bad eating. Helps the men to keep up their strength before their long rides. Up here you never really know if you'll come back, so it's wise to fill up with fresh meat and make sure you take waterbags with you.'

'I saw bags of potatoes and onions being loaded on board at Port Adelaide, but I'm wondering if you have any other vegetables?' asked Leopold.

The crew man looked at Leopold and replied, 'Not much will grow here. Thought you would've known that ... the government, though, have set up a ten-acre plot to grow vegetables and fruit trees two miles out of Palmerston.' He stared at Leopold, waiting for his response, but none was forthcoming. 'The Chinese came over here to help on the Overland Telegraph Line, and when that was completed a year ago, they helped set up vegetable gardens. The fences aren't very substantial, a few fork-shaped branches and sticks. Cows wander in at times and destroy what's there.' The crew man paused for a moment. 'Bananas, pineapples and sweet potatoes grow here like weeds, so it's not too bad if you like that kind of food. The only thing is that you can only grow up here for eight months of the year.

'Oh! And if you want water and can manage to find yourself a bucket, there's Peel Well about a mile out of Palmerston,' he continued, happy with the shocked reaction Leopold gave him. 'And while we're on the subject, I hope you brought boots with you, because they haven't sent us some for months ... and with all these stones, your feet won't feel too good by the end of the day ... you really got to have boots.'

And after a moment, 'What are you doing here? Trying to get some gold, are you?'

'No. I'm one of the police troopers sent to replace the ones that took off to stake a claim,' said Leopold. 'We're yet to unpack our uniforms, and our weapons. They are under lock and key. They'll be marked with our names and contain our breech-loading revolvers, 2,000 rounds of ammunition, swords and our pouches. Our uniforms are the same as we had in South Australia, and they are too hot for here ... heavy blue jackets and pants, and boots.'

'Well, in that case then, you'll be looking for the Government Departments. See up there on the hill just past Fort Hill ... that's Palmerston,' said the crew man as he watched Leopold trying to locate it. 'Look a bit more to your left ... see up there ... by the Howitzer cannons.'

The crew man started laughing. 'Those police men that left and said they were going looking for gold, I think they lied to you. Look up there. I reckon trying to get up there from the beach is what really made them leave.'

Leopold strained to see the buildings perched precariously on the edge of the cliff a hundred feet up.

'Look straight ahead,' the crew man said, pointing to the cliff. 'And now look up a hundred feet along the edge of the cliff.'

'Yes, up there. I see it,' said Leopold.

'That's where you have to walk to get to it … you can go through the tradesmen's quarters, but they're a rough lot. Their horses are well looked after though. Further on, there's about thirty stables for the police horses just by the government buildings … What are you doing?'

Leopold was expecting to be one of the first to get into the boat.

'Nah! You can't get in. You got to wait with the others. There's not enough room. I'll be back after I empty this lot. If I don't make the tide, I'll have to come back tomorrow. It's far too dangerous to do this at night, although Dixon and his mates do.'

'Who's Dixon?' asked a curious Leopold.

'You ask a lot of questions, don't ya,' said the crew man.

'Dixon's the butcher! He and his mates get in a boat and row out to Melville Island to get fresh meat. It usually takes them a few days. Just rowing there takes them twelve hours at times. The waves can be strong, pulling them back towards shore … On the island they go out and catch bullock, turkey, kangaroos, pigeons, quails … tastes bloody good,' said the crew man.

'I heard the natives are ferocious?' said Leopold.

'Yeh ... but you haven't seen Dixon if he doesn't get his meat,' the crew man replied, laughing. 'Then Dixon and the others cut the meat up on the island and pack it into bags to bring back: makes it much easier to transport. Usually spend a couple of nights there. More than likely they head off at midday and don't get back here until midnight. I have to go ...'

The crew man stopped for a moment, stood up, and looked straight at Leopold, his dirtied hands on his hips.

'Before I leave, I want to give you a tip. Don't trust those bloody crocodiles. Can't trust them as far as you can throw them ... A crocodile took one of you guys in January. Found his body upstream a week later with teeth marks through one of his eyes and the back of his head. Must have been a large crocodile to do that sort of damage.'

'Are they the same as alligators?' asked Leopold.

'Similar, but we don't have alligators in Australia. I think crocs, though, are sneakier. They'll watch you go down to the river for three weeks in a row, every day, and not bother with you, and then, one day, just when you think you're safe, they'll take you ... and you haven't got a chance. Next thing you know, they grab you with those strong jaws, and they'll take you down into the water, and roll you over and over, till you don't know what's up or down ... you can't get a breath ... then they tuck your body under the roots of the river gum trees in the water, and wait for your flesh to get soft enough to eat,' said the crew man.

Leopold was speechless. He had only agreed to the position in Palmerston, a town that he now feared was a God-forsaken place, because the wages were better than in Adelaide. Leopold missed his family dreadfully. His mother was growing older, and the children were making their own lives, so he was hoping that once he got settled into his eight by fifteen-foot log house at Palmerston, things would get better; but from what he had seen and heard, he would be happy to get back to Adelaide.

'I'll make sure I carry my rifle with me at all times,' said Leopold, scanning the water for crocodiles.

'Better make sure it is loaded and ready to go … those crocs won't wait for ya to load and take aim,' the crew man laughed. 'Oh! And better make sure your gun's breached, so you don't shoot yourself in the foot.'

Leopold was too caught up in the story to be offended by the crew man suggesting he was stupid and had no idea how to carry a gun.

A few minutes later, two of the other boats had returned to pick up passengers and their luggage.

'Fast as you can, so we can beat the tide,' said one of the crew men. 'Some of the crew will remain with the Gothenburg to look after the animals until they get picked up tomorrow,' he said in response to Leopold's concern about his horse.

As the boat carrying Leopold moved closer to shore, he cast his artistic eye over the landscape. He looked in awe at the beauty and the colours that lay in front of him, beholding the texture and colours of the bush and the details in the rocks. Beautiful blue skies, red ochre landscape covered in round green bushes, and beaches covered with white stones, tall green grasses and roughly built brown huts captured his attention.

'I'll be pleased to put my roots down for a while,' said Leopold to the passengers nearest to him; then, looking around the boat, at the many weary faces, he added, 'I think we all will.'

# Twenty-Six

The officers looked out from the police headquarters at the vast, rocky, orange land and the various poorly-built houses scattered around Palmerston. There were some Aboriginal children digging in the dirt near a gum tree and the doctor's wife walking toward the makeshift hospital.

'I can see why they chose this particular spot to build the station,' said Leopold, turning to Foelsche, his supervisor. 'It's a clear view of the ocean, and of the town centre, for want of a better name. But how are the actual town locations chosen initially?'

'Police stations have been set up close to Aboriginal communities or where they can serve as a base for us to carry out our duties effectively,' said Foelsche. 'Other stations have been built closer to goldmining activities or where cattle have been killed or stolen by the local Aborigines.'

'Apart from our usual duties, what else will we be doing up here?' asked Leopold.

'Well ... as a trooper you've been better trained than the men already here, but there'll be anything from acting as clerks of the courts, assisting the bailiffs, clerk of the licensing bench, registrars of births deaths and marriages, registrars of dogs, commissioners for affidavits, labour bureau agents and issuers of miners' rights,' explained Foelsche.

'No *real* trouble up here, then?' noted Leopold.

'Not really. I wouldn't exactly say that it can get boring, but there's not much you'll have to do in a hurry. The heat and the flies will make your life up here hell, though. And the drink will tempt you just to get through your day,' explained Foelsche.

Foelsche continued explaining about the duties Leopold might be involved in. 'Some of the police have undertaken duties like fisheries inspectors, issuers of Aboriginal rations, inspectors of brands, stock inspectors, slaughterhouse inspectors, inspectors of public houses, customs and excise officers, wide tyres inspectors, and rabbit act inspectors.

'Police were also public vaccinators, gaolers, crocodile and lands rangers, electoral registrars, and destitute department officers. You might even escort gold from the diggings.'

Leopold looked around the police office, a makeshift log cabin made from local gum trees cut down by the police officers and put together by Foelsche and his men. No windows or doors: just big gaping holes, with a bark roof.

'How many people living in Palmerston?' asked Leopold, still coming to terms with what he was seeing.

'Last count would have been five hundred, mostly single men, but a few with their wives and children,' Foelsche answered.

'The loneliness gets to some of them up here. Not much to do, people wandering off and getting lost, others missing their families ... and they end up turning to drink,' warned Foelsche. 'I don't condone it, mind you, but I can understand it. Seems like they've come up with a new concoction … they call it "Sunset Rum".'

'Sunset Rum,' Leopold repeated. 'Sounds interesting.'

'Hope you don't smoke? Light a smoke or anything around the drink, and it's likely to explode,' said Foelsche. 'Made from methylated spirits and kerosene!'

Leopold stood dumbfounded. 'Is it meant to make them feel better or kill them?'

'Kill them, I reckon. They mix half and half of the explosive spirits, add Worchester sauce, ginger and sugar. Then, of course, if you want something stronger, they have a drink with gin, vinegar and saltpetre. Burn the bottom of a bucket, they reckon,' said Foelsche. 'Never tasted it. Don't intend to.'

'What was it like when you first came here? I mean … you set up the first white settlement, didn't you?' asked Leopold, admiring Foelsche's bravery in this wild land.

'We were first sent here just to reside without any particular objective. Keep order, of course, for those who bought land, but no real orders, except to settle the place,' answered Foelsche, thinking back to his first encounter with Aboriginals.

'Relied on the Aboriginals … and yet there were times we didn't know if we could trust them. Aboriginal trackers helped us out a lot. Taught us how to find water, make damper … that sort of thing. One of the trackers was Dingo Mick … he's a good tracker. There were no roads or landmarks, so we had to learn new skills. That Dingo Mick was a steady fellow, and without him life would have been very different.'

'I can't begin to imagine how primitive it was! The only reason I'm up here is to make enough money to get back to Germany, to be with my family as quickly as I can. Like an adventure, but this one I think will be very different to adventures in Europe!' said Leopold.

Foelsche continued, 'It was harsh, and there were killings between the Aboriginal people and the whites. The Aboriginal people saw us as taking their land, and we were up here to try and stop any cultural clashes. I think we were all scared of each other at first, but we get on well enough these days. Well, most of us do; some are still scared of them. I think it was hardest for the black trackers, the way they were seen by their own people. You see, the trackers had more liberties than the rest of the Aboriginal people, and so it caused friction amongst them.'

'Sounds like a harsh, unforgiving environment,' suggested Leopold.

'Bloody harsh,' Foelsche agreed.

# Twenty-Seven

A couple of months had past, and Leopold was stationed in Southport and starting to become familiar with his environment and its conditions, so his superior, Trooper Lewis, thought it was time he travelled further afield.

That morning, Leopold and Lewis packed their saddle bags with drinks, dehydrated meats and vegetables, hitched up their horses and headed out of Southport. It was hot, so they each had two horses, to rest them, one walking alongside the other. As Lewis thought it might take a week to patrol the area, they took extra ammunition to shoot fresh meat for themselves. The trip would take in some of the most beautiful scenery, and some of the most isolated and dangerous, in Australia, and they would cross wide rivers and creeks. They would have to pay particular attention to landmarks, so they could find their way back to Southport, particularly in case something happened to one of them and the other would have to find their own way back alone.

On the second day, they came to Adelaide River, only to find it was flooded and too difficult to cross. They had to travel for hours in search of a narrow crossing.

Lewis yelled out to Leopold, trying to be heard above the sound of the gushing water.

'Think we'll cross here ... as good a place as any, and if we go too much further the horses will be tired, and it might be just as bad as it is here … and if they're tired we might end up drowning them.'

Leopold was uncertain of the crossing, but his training in the Prussian Army had taught him not to question the command, but follow it.

'Take our clothes off except for your underclothes, and pack them into your saddlebags,' he suggested to Leopold. 'If they get wet, it will weigh you down and make it harder for you to cross.'

Leopold began to undress, becoming more uneasy at crossing the gushing waters with his horses.

'How are we going to manage the horses? One at a time?' asked Leopold.

'Nah! We'll take them both across. Horses are funny creatures, and might get spooked if their partner horse is on the other side of the river … undo the buckle on the reins and thread them through the stirrups of the front horse, and then do them up again. Only way I can see it working,' suggested Lewis.

'Let's hope they cooperate,' said Leopold, agreeing that looking after two horses if they got spooked would surely end badly.

At first the horses were reluctant to enter the water. They splashed at the river's edge for some time, as though stomping on a deadly snake to kill it. The water splashed up around the horses' legs, and the men became wet and began to struggle.

Lewis found it hard to pull his grey mare further into the water. With each gesture to get her to walk into the water, she strained, and pulled her head up high, tugging against his grip on the reins.

'Hop on your horse, and maybe she won't feel so frightened,' suggested Leopold. 'Once you're in the water you could slide off and then walk her through the water, and if she can't reach the bottom, she can swim? And be careful she doesn't kick you with those hard hooves of hers if you can't get by her side, or far enough in front. We'd be in trouble then … If you got injured, I wouldn't be able to manage four horses and an injured person.'

'Might have to … she can be stubborn at times,' agreed Lewis, the sound of the water thrashing over the creek bed dampening his deep voice.

Lewis and his beloved grey mare walked forward, and after some splashing entered the river and started to cross against the strong current. Lewis slid off the horse and took the reins, moving forward as best he could until the current was too strong. He was forced to place the reins in his mouth, so he could swim to avoid being dragged downstream. He winced with pain as the reins tore at the corner of his mouth.

Leopold followed into the river with his horses.

About half way across, after Leopold had dismounted and taken the reins in his hand, he yelled out, 'Crocodile,' and, with that, both Lewis and Leopold swam as fast as they could until they reached the other side of the river, breathless.

'We can't stay here, Leopold; crocodiles have been known to come up out of the water. They may look sluggish and awkward but believe me, they can still get you … let's go,' said Lewis, as they led their horses away from the river.

'We can get dressed over there,' said Lewis, looking for a safe place far enough away from danger. As he looked back towards the river and to where Leopold had sighted the crocodile, he realised that Leopold's crocodile had been nothing more than a half-sunken tree-trunk with a jagged branch attached to it.

'My God! I did think it was a crocodile,' said Leopold, embarrassed.

'You stupid man! Even if it was a crocodile, you ought to have kept quiet. You had the horse between you and the crocodile, and it would've taken the horse first,' said an infuriated Lewis.

'I've heard how dangerous they are, and I wasn't taking any chances,' explained Leopold, trying to get Lewis to understand his mistake.

They dressed and headed off in the direction of Mc Minns Bluff on the river flood plains, where they planned to make camp for the night.

The rains that had caused the river to flood had also brought with them new hope. New shoots were growing on various plants, the green foliage contrasting with the orange-brown soil. The birdlife was plentiful and noisy, with small, bright-green birds screeching across the open, blue skies.

'Those are Budgerigars,' said Lewis. 'The Aborigines call them "betcherrygah", which means "good eating". Mind you there's not much meat on 'em. You need to eat about sixteen just to know you've eaten anything at all, but believe me, if you're hungry, they taste damn good.' He laughed.

'I think I'd settle for anything to eat right now,' said Leopold. 'Over there, under the ledge of that mound, seems like a good spot to camp. It's quite protected by the trees, and we won't have to watch our backs all night.'

They had travelled through countless valleys and gullies, and were too tired to travel further in search of a more suitable campsite.

They tied their horses to the tree under the little shade that was available, and emptied their food supplies from their saddle bags. Leopold began to dig a wide, shallow pit in readiness for the fire to cook their meal, while Lewis went off to find the fuel to burn. Leopold then put a tin of meat into water while he waited for Lewis to return with the wood. He broke the bread into fist-size pieces, and planned to throw the potatoes into the fire the way Aboriginals had shown him. Within the hour, the men were peeling the charred skins from the potatoes, and tucking into a healthy, much needed meal.

While they had been eating, Lewis' grey mare had come loose and had wondered off from the other horses. Leopold could see from a distance that it seemed to be in some sort of trouble.

'I'll go and get her, Lewis. You might as well finish eating while your food is still warm,' said Leopold, as he stood and headed down to get the horse, not realising the degree of difficulty the horse was having until he got closer.

'Lewis quick ... get here now,' yelled Leopold. 'Lewis, now or it'll be too late!'

Lewis dropped his plate of food and ran. 'What is it? Has she been bitten by a snake?'

'No ... your horse is stuck in quicksand. We need to get that pack off her back. It's dragging her down,' said Leopold, trying to help the frightened horse.

Leopold was straining on the reins to help the horse, while Lewis tried to reach the pack, but he couldn't. Leopold held her reins firmly, hoping to help her keep her head above the quicksand.

'She's sinking fast,' said Lewis. 'She's sinking too fast,' he said, as the horse continued to slip further and further down into the bog.

The horse's nostrils were flared, and she was neighing with fear.

'If she would only stop thrashing around, she'd have a better chance,' said Leopold.

Lewis ran with great speed back to their camp, and, returning just as quickly, he held out his rifle.

'You will have to shoot her, Leopold.'

'Surely we can get her out. Grab her bridle, and we'll pull.'

'Shoot. For God's sake, man; you're a better shot than me, and I can't bear to do it. Shoot her,' pleaded Lewis, who was growing more and more distressed the longer he saw his mare struggling.

'Surely ...,' started Leopold.

'I've seen this before ... She won't make it, and she's scared. You have to do it for me.' Lewis shoved the gun into Leopold's hands. 'She's terrified, man. Shoot her.'

Leopold took the rifle and looked through the sight. The grey mare's eyes were black and dilated with fear. He looked down the barrel, took aim, and fired.

The sound echoed, the job was done, and the men stood motionless and exhausted, watching as the grey mare's limp body disappeared into the quicksand.

They walked back to their camp and checked that the other horses were tied securely, and then sat, staring into the fire. Not a word was said. The horse, along with the pack containing the rest of the food, were gone. They would have to return to Palmerston earlier than expected.

# Twenty-Eight

Sundays had become race days in Palmerston. The Aboriginal and the white communities had great fun competing against each other. They would often raise money for a much-needed service or facility like a new hospital, and as a prize, race winners would receive bags of flour and sugar. The races would begin early in the morning before the heat had had a chance to penetrate their skin.

For some reason, this Sunday, Leopold felt the heat more than usual. At first, he put it down to having a restless night, after he and Trooper Howard had spent most of Saturday in ninety-eight-degree heat, apprehending a horse thief by the name of James Henretta. However, as the morning progressed, Leopold was starting to sweat more than he would have expected.

'I hope I'm not getting sick,' thought Leopold. 'Maybe Foelsche was right when he chatted to all of us about being out in the heat too long and getting sick if we didn't drink enough?'

He wiped the sweat from his sun-burnt face, and suggested to the other troopers and a few of the locals sitting next to him at the local park that they take their horses and ride down to the river to cool off after the morning's events had finished.

'Your face sure is red,' said Trooper Howard to Leopold. 'You look like a beetroot. And, yeh, the river sounds like a great idea, I know I could do with a cool off. Anyone else coming with us?'

he asked those around him. 'We can buy a bit of tucker from the women over there,' he continued, 'seeing as we saved our entry fee by not competing in the races.'

'Good idea,' replied one of the police troopers. 'And every bit they make helps towards building the hospital.'

'The women put a lot of work into preparing the food. I know some of the wives stay up until late at night, after the sun's gone down and the houses have cooled off a bit, before they start cooking,' said Trooper Howard.

With the formalities of the morning over, two of the police troopers went over to the women and chatted to them about their plans to head to the river, and to purchase their tucker. Leopold and the others in the group, eight in all, packed the food into their saddle bags, and then hooked their waterbags over the pommel of the saddle. The tucker consisted of homemade cakes and biscuits, bananas, bags of nuts, flour to make a bit of damper, sugar and beef jerky. Plenty of food for the afternoon, but it was always wise to take more food than they needed as people had been known to get lost and to be stranded overnight.

The police troopers packed their rifles and ammunition in long pouches underneath the pommel, and each of them also carried a knife tucked in their boot, as did Dixon, the butcher; Carter, the builder; and a friend of Carter's, named Bill. Even though there had still been clashes with Aborigines near the camps and water holes, they had no intention of using their weapons for anything other than hunting for fresh meat if they saw a kangaroo, but, nonetheless, they had been advised to take weapons with them whenever they left Palmerston.

'Let's hope we don't see any crocodiles,' said Trooper Howard to the rest of the men, as they headed off in the direction of the river.

'Let's hope they don't see us, more likely,' laughed Carter, the youngest member of this group of adventurers. 'One look at our ugly faces, and they'll swim up the river quick as they can, to get away from us.'

'Speak for yourself, Carter,' said Dixon, laughing at Carter's joke.

Less than an hour into their journey, in the hottest part of the day, they could feel the sun burning into the back of their necks. They wore hats, which protected the tops of their heads, and scarves wrapped around their necks, which they had soaked in water before they left Palmerston.

'Don't know if this was such a good idea, to come out this far after all, Leopold. I'm hotter than before!' said Trooper Howard.

'A few hours cooling off in the river will be well and truly worth it. We'll have a few hours to soak in the water if we want, and still make it back to Palmerston before sunset. Trust me,' replied Leopold, who had also started to question his idea of going to the river.

They knew it was madness leaving after lunch, but they also knew there was not a lot of shade in Palmerston, and their homes were already hot from the previous days' heat and showed no signs of cooling off.

The horses walked at a slow pace with their heads hanging down.

'We're almost there, girl,' said Leopold, who leaned forward and stroked his horse's neck. Then he turned to the others and called out, 'Almost there. I can see a line of trees by the river.'

The countryside between Palmerston and the river had changed very little—the same soft brown and ochre-coloured soils, spindly grey bushes, gum trees, and termite hills. The line of trees they saw a few miles ahead, marked the outline of the river which buoyed their excitement and gave them renewed energy.

As they neared the river, the undergrowth became denser and somewhat matted, making it difficult for the horses to get a foothold. The men made their way carefully to the edge of the river, ducking under the lower limbs of trees.

The river red gum trees that ran along the edge of the river showed signs of distress, with peeling bark and cracked limbs.

Dixon was the first to arrive at the river. 'I wouldn't have expected the trees here to be in such poor condition,' he said to the others when they joined him.

The men dismounted and left their horses to drink at the water's edge, as they pulled their boots and socks off and plunged their feet in the water. It was cold and soothing.

'Ahhh. It was worth the effort,' said Leopold as he continued to remove all his clothing with the exception of his tight-fitting, knee-length flannel drawers.

'Carter, you're the youngest one here. Can you and Bill take the horses and tie them up by the trees over there?' asked Dixon. 'We don't want them over here stirring up the water too much and attracting the crocodiles, do we? And take their saddles and blankets off, too, will you. They might as well cool off as much as possible.

As Carter and Bill walked towards the trees, a creaking sound was heard, and then the sound of a branch as it cracked and broke free, falling to the ground with a whoosh, right beside the two men. The horses reared up, and tried to pull free, but Carter held on firmly to their reins. He looked at his hand, and saw a deep-red burn etched into the palm of his hand.

'That was lucky. I could have been hit, or smashed in the face,' said Carter. 'Look at the size of that branch.'

'Don't know that anyone would have noticed if it did! You said before that you'd scare the crocs up the river,' said Bill, who started laughing.

Carter laughed with him, then his stinging hand demanded his attention again.

Dixon went over to see if the men were alright. He saw Carter looking at his hand, and wondered if the branch had hit him and broken his hand.

'Let's have a look at it,' Dixon said. 'Nice clean burn. You'll be right. Bit of aloe vera on it, and in a couple of days, it'll be gone. Learnt that little trick from a friend of mine who went off exploring Africa and used to write to me every month telling me about his adventures. Seems to grow up here wild, too.'

Carter grimaced.

'Oh, it might sting a bit for a while, but I wouldn't worry about it,' said Dixon, snapping open the gel-like contents of the plant and letting it drip onto Carter's wounds. 'Here,' he said, pulling Carter's hand closer to him, 'I'll bandage it up, so it gets a chance to heal. At least you weren't hit by the branch; we're already short of builders as it is.'

'Why'd the branch break?' asked Carter, who had only been in Palmerston for six months.

'They'll do that. It's the way a gum tree can keep itself alive: it drops its branches so it doesn't need as much water to survive …

should have warned you, I suppose,' said Dixon. 'Just be aware of it from now on, and you'll be alright.'

Leopold was looking at the water in the river, at the reflection of the trees and the blue sky, watching ripples travel across its surface as a gentle breeze picked up. He stepped out of the water to collect some twigs lying around on the ground, and one by one he tore the gum leaves from their stem, releasing a refreshing smell of eucalyptus into the air. He dropped the leaves into the water and watched them follow the current. They swirled around and then dipped down, sliding over the small rocks and down a small waterfall. Small frothy bubbles from the water gathered around the rocks and swirled around in circles.

Leopold saw the other men watching him. 'We used to do this when we were children. We'd drop pieces of grass or leaves into the moat and then watch the carp as they'd come up to the surface of the water, thinking it was food,' said Leopold. 'What care-free times.'

The other men smiled, recollecting their own memories of childhood.

The ochre-coloured landscape by the river, and the soft brown soil and shrubs, spread as far as the eye could see. They were a stark contrast to the green pine and beech forests Leopold could remember from home. He looked over to the horses to see if they had settled down after their scare, and noticed a large termite hill. He had seen Aboriginals break off chunks of termite hills, to expose the termites, which they grabbed by the handful and then squashed between the palms of their hands, rubbing in a circular motion, to kill them and eat them to cure digestive problems.

Leopold walked back into the water and submerged himself fully, singing out to the others who had gathered around the horses. 'Anyone else getting in?' he shouted.

'After we've eaten … We're starved,' replied the others.

'Thought I'd try me hand at catching meself a fish or two, while the rest of you unpack the tucker we brought with us,' said Bill.

'Wait up, Bill. I'm coming, too,' Carter said, who had been keen to catch fish. They both looked around for suitable slender branches that could act as spears, and Bill began shaving one of the ends to a point.

'I can do one for you, too, if you like, Carter. Don't know that'll do you much good what with your hand,' said Bill.

'Don't know meself, but I'm gonna give it a try. If you can shave a nice point on that for me, I'd be grateful,' said Carter, trying not to show he was in pain.

Leopold watched them jabbing at the water with their handmade spears, further up the river. Having cooled off enough, he decided to get out. 'Maybe it was the heat that made me feel sick. Thank God I feel a bit better now,' he thought.

'Caught any fish,' he called out to Bill and Carter after he had got dressed.

Bill held up a handful of fish, strung together using a piece of wire that the men often kept in their belts in case they saw snakes.

'Not bad at all!' Leopold said. 'I might head over to the others.'

Bill got out of the water to dig a hole at the edge of the river, to put the fish in to keep them cool and wet. He made a small ridge from the hole to the river, so that the water could flow into the hole without the fish flowing back into the river.

Trooper Howard joined Bill and Carter spearing fish. What looked like a broken branch was floating on the surface of the water behind the trooper, but given the direction that the river was flowing, Bill knew that the branch would continue to float away from the trooper, so there was no need to worry.

Bill picked up some flat stones and skimmed them across the surface of the water, counting how many times they bounced before sinking. Carter decided to join him.

Carter and Bill competed to see who could make their stones bounce across the surface of the river the most. As they watched, Bill suddenly noticed that what he had thought was a broken branch was suddenly moving towards Howard.

'Howard, swim, swim!' shouted Bill. 'Crocodile!'

When Leopold heard Bill's cries, he grabbed his rifle from his saddle that was resting against a tree, loaded it as quickly as he could, and ran back to the river.

He saw Carter and Bill unable to assist as the crocodile, its mouth opening, swam at speed toward Howard. 'Move yourselves. Fast!' he yelled out.

The crocodile had increased its speed, and almost stood up on its back legs as it grabbed at Howard. It swung its head sideways, Howard's leg between its teeth, pulling Howard back into the water.

'JESUS!' yelled Dixon, who was rushing to the water with the others to help.

'Poke it in the eye. Punch it if you can on the nose,' yelled the others.

'Out of my way,' yelled Leopold.

The group of men were now standing near Carter, watching

at the edge of the river, as the crocodile thrashed around and started spinning in circles, half drowning Trooper Howard. His arms came up out of the water trying to get a grip on something to save himself, but he was growing more and more breathless. He seemed to lose consciousness, and then the crocodile, still holding Howard, quietly slipped into the water without a trace.

Then, suddenly, the crocodile appeared again above the surface of the water.

A loud shot was heard and the crocodile released its grip on Howard. As the crocodile sank into the water, Carter rushed in, grabbed Howard, who was now unconscious, and pulled him out onto the bank of the river. The cold water seeped through the bandage on Carter's hand, making his wound sting, but he had to keep going. He lifted Howard up and threw him over his shoulders, so he could get him away from the river faster. The force of falling over his rescuer's shoulder, pushed some of the water out of the young man's lungs, and he started coughing up water. He gasped and coughed several times, almost losing consciousness again. Straining to inhale air, it took him several minutes to catch his breath properly and for the pounding of his heart to subside. He kept falling in and out of consciousness.

'Betta get him up to the shade in case that beggar's not dead,' said Bill, who had swung back into action. 'He might come up out of the water and try again.'

'Think I got him with that shot. Don't think he'll be going too far,' said Leopold.

Back at the camp, the men covered Howard with their jackets to keep him from going into shock. The others stood around and watched in disbelief.

'Get me my saddlebag, will ya …,' said Bill to Dixon, who went and grabbed it for him. Bill withdrew a bag needle and a pouch of tobacco, and asked someone to get him a bowl or a flat stone.

'No time to smoke!' snapped Dixon.

Bill looked up at Dixon and said, 'I keep my leaves of Emu Bush in there; helps to keep them moist. The Aborigines call it "ngawil", and it's really good for burns and wounds. Keeps the bacteria out, the Doc' told me.'

Bill took the long skinny leaves from his tobacco pouch and put them on the rock where he bashed at them with another smaller rock to get the juices out. 'I won't have enough to do the job, but it'll be better than nothing.'

Trooper Howard regained consciousness and was grabbing at his leg, and squeezing it to stop the pain. Bill mixed the Emu Bush juice with water and carefully dropped the juice into the wound.

'We can hardly leave him bleeding here. He'll be getting weak … we're going to have to stitch him up,' said Leopold.

'You're right,' agreed Dixon. 'And rip up a shirt or something, men. It will need to be bandaged and bandaged tight.'

'Someone grab some horse hair from my horse's tail and boil it up for me. The water from the billy will do,' said Bill.

Bill started stitching Howard's leg with the bag needle and boiled horse hair, while Dixon and some of the police troopers grabbed their rifles and headed back to the river to see if they could find the crocodile.

'Be careful. Make sure it's really dead. Those beggars will pretend til ya close up and then you're done,' Bill called out after them.

After scouring the river, Dixon called to the others, 'Over here, and get your guns ready.' He had spotted the crocodile under a tree by the water's edge. 'I'm going to grab its tail and pull hard. If that beggar turns around to grab me, shoot it ... and make a bloody good job of it. If it kills me, I'll come back and haunt the pair of ya.'

'On the count of three,' said one of the others. 'One ... two ... Don't know if this is such a great idea.'

'Grab the tail and pull it out. I reckon it's dead ... Go on,' said one of the police troopers, who was keen to see what was going to happen next.

'Three ...'

Dixon pulled at the leathery creature and started to drag it. 'The croc's too heavy for just me. Come on you two, give me some help. Looks pretty dead to me.' After a lot of heaving and working together, the crocodile was up on the bank, leaving behind a deep groove in the mud from the weight of its flesh.

Certain the crocodile was dead, they left it lying on the bank to start packing up their camp site.

'Where are you going, Dixon,' asked Carter a while later.

'Off to skin that thing,' he answered, referring to the crocodile. 'Never seen anything that big. Not up here or on Melville Island.'

'Come on men. We've gotta get moving if we're going to make it back while there's still light,' said Bill, who had noticed Leopold looking pale and sweaty again, and Howard grimacing with pain.

'Bill, it looks like Dixon's determined,' said Carter to his friend. 'Do you mind helping him? But be quick.' And to the others he said, 'Anyone who hasn't eaten yet, have a quick bite while we finish packing up, plenty of tucker left. No good riding back on an empty stomach.'

After Dixon and Bill came back with the crocodile skin, they rolled it up tight, and placed it in a hessian bag to make it easier to carry.

When the men had finished packing, they helped Trooper Howard onto his horse, and then started their journey back to Palmerston, a couple of hours away.

# Twenty-Nine

Even though the late afternoon sun was sinking, the heat made their journey back to Palmerston a slow one. It was an agonising ordeal for Howard, the injured trooper, and to make it worse, flies were following the scent of blood from the crocodile skin and were buzzing around Howard's wounds. Out of the others, Leopold, the most unaccustomed to the heat, was suffering most.

'It won't be too long now,' said Dixon to Leopold. 'Howard's having a hard time of it. How are you feeling?'

'My eyes are hurting, and I'm feeling sick,' he replied. 'And I keep breaking out in a sweat.'

'By the look of the sun, we don't have much light left. We should probably camp overnight, but with the look of you two, I think we'd better keep moving. Let's hope we can make it back alright. If one of the horses stumbles, that'll be it … break a leg or something, and we'll have to shoot it … put it out of its misery,' said Carter. 'And go on foot.'

Night had begun to fall and their vision was growing worse as their landmarks began to disappear into the darkness.

'We'll have to rely heavily on our hearing now,' said Bill.

'What if one of us gets off our horse and walks with a small branch with a fire on the end of it, like a lantern?' suggested

Carter. 'Dixon's got kerosene in his bag, and I can rip a bit of me shirt and wrap it around the stick.'

Dixon and Bill chatted to each other about Carter's suggestion. They looked across at Howard still losing blood between the stitches, and at Leopold.

'I think we have to take the chance,' said Dixon. He knew the look of death, and the sheer exhaustion they showed in their eyes. He had seen it too many times.

'Thing is,' said Bill, 'horses are scared of fire, might become frisky, and tire themselves out even more; they might even bolt. And the scrub is so dry, that if you drop the flame, we could start a bushfire.'

'Fair enough,' agreed Dixon. 'Best just to go slowly, then, to keep this lot going, or they might not make it in the morning.'

Not much was said for the next gruelling hour; they simply listened for any sign of danger, the men's heads tilted towards the ground, swaying to the rhythm of the horses.

When they finally made it back to Palmerston, no man or horse was free of exhaustion. They rode straight to the makeshift hospital. Bill and Carter got off their horses and mustered what strength they had left to help Howard, who put his arms over their shoulders and was virtually carried into the ward.

'Is there a medico on duty? This man's not too good. Got taken by a croc, and if that fella out there hadn't shot the croc, he would surely not have lived long enough to get back here,' said Bill, pointing to Leopold.

'The medical officer's wife was on duty. As she moved forward to assist, she looked out through the entrance towards Leopold. Is he alright? He doesn't look too good either.' She had no special training as a nurse, but was only too pleased to be able to help her husband at times like this.

'He'll be okay,' said Dixon. 'I'll go with him to his cabin if you're okay in here now.'

Dixon climbed back on his horse and took the reins of Leopold's horse.

'Come on then,' he said, and the horses walked on to Leopold's cabin.

Once Dixon had helped him inside, Leopold pulled off his dusty boots and lay down on his bamboo bed.

'Can you get me a drink, and then pull this mosquito curtain around? I just need to sleep … my eyes are so tired and sore.'

'Probably just from the dust,' said Dixon, handing Leopold a drink. 'You'll feel better after a rest, a long one by the looks of it. We all need a rest.'

During the night, Leopold awoke, delirious and with a fever. He had muscle pains, especially in his back, and a severe headache. For the next three days, he continued to shiver, and had diarrhoea and vomiting. Bill had been calling in to check on him and asked the medico to come and see Leopold. He drank as much water as he could, to ward off dehydration, but it did little good.

Leopold tossed and turned in his bed, dreaming of his home and family, colourful dreams that twisted around in his groggy mind.

'Mama, where are you, Mama? Can't one of the girls … no. I don't want to go. Alhard had it before I did. I asked him not to … why did you go there anyway? Is anyone there? I'm here all alone?' Leopold began shouting, 'Is anyone out there or am I all alone?'

While he seemed to improve at times, and with Bill coming to check up on him every day, he still couldn't manage to pull out of his illness. He eventually experienced the worst twenty-four hours since his illness began, developing a dangerously higher fever and yellowing of his skin.

An Aboriginal man, Mick, had come into Palmerston in the early hours of the morning, before sunrise, and heard Leopold shouting out in his sleep. He had been out with Leopold and another trooper some weeks ago, and they had got on well together.

When Mick walked into Leopold's cabin, he was immediately concerned about Leopold's sweaty brow and his rantings. Mick tried to help in the only way he knew. He lifted the calico curtain up and away from the bed, sat on the edge of the bed, close to Leopold's head and shoulders, took a deep breath, and then blew air over Leopold's face. He placed his hands around the back of Leopold's neck and began massaging his knotted muscles.

'STOP!' yelled a curious neighbour who had heard the commotion. 'Get away from him, now ... go on. Get.'

Mick ignored him and went on trying to help Leopold get rid of the evil that had made him so sick.

The neighbour rushed to get Bill, who understood the Aboriginal ways.

Leopold seemed oblivious to what was going on, merely continuing his delirious rantings. 'I told you ... *Ich habe nichts getan ... WAS. Tag, Therese, wo ist Mutti? Ist sie mit Papa? Ja, Mutti, ich habe viel Hunger. Mutti, du musst mit Papa sprechen.*'

Bill entered the room with the neighbour, and as soon as he recognised Mick sitting on Leopold's bed, he said, *'Mamu'*.

'It's the Aboriginal way,' explained Bill, turning to the neighbour. 'When any of them have a fever, they think that a bad spirit, *mamu*, has entered the body. They blow in their faces to blow the bad spirits away, and then they massage their necks to help the blood flow and to push away negative energy ... Mick's not trying to strangle him like you thought, he's trying to help.'

The neighbour was incensed by what had happened, and was still suspicious of Mick.

Mick lifted Leopold's head off the pillow, and gently poured some water into his mouth.

'They think that his heart's hot, and that they have to cool it off,' Bill said, as Mick stood and left without a word, merely patting Bill on the arm as he passed.

'Don't know I'd have one of 'em helping me,' scolded the neighbour.

'When someone is in trouble, it's natural for them to want to help. They might believe in different things, but they value family and share whatever it is they have ... and if someone is sick, they don't think it's right just to leave them that way,' explained Bill.

Bill stayed with Leopold, listening to him rambling in German, until the sun came up. The neighbour had left not long after Mick to fetch the medical officer. By the time the medical officer arrived, Leopold was bleeding from his nose, his eyes, and his mouth.

'By the look of his yellow skin and eyes, I reckon he's got yellow fever,' said the medico. 'We better move him to the ward. If we don't, he'll surely die.'

# Thirty

Endless bowls of potato and onion soup, tough buffalo and kangaroo meat, and bananas and pineapples for sweets were helping Leopold grow strong again and put on weight after his ordeal with yellow fever.

It was a long, tedious recovery that made Leopold all the more determined to get back home soon to his family in Germany. He had written to his brother about his harrowing time and his near-death experience.

Leopold leaned out of bed and reached into the wobbly, hospital bedside table to extract the letter he had written to Alhard. He unfolded the pages and began to read it again,

*Dear Alhard,*

*I am writing to ask if you and the family could write to me more often, as I have not heard from anyone for months. The mail only comes up here four times a year, so if your letter arrives in Australia after the ship has sailed, it can be eight months with no news from home. I hope you have not forgotten me.*

*I have been here in the wilderness for some time now, and I have been desperately ill, losing almost forty pounds in weight. I look like a skeleton. We don't have a proper hospital here yet, and I am in this dreadfully hot wooden ward and have been for some weeks. The*

*doctors think I may have caught yellow fever. Apart from the muscle pain and everything else that happens to your body when you are so sick, I was told I was bleeding from my eyes and mouth ... I was too sick to really care if I lived or died. Who would believe that a miniscule insect like the mosquito could be so dangerous?*

*This experience has made me miss home and my family more than anything else, and I feel so far away. I want to come home, dear brother. I want to come home more than anything else in the world.*

*One of the doctors tells me that I may have to leave the police force, and expects that I will possibly have problems with my liver and kidneys for the rest of my life. I must certainly leave the Northern Territory, and so my two-year contract will be terminated early.*

*It was a shock to arrive in a country so different to Germany, but to come up here, to such a remote and harsh environment has been very difficult. The people are friendly, and we try to help each other, but water is scarce, and the days are long and hot under an unforgiving sun.*

*My home is a log cabin, eight feet by fifteen feet square. It is my castle.*

*There have been problems up here between some of the Aborigines and the white men. I think there always has been. And often the Europeans refuse to listen and learn. Back in the early Eighteen sixties, not long before I came up here, two explorers, Burke and Wills, ventured into the centre of Australia. It was before the Overland Telegraph was put down, and the Aborigines and the explorers crossed paths. Burke and Wills were scared of the Aborigines, and even though the Aborigines offered to help, Burke and Wills refused. I think their arrogance or fear lead to their deaths? Another explorer, by the name of Stuart, had such a different attitude to the Aborigines when they offered him help, and he survived.*

*Right now, I would be happy to have somebody to help me.*

*I don't know if the Aborigines and white people will ever be able to work together. The Aborigines are an interesting people with a strong sense of family, yet they are still quite innocent and naïve. They know this land so well and tell interesting stories about it. If I was ever lost in this wilderness, which is easily done, I would trust that they would help me, as they tried to do when I was first so ill. Mick, one of the Aboriginal trackers, helped when I was ill.*

*I end this letter, dear brother, by letting you know that I shall be going back to live in Adelaide and will forward my address to you when I have it. Once again, I want to come home.*

*Give my love to the family.*
*Don't forget me*
*Your loving brother*
*Leopold*

'Who are you writing to?' asked the medical officer's wife, inquisitively, as she stepped into the room. 'Family?'

Leopold looked up. 'I thought I would write to my brother, let him know how I am.'

'I suppose you miss everyone. Are they down in Adelaide? I hope you don't mind me asking you, only I feel I know you a bit. Funny, isn't it? An odd way to get to know someone. I was here every night and most days, and they thought you were going to die ... you were so, so sick. Good to see your colour is more normal.'

Leopold smiled at her. 'I used to have people to look after me, when I was younger, but, since I've come to Australia, I've had to look after myself in every possible way. At least I had a good life once ... back in Germany it was a good life, and an easy one. Don't know that I ever really appreciated it til now.'

'I thought your accent might be German. I had a bet,' she said, smiling, 'with one of the younger girls that helps here. I said I thought you were German, and she thought you were Dutch.'

'Definitely German, although my grandfather was Dutch, so I suppose you're both right to a degree,' said Leopold, trying to be diplomatic.

'One of the troopers, Lewis, I think he said, told me you're a Count or something. Lived in a castle back in Germany. Is that true? I can remember when I was a little girl, and my mother would read me stories about princesses ... always wanted to be a princess when I was little ... or a fairy, and have a magic wand. Suppose all little girls do really.' She laughed, looking at him in the hope he would answer her questions.

She went over and sat on the end of his bed, holding the clean sheets that she had brought in with her, waiting to hear what he would say. 'What is it like? To be a Count ... to be someone special that others watch and look up to?'

'It is quite different. My grandmother was a princess, and she was such a beautiful person, and with titles like hers come a lot of expectations and demands. Her full title was, Her Serene Highness Princess Therese Bentheim-Tecklenburg-Rheda. And I loved her dearly ... I think people forget that royals live real lives ... even though they may be remarkable lives.

'The life I've had here is certainly different ... my grandfather was a count, but I'm a baron, and come from many generations of titled people.'

'Really,' she said.

'We never really talked about it at home, never thought we were special or anything like that. And everyone back in Germany knows our history. It's unsaid. I suppose we don't really have to explain ourselves. It's just a way of life, and it's accepted.' Leopold let his mind wander for a brief moment. 'The most enjoyable part of it is the many people you get to meet, and all the places you get to travel to. The worst of it is that if you do the wrong thing, you're sent to Australia!'

'Really,' she said, with a little sigh. 'Did you do the wrong thing?'

Leopold did not really have the energy to explain everything, and he didn't feel right telling someone he hardly knew about his ordeal.

'I appreciate you looking after me … you remind me of my sister … when I was sick I heard your voice in my foggy brain, and it was soothing … just for a moment I thought it was my sister, and that I was back in Germany. It made me feel that I was being cared for again. That was nice.'

Emily, one of the other women who helped out, came in with a tray with a pot of tea, some milk and sugar, and a slice of home-made cake that the medical officer's wife had made.

'Thank you,' he said. 'I don't seem to recall your name?'

'Emily, Sir,' she replied.

'Please, call me Leopold. Would you like to take tea with me? It's the least I can do for the wonderful care you've given me,' he said, smiling at her. 'I shall be going back to Adelaide when I've recovered.'

'That'll be a few months, probably. You've lost so much weight, and your condition isn't good. It'll take a while to fatten you up again,' said Emily. 'Besides, I don't even think there's a steamship for months.'

Leopold just nodded in agreement, not fully paying attention. He was thinking about Germany.

# Thirty-One

'How long do you think it will take you to get back to normal?' asked Ernst, who had picked up Leopold from the wharf at Port Adelaide. 'You look thin enough to get blown away in a strong wind.'

'More than likely you could thread me through one of those bag needles they use for sewing up the hay bales,' responded Leopold, able to laugh at his situation as they put his bags and a few items of interest he had gathered on his journey into the carriage.

'I'll take you home to freshen up before you meet the Governor at Government House later today,' said Ernst.

Compared to Palmerston, Adelaide seemed so large and hectic to Leopold. There were clean city streets, people riding on trains, and people flitting in and out of the stores to buy their goods. And instead of having to walk a mile in the heat with a bucket to collect water from Peel's Well, there were water fountains. 'Such luxury,' thought Leopold.

Leopold had been introduced to the Governor through a mutual friend, George Kingston, who had held the position of Deputy Surveyor to Colonel William Light, and who became the first speaker of the House of Assembly.

Leopold gave his name, Baron Leopold von der Borch, to the guard on duty at Government House in the new guard house, and he was directed to enter by the State Entrance which fronts on to North Terrace.

Leopold looked at the two distinctive facades of Government House, each built around Eighteen forty and Eighteen fifty-five respectively. The Eighteen-forty east facing arc-like bow fronted wing had shuttered windows. The Eighteen-fifty-five wing, facing south, he thought looked more regal with its Italianate-features and portico. He cast his eyes to the roofline and the craftsmanship that went into building it with slate.

He marvelled at the surrounding grounds, and thought to himself that it was probably the most prestigious site in Adelaide, with its park-like setting and extensive lawns and gardens, reminiscent of some of the English gardens he had seen in London.

Leopold was greeted at the front door by the footman, and led into the State Room where Governor Musgrave's was waiting to greet him.

It was one o'clock exactly, and the men launched directly into a conversation about the garden.

'It's rather beautiful, Musgrave,' said Leopold in an animated manner.

'Yes, very relaxing here, and there have been many changes over the years, and I'm sure there will be many more,' replied Musgrave.

'The garden for a start, had a number of gum trees removed a couple of years ago, and a fellow by the name of Richard Schomburgk, Director of the Botanic Gardens, he was responsible for providing the pines, cypresses and shrubs. One of your kind, Schomburgk, over here from Germany. But, I mean, he would be, wouldn't he, with a name like that. Be from Germany!' said Musgrave, feeling a little awkward and not wanting to offend.

'The palms you walked past are from the original planting, and, of course, so are the Hoop Pine and the Morton Bay Fig,' Musgrave explained. 'And, of course, the Hoam Oak's been here so long, I'm not sure when that was planted, possibly at the same time?'

'How long have you been Governor?' asked Leopold, as they walked through to meet the other invited dinner guests. 'I know when I first met you, before I left for the Northern Territory, you were Governor.'

'Not long ... Eighteen seventy-three I became Governor, I was here when they authorized the connection of the telegraphic circuit to Western Australia, and when the University of Adelaide Act was passed to encourage the formation of a university.'

Governor Musgrave stopped in the passage before they had a chance to meet the others, to focus on his conversation. A framed gold-picture of Queen Victoria hung on the wall behind his head, and distracted Leopold for a moment.

Leopold was about to speak when Musgrave interrupted him. 'And of course, I was here when the Civil Service Act was put in place. The servants working for the government needed an incentive to stay with us, so we had to do something to improve their status to get them to stay with us.' He almost sighed with relief that he had remembered it all.

Musgrave continued. 'Let's talk of something a little closer to the point, to the reason why I invited you to come and see me today ... your time in the Northern Territory, and how you recovered from yellow fever in those primitive conditions.'

Before Leopold could speak, Musgrave again continued his speech. 'I hear they've named a river after you, after you killed that retched crocodile that took that chap. One of the men sent the skin down to Adelaide, and we're planning to put it in the museum.'

'Certainly not an easy posting ... very primitive setting, and like nothing else I had experienced. I found the Aboriginal people easy to get along with, especially once we had time to adapt to each other. They certainly helped us to establish a settlement up there, find food and water ... and yet we had problems, like the Barrow Creek Massacre. Apart from being over a hundred miles away, I had only recently recovered from yellow fever and didn't have the strength to do anything much except recuperate. Both natives and whites were killed as troopers were trying to protect the overland telegraph and our communication with the world. Troopers Gason and Born dealt with it mostly, along with some of the station owners, but a dreadful thing for everyone. I haven't spoken to them personally and I don't like to speculate, so I'll leave it at that,' explained Leopold.

'Dinner will be served momentarily, Sir,' said the butler to Governor Musgrave, looking very formal in his black suit, stiff white shirt and black tie.

'Thank you,' answered Musgrave, then turned to face Leopold to continue the conversation.

'Now, where were we ... Yes. A dreadful thing that massacre. There was talk of two white men being killed. Something about a waterhole being blocked off from the Aborigines. Or was it to do with the way the white men treated the Aboriginal women?' said Musgrave.

'Not for me to speculate,' answered Leopold, who, as an aristocrat, had been taught not to get too involved in political discussions.

'True; very diplomatic of you.' Musgrave paused for a moment, then continued. 'It's been told to me, young Leopold, that you will no longer be able to go to places such as Palmerston, as your health is still rather poor. Is that right?'

'From what the doctor has told me they think I should take it easy for a while. Possibly a desk job. I'll wait and see. They say I was lucky to survive, and as I did, they think I'll have some problems with internal parts, my liver and kidneys, possibly for the rest of my life.'

'You look such a healthy young specimen, though. Very athletic!' said Musgrave. Perhaps in need of some good food, that's all.'

'Yes, I look forward to getting back some weight and gaining some strength,' replied Leopold.

'Paul Foelsche … you would have certainly met him at Palmerston? Decent chap, and doing a good job up there. Been there since Eighteen sixty-nine I believe, first lot of chaps that went up there to settle things when they put the overland telegraph line in. Good police officer if ever I saw one.'

'Yes, of course …,' said Leopold.

'Yes, Foelsche's taken some damn good photos in Palmerston, and of its surrounds, and of the natives, etcetera, so that got me thinking … we could do with something like that here,' said Musgrave, looking intently at Leopold.

Leopold nodded his head.

'Well then, what would you think of being the first official police photographer, Leopold?' said Musgrave, looking very pleased with himself. 'All the other photographs have been taken by anyone who happened to be around, and we paid them, but we haven't had someone who was dedicated just to police work, and someone who was a member of the police force ... so what do you think? Interested?'

'I'd be honoured, though I'm not sure what I would photograph?' said Leopold.

'It's my opinion that what we need is someone to photograph the criminals before and after they go to jail. We've had escapes, and it's almost impossible to recognise them once they grow beards or grow their hair back ... the Kelly Gang in Victoria is a good example, they get away with blue murder. The eldest one, Edward, spent three years in Pentridge prison, around Eighteen seventy-three, for receiving stolen goods, and his younger brother, Daniel, was suspected of being a part of the Mansfield murder. Mark my words, we don't want people like the Kellys roaming around here. It's all very well shaving their heads when they go into jail, but when they come out and grow back a head of hair and a decent beard, we wouldn't know who they were. I believe we need photographs to identify criminals like them.?' asked Musgrave.

'It sounds interesting and not too tiring. I'm ready to sleep early these days, but the doctor tells me that this will improve,' answered Leopold, pleased at the prospect of work, and the hope of saving enough money to go home. After the initial hiccup of arriving in Adelaide with no money from Schönebeck, Leopold was grateful that the problem had been sorted out, and he was now receiving a monthly income. The cost of living in Australia was at least three times that of Germany.

'Did you know I could make three times the amount of money as a bricklayer in Germany than I can as a police officer in Adelaide? Not that I'm complaining; it's just an interesting aside,' said Leopold.

'The government will pay for the camera and everything you require to set yourself up. I'll be most interested to see how it goes … I have an amateur interest in photography myself,' said Musgrave, feeling that he was sharing something personal with Leopold.

'Excuse me, Sir,' said the footman to the Governor, 'your other guests are waiting for you, and dinner is about to be served.'

'We'd best get moving then, young Leopold. Now what was it you started to say,' asked Musgrave, as they walked to the door of the dining room.

'Can you recommend where I can get the equipment?' asked Leopold.

The dining room door opened as if by itself. The other guests stood up as Musgrave and Leopold entered the room.

'Here, young Leopold. I've asked them to sit you to my right, so that we may continue our conversation.'

Slowly the noise from the various conversations around the table started to grow.

'Leave it with me, and perhaps between us we'll sort something out. The government will pay you a regular wage of course, so there's no bother there … Yes, so that should be it. Done.'

'Thank you. I'd indeed be most interested,' replied a cheerful Leopold, as the two men shook hands to seal the deal. 'And what about your other interests, besides photography, Musgrave? As Governor?'

'Glad you asked. During my time as Governor I've become quite interested, I must say, in extending the railway service, but that of course means raising taxes, and I'm not sure that others are in agreement with me. Then of course I think we should be getting more migrants coming in. A third of all the men have left, gone up to the goldfields, so we have a shortage of workers,' Musgrave replied, bouncing up and down on his heels. His bald head, with a light sprinkling of hair, and his scarecrow beard, amused Leopold.

'Excuse me, Gentlemen, dinner is ready to be served. If you could take your seats,' announced the butler.

The men walked into the State Room, greeted the other guests, and sat at the highly polished wooden table.

For the first time in five years, Leopold was happy to sit at a formal dining table, with place-names for each guest, beautiful china, and staff to serve the meals and drinks.

The china plates were white, with the letters SAGH, the initials for South Australian Government House, emblazoned on them in blue.

Silver cutlery, also adorned with the SAGH letters, had been placed on the table, and measured with a ruler, so that the handles of the cutlery were exactly an inch from the table edge. There were also three glasses for each person: one for water, one for white wine, and one for red wine. In the centre of the table, a beautiful glass vase filled with a flourish of coloured flowers and greenery.

'For starters,' the butler announced, 'there will be a *potage à la duchesse*, asparagus soup thickened with egg yolks and cream; and *merluchons fleur de sel au beurre fondu avec une sauce d'anchois liée,* salted Hake in butter with creamy anchovy sauce.'

As the meals were served, Leopold was delighted at how beautifully they were presented and how delicious the food tasted. Wine was savoured throughout the courses, and the conversation flowed.

'*Chevreuil rôtie à la gelée de groseilles,* roasted venison served with redcurrant jelly,' announced the butler, as the main course arrived. And later, for dessert, '*Glace à l'orange,* orange sorbet.'

The evening ended in the drawing room, with discussions about the future of Adelaide, a few glasses of port, and a cigar.

# Thirty-Two

'Collodian photography is both difficult and somewhat dangerous to do,' said Leopold's instructor, 'and the room can smell heavily of chemicals. But it certainly shows much more detail in the photographs than the dry plates.'

Leopold looked at the bottles of chemicals and other paraphernalia on the shelf: collodian drain, collodian, collodian positives, varnish drain, pure alcohol, glass tubes and rods in glass beakers, silver salts and ferrous sulphate and other containers of equally dangerous chemicals tucked in behind the bottles.

'What is it that you have to photograph?' asked the instructor. 'The Governor sent a message that I needed to train you, but said nothing about why?'

'Criminals. Men mostly, but a few women as well, who have committed larceny, murder, anything that requires them to be incarcerated,' replied Leopold. 'The idea is to photograph them when they arrive to go to jail, and then after they've had their heads shaven, so that if they escape, we can track them down more quickly.'

'I thought they had people to take photographs like that?' commented the instructor.

'Yes, there have been, but none of them have been in the police force, and the Governor believes that this will be an important step for the police department to take, in order to improve their resources,' answered Leopold, wondering why the instructor asked so many questions.

'Very well then ...,' replied the rather droll photographer, before returning to the job at hand. 'There are two solutions that have to be made a day or so before we need to use them, and once they are made, we then combine them and let them cure overnight.'

Leopold took a quill, ink and paper to write down the instructions as he was shown what to do.

'The two solutions are collodian and silver nitrate. We'll start with the collodian first as it takes a little longer to make.'

The instructor asked Leopold to hand him the various chemicals as they were needed.

'To make the collodian solution, we'll need potassium bromure ... up there to your left ... and potassium iodine ... that bottle of pure alcohol next to the nitrate, and of course distilled water, which I'll get. The chemicals we use to mix with the collodian is what helps to make it photosensitive, and the collodian itself helps the silver nitrate to adhere to the plate. And, of course, it's the silver nitrate that makes the plate sensitive to light. But first things first. Let's concentrate on the collodian solution for now.

'What about the silver nitrate?' asked Leopold.

'Be patient, I'll explain it more as we go along, otherwise it'll be confusing for you. Now, let's get back to making the collodian solution.

The instructor carefully measured out the potassium bromure, potassium iodine, pure alcohol and distilled water, and stirred them together with a glass rod.

'Looks simple enough,' said Leopold innocently.

'It may look simple, but if the ingredients aren't measured correctly, you won't get the detail you need … And that's only one part of what we need to do,' said the instructor as he continued stirring.

'Right … looking good. Now, once we've mixed those, we pour the collodian into the potassium bromide-iodine solution we've just made, and mix them together.' He was hoping that Leopold was taking in all the information, and, in the correct order.

'Now that we have our collodian solution, we'll put a glass lid on it, to prevent it evaporating, while we get a glass jar to put it in,' continued the instructor. 'Some photographers use cork to seal the mixture, but I've found that very small fragments of cork tend to fall into the solution, and then of course, the photographs end up looking very poor. I prefer glass. It might evaporate a little, but I allow for that by making a little more than I need.'

Leopold wondered if the instructor would stop to take a breath, and why he had not organised a jar for the solution before he had made it.

Outside the rain began to fall on the iron roof. It was a soft, gentle patter of rain that delighted Leopold, such a contrast to Palmerston that had been so hot and dry, with little or no rain at all.

'It's raining!' Leopold declared excitedly, and for a moment he thought of escaping outside just to feel the rain on his face.

'The colloidal solution might look cloudy now, but I can guarantee, that in twenty-four hours, it will be clear and the colour of golden honey.'

'Can you not hear me, you intellectual, boring man,' thought Leopold, as he watched the instructor pour the collodian solution into a glass jar, place a glass lid on top, and label and date it.

'And that's the collodian process,' said the instructor.

'Now we need to make the silver nitrate. We need to be much more accurate with our measurements with this one.'

'Are there any ill effects from using all these chemicals?' asked an enthusiastic, but cautious Leopold.

'No, I don't think you need to worry too much about that. The ether can make you feel a bit tired if you don't watch yourself. If that happens just go outside and get a bit of fresh air. Other than that, I can't really say.'

'It's raining,' said Leopold again, hoping to incite some enthusiasm in the instructor.

Leopold had not remembered the instructor's name, nor did he intend to ask him. He wondered if the instructor thought he was stupid, considering the way he talked to him, and the way he completely ignored his comments about the falling rain.

'What about the silver nitrate?' asked Leopold.

'The silver salts that we use to make the silver nitrate are relatively harmless, and in fact some of the scholars believe they can be used as an antiseptic, although no-one has proven it yet … I suppose about the worst thing that can happen to you, with brief exposure, would be that you'd have purple, brown or black stains on your skin … mind you, longer exposure, or a more concentrated exposure, might cause burns or eye damage. Silver nitrate is known to be a skin and eye irritant.'

As the instructor became more relaxed, Leopold was wondering if he had made him feel nervous. It had happened before, when people knew about his title; and although he tended not to tell everyone, others had done it for him, in spite of Leopold wanting to make his own identity and reveal himself if or when he felt it necessary.

'Thank you for making the time to guide me through this process. It's quite a bit more intense than I expected,' said Leopold.

But again, the instructor seemed to take no notice of him.

'Thank you for making the time to guide me through this process. It's quite a bit more intense than I expected,' repeated Leopold, this time touching him on the shoulder.

'Were you talking to me, young man? You see, I'm deaf on that side, consequence of my brother firing off a shot when we were children. I should have put you on the other side of me, only the bench isn't big enough, and I can't work it that way,' explained the instructor.

'You stupid man, Leopold,' thought Leopold. 'You hate people judging *you*. You should know better than that.'

'Forgive me. I can't remember your name?' said Leopold, still feeling a little annoyed with himself.

'John Hazen Garden. John is fine.'

'Right then,' John continued. 'Let's make the silver nitrate.' He was pleased that the young man appreciated his time and the difficulty and accuracy required to make successful photographs.

This time as John talked and made the silver nitrate solution, Leopold looked on with great interest.

'We need scales and a glass beaker. Measure 90 grams of silver nitrate crystals. Put that aside and then get a glass bottle. Use a funnel and pour the crystals into the bottle … add a litre of distilled water ... stir until the crystals dissolve. If the water is cloudy, it is not pure water. Rinse the last of the crystals out of the measuring glass ... and use a glass rod to stir. This usually takes a couple of minutes ... Next we measure the gravity level. We do that by stirring the mixture, and then we see if the glass rod will stay in the centre, or near the centre of the solution, without falling over and touching the sides of the beaker. If it stays, then we're on the right track. Put the lid on, label and date it. That's very important ... In fact, I don't think I told you to do that with the colloid? Would you mind checking for me,' asked John.

'Certainly. I'd be only too happy to help,' answered Leopold.

'Now you have the basic ingredients and solutions made up, I can show you how to take the photographs and process them,' said John.

'Would you mind if we take a break from this for a short time?' asked Leopold, who was feeling a bit light-headed. 'I think I need to step outside for a moment.'

'Not at all. While you're doing that, I'll cut the glass and burr the edges ... I'll explain why I do that when you come back.'

Leopold went outside and took a few deep breaths. The cool wind was refreshing, as it blew over his face and up into his nostrils, while the rain fell on his face.

To his surprise he felt a little unnerved by the experience. The chemicals had made him feel a bit strange in the head. He could not explain it, but he felt a bit foggy, unclear of his thoughts. It reminded him of watching his horses being lifted onto the Gothenburg, and the fear they showed when their feet were lifted up off the ground. That same sense of struggling to break free.

He breathed in several more deep, cool breaths of fresh air. 'Agh! That feels better,' he said, as he relaxed himself more and more. He hoped he would soon get used to the smells, as photography seemed his best opportunity for work.

After a few more minutes had passed, he could smell the lemon-scented gum tree again and the scent of roses from the garden next door. He watched as the raindrops fell from the rose petals and plonked onto the leaves of the agapanthus below.

It was a welcome relief, as Leopold had felt a little claustrophobic indoors, almost as though he could taste the chemicals as well as smell them.

'I suppose I'll get used to it,' he decided, and went back inside to learn the next stages of taking and developing the photographs.

'Thought I might have lost you?' laughed John.

Leopold looked at him with concern. 'What do you mean?'

'Thought you might not be back,' he replied.

'Oh! No, just made me feel a bit light-headed,' explained Leopold. 'I think all those months at sea being confined have left me a little claustrophobic.'

'Happens to the best of us. Nothing to worry yourself about,' said John.

'Right then! Back to work. If you look over there you'll see some glass I've cut. I use the clear glass for negatives and black glass for positives.'

Leopold picked up a piece of the glass without thinking.

'That one's quite alright to pick up, but careful of those over there. I haven't burred the edges. The burring has two purposes, it helps to keep the solution on the plate because it makes a sort of ridge. It also prevents us getting any cuts while handling the glass, which is important considering some of the solutions in photography contain cyanide.'

Leopold carefully placed the glass square down.

'Once the glass has been burred with a sharpening stone, one of the most important things we need to do is thoroughly clean and then polish the glass with a glass wax, otherwise the collodian solution will peel off.'

Leopold looked surprised. 'How amazing. Imagine coming up with an invention like this? It's an amazing time to be born … so many advances taking place around the world.'

'Speaking of that, try this,' said John, taking a piece of chewing gum out of his pocket. 'Fairly new invention itself, and it helps me to keep my ears unblocked, and stops me feeling nauseous when I'm working.'

'Thank you. I have tried this once before. Someone on the ship coming out here gave me some to try.'

John then took a jar of collodian solution, that he had made the previous day, from the shelf. 'Perfect,' he said, 'Nice and clear.'

'This part of the process is called "flowing". This is where you pour the collodian onto the plate. It takes a lot of practice. Flows like watered-down honey,' he said, pouring the solution onto the middle of the piece of glass. 'Then you tilt the glass at various angles so that the solution flows into the corners, and then keep tipping and tilting until all of the surface is covered with the solution … this is where technique will show … if there are ridges or other marks on the glass, you'll lose detail in the finished image. After the solution has gone into all the corners, and has completely covered the glass, you pour any excess back into the jar … how are you going. Keeping up?' laughed John.

'That done, we now do what we call "sensitizing the plate" … Come over here, and I'll show you the bath, or box, it goes into, which is where the silver nitrate is … does its magic for three to four minutes.'

Leopold came close to get a better view of the box. It was charcoal in colour, and inside the box were several divisions for the glass plates to fit in.

'Put the lid on to prevent evaporation.' John paused for a moment. 'Now you're ready to take a photograph!'

'So much preparation, isn't there? I'd certainly need to prepare the solutions the night before! Imagine if I had the criminals waiting for this to be done? They'd escape in no time,' laughed Leopold. The two men had started to feel more relaxed in each other's company.

'Now, if you sit over there, I'll take your photograph … This is what we call "exposing the plate". It's the technique of allowing light to fall onto the plate … it can be the sun or any form of light. It may take a few seconds, or a few minutes, depending on the technique used and the lighting.

'The last stage is called "developing the plate", and it only takes about fifteen seconds … This is the important part of taking the photograph, and you need to know what you're looking for, so it's not underdeveloped or overdeveloped. We use potassium cyanide to fix the images.'

John pointed to a chair where he wanted Leopold to sit.

After he took the photograph, they took the glass plate into the dark room. 'Watch Leopold … you'll see it change from a bluish negative to a warm amber.'

Leopold watched as his image seemed to come from behind the glass plate and then somehow push itself through the glass to the front. He watched the colour change with great interest.

'This is when we pour the potassium cyanide over the glass plate, to "fix" the image,' explained John. They both looked at the image of Leopold. 'You're quite a handsome, photogenic young man, Leopold.'

# Thirty-Three

It was a summer's day, late in the afternoon, and the trees and buildings cast long shadows across King William Street.

Leopold had gone to the city to meet Ernst for lunch and had done a bit of shopping while he was there. On his way back from shopping, he noticed a man who looked oddly familiar. He turned and followed the man for a while, crossing over Rundle Street and continuing along King William Street.

'What is it about this man that makes me think I've seen him before, and yet I know I haven't?' thought Leopold, as he studied the man's dark hair, neat clothes, long gait and shiny black shoes.

Leopold increased the pace of his walking, keen to get a closer look, but the man seemed to be aware of Leopold and quickened his pace.

'Excuse me,' Leopold called out, but the man continued to walk faster.

'Excuse me. Could you stop for a moment, please?'

The man put his hands in his coat pockets and turned around to take a look at who had been following him.

'Can I help you?' asked the man.

Leopold looked at the man's face more closely. 'Now I know why he looks so familiar,' thought Leopold. 'The same nose, brown eyes, high cheek bones, even the attached earlobes.'

'I'm sorry if I gave you a start, but I had a feeling that I knew you from somewhere, and now that I can see your face, I do recognise it, or at least I think I do,' explained Leopold to the rather perplexed man.

'What is it you want?'

'I don't want anything from you ... well, I suppose I do really, I'm not exactly sure how, or where to start ... I suppose I should introduce myself. I'm Police Officer von der Borch, and I was wondering if you've read the papers during the past two weeks?'

'Well, I can assure you, Officer, I've done nothing wrong. My name is ... well, just call me Wachter ... everyone else does ... yes, I usually keep up with the news. Why?'

'There was an article in the paper about a man who bears a strong resemblance to you, and I wondered if you'd seen it?' asked Leopold.

'I haven't actually read the papers myself for a while ... I've had sore eyes, and the doctor gave me something to get rid of the infection. It made everything look blurry. But I've come good the last day or so, particularly today. Why do you ask?'

'Bear with me ... As I said, I'm not sure how to go about this. I'm more of a police photographer, and when I saw you, I didn't want to miss the opportunity to talk to you. I'll get straight to the point. Do you have a brother?'

'Yes, I have a couple of brothers, although I haven't seen one of them for a few years, maybe never will again, I reckon. He was always a bit different to the rest of us. Always wanted to see other places, do his own thing ... you know the type ... heart of gold, but have to be their own person ... if you know what I mean?'

Leopold nodded his head. 'As a police photographer I get asked to go out to take photographs of criminals and—'

Before he could finish, the stranger interjected and said, 'Wouldn't surprise me. My brother could get up to anything … think that's why he left home in the first place … Nothing he did would surprise me.'

'No, he hasn't done anything wrong. Well, not as far as we know, but … could I get you to have a look at a photograph for me? I've been carrying it around, hoping I might find out who he is. As I was saying, I get asked to go out to visit places where a crime has been committed, or if there's someone we need to identify…,' said Leopold trying to be subtle, 'who's … unable to tell us who they are.'

'This person had some kind of an accident then, did he, hit himself on the head or been kicked by a horse, and he can't remember anything? And you think it might be my brother?'

'Let me show you the photograph first; hopefully you can make it out well enough,' said Leopold, handing the man the photograph.

'It's my brother, I think,' said Wachter, focusing on the image, 'but he looks so strange, so unwell. Yes, it's him, but what … what happened to him?' Wachter feared the worst. 'Can I go and visit him?'

'Unfortunately, your brother met with an accident, or at least we presume it was an accident, and as a result, he died. He was found at Glenelg Beach; apparently, he drowned. I'm sorry I have to be the bearer of bad news.'

Wachter was silent, staring at his brother's image.

'We had no way to identify him, no watch, nothing to follow up. The Governor asked me to take his photograph instead of relying on the usual paperwork, which often doesn't return any results in cases like this.'

'I'm glad you followed me, and followed your instincts, otherwise I would never have known what became of my roaming brother,' said Wachter, handing back the photograph.

'I am, too. I genuinely feel for the loss of your brother,' said Leopold, comfortingly. 'I guess, we can also thank the Governor for his decision to take photographs like these. They will soon be part of the standard information that police will have on file, in the city at least.'

'Where's my brother buried? I'd like to put some flowers on his grave.'

'Would you mind coming to the police station first, to formerly identify the photograph of your brother? And then I can personally take you to see where your brother is buried, if you like. I'd like to pay my respects to him, too,' said Leopold.

'Thank you,' said Wachter. 'Thank you so much. I'll be able to put my mother's mind at peace now, and we'll know where to find him if she wants to visit,' and he shook Leopold's hand.

# Thirty-Four

The proprietor of the Hamburg Hotel, Thomas O'Leary, chatted to Leopold and Meyer when they arrived at his hotel before showing them to their usual Friday-night table. It was a place frequented by both businessmen and most of the German population of Adelaide. The Liedertafel and the German Club were a big part of the hotel's attraction, as they provided the men with a chance to speak their own language, and to enjoy the culture they missed.

Leopold followed O'Leary to the table by the front window, while Meyer went off to order two beers. When Meyer returned, he said, 'When we came in you were starting to tell me about a case you'd been working on in Lobethal?'

'Yes … It's a very curious case indeed,' said Leopold. 'I was acting as both a detective and the interpreter of the case. It happened over three months ago now, but has just begun to spark interest again.

'A man by the name of Gottlieb Schulz died on his property and was buried without an inquest, and now they think he may have been poisoned, but they can't prove it. One of the witnesses giving evidence at the time was Edward Hunold, the ex-suitor of Schulz's daughter, Julia. Julia had apparently been destitute for months. We later discovered that it was Edward who had found a bottle, four or five weeks after Schulz had died. But apparently, Julia wasn't very happy about him finding it. It was his evidence that made them question Julia again.

'Apparently, Julia had asked the local brewer, Conrad Diedrich Engelking, to help her put her father's body in a coffin, before she had sent a telegram to the doctor, and before an inquest. When Engelking found that out, he refused to help.

'Captain Rollinson asked me to assist him with the investigation, and we gave evidence to the coroner. Prost!

' Leopold clinked glasses with Meyer and took a sip of his cold beer.

'Prost,' said Myer, 'I remember reading about him and that case in the paper. Something about the man committing suicide, or so they thought, until someone suggested he might have been murdered, by his wife.'

'Yes, I think most people thought the same thing, that it was the wife,' said Leopold. 'But the wife's blind, so it would have been difficult for her to have altered his medication, and then make the whole thing look like a suicide or an accident. Interestingly enough, the wife had called the station a week before, and I was asked to be her interpreter. She said that she thought her husband was dying, so I went out to their home, but by the time I got there I thought he had died. My first instinct was to feel for a pulse, but I couldn't find one. So I put my hands on his shoulders, to see if that would wake him, but he seemed lifeless. I even knelt down and said a prayer for him, and that's when I heard him grind his teeth.

'He must have just been in a deep sleep, so at that stage we had no reason to suspect anything. A couple of days later, when

I saw him, he told me that he suffered from rheumatics and had pains in his muscles and joints, which slowed him down, and he couldn't walk further than the well, and that it got him down, but apart from that he was strong and healthy.'

'So what happened? What did the daughter and the wife have to say about it?' asked Meyer.

'Either of you men want another round of beers?' asked the waiter. The men nodded their heads at him to indicate they would like another beer, and Leopold and Meyer went on talking.

'According to the wife's report, the husband seemed fine enough the day before he died. He'd gone down to the well to fetch water, had dinner, but then went to bed early, saying to her and their daughter that he felt a bit strange in the head. Both the daughter and the wife continued with their meal, unconcerned. The next morning, the daughter left for the day, without having breakfast, and didn't return until after the father had been found dead.'

'Was that usual for the daughter, not to have breakfast? Or to be gone all day?' Meyer asked.

'It seems as though it was quite usual for her to do that on occasion, so they just had to take her word for it. And as for the jilted suitor, they didn't know whether to believe him or not when he said he thought the daughter was involved. What was really interesting, however, was that the day I first saw the father, when he had begun to feel a bit better, he told me that he was tired of life, because of his rheumatics. Later I heard that he had threatened to shoot himself about six years earlier. That's where the case is a bit confusing. Did he commit suicide? He had a history of wanting to shoot himself. But then, instead of a gun, the question is, did he take an overdose, or did someone try to poison him? And what also makes them question it, is the way they found his body, all curled up on his bed as though he had stomach pains.

'And another puzzling bit of information is that the bottle was found hundreds of feet away from the house, so it would have been unusual for him to have done that.'

'So, that leaves the daughter and the wife,' said Meyer.

'And Edward, the daughter's suitor!' said Leopold. 'A hawker named Pfeiffer said that Edward had found a bottle with the label almost completely gone, except for a few letters. The letter 'L' was intact and the letters 'an', so it was presumed it was a bottle of Laudanum. Same shape and size. But I wonder whether he found it, or whether he was the culprit and took the bottle with him to hide the evidence, and then, worried about being caught with it in his possession, made up the story about finding it?'

As the men in the Liedertafel started singing, Leopold and Meyer's voices were gradually drowned out.

'So, who did it?' asked Meyer, having to speak louder. 'You were saying that the bottle had been thrown a hundred feet away. That makes me wonder why they would have thought his wife did it?'

Leopold was delighted that the case intrigued Meyer as much as it had him. 'I agree,' he said, 'they knew the wife was blind, so if she wanted to get rid of a bottle, surely she would've hidden it somewhere rather than just throwing it away, not knowing for sure if it was out of sight or not.'

Meyer nodded, anxious to hear more.

'We may never know the truth. Schulz's body was finally exhumed, but it was too decomposed to be able to confirm the cause of death.'

'So, somebody got off with the perfect crime, it would seem?' said Meyer.

'That's what I suspect, but the judge concluded that Gottlieb Schulz died of natural causes.'

'But surely somebody killed him?' said Meyer. 'What if the daughter did do it? Then again, maybe the father took the Lauda … whatever it is, and she just got rid of the bottle for him?'

'The thing with Laudanum is that it's very bitter, so it would have to be mixed with food or something very sweet to disguise it. Of course, the fact that a burial certificate was written out by the registrar rather than a medical certificate made the whole case more suspicious. The Act of 1852 requires that a medical practitioner is in attendance of the deceased body, and that didn't occur. So that also added to the confusion. The conclusion, it would appear, after weeks in court, and weeks of interrogation, is that the daughter's ex-suitor simply fabricated the whole thing about the daughter murdering her father, when in fact poor old Gottlieb died of natural causes.'

At that very moment, Meyer was distracted by O'Leary's auburn-haired daughter walking across the room. 'Look over there, Leopold. That's her. Remember me telling you about her?'

'Yes, she's certainly beautiful,' said Leopold. 'But she looks nothing like O'Leary.'

'Well, she's his adopted daughter. Her mother died when she was only nine, or so I heard, and her father re-married, and they went back to live in New South Wales. Apparently she was very unhappy, so she came back to live with her aunt and uncle, with O'Leary.'

'So, what's her real father's connection to O'Leary?'

'Her real father is O'Leary's brother-in-law ... his wife's brother. That's why O'Leary and his wife adopted her.'

'I know what that's like. I lost my own mother when I was only twelve. It was certainly difficult enough to get through. My stepmother was my mother's sister, and she was so kind to us.'

'You two have something in common, then. Good excuse to say hello to her,' said Meyer, laughing.

'I was thinking it might be less conspicuous if I joined the Liedertafel Wednesday nights,' laughed Leopold. 'Do you know her name?'

'Sarah,' said Meyer.

Leopold watched as Sarah walked upstairs to the living quarters of the Hamburg Hotel.

# Thirty-Five

It was a typically balmy summer evening in Adelaide, and Meyer and Leopold met at the Hamburg Hotel at eight o'clock, as they usually did on Fridays. Carl Bosch, Leopold's closest friend, actually, more like a brother than a friend, also met with them.

It would be Christmas soon and Leopold was feeling homesick.

The Liedertafel could be heard practising their Christmas carols upstairs, but when 'Silent Night' began, everyone downstairs stopped to listen.

*'Stille Nacht, heilige Nacht!*
*Alles schläft; einsam wacht*
*Nur das traute hochheilige Paar*
*Holder Knabe im lockigen Haar*
*Schlaf in himmlischer Ruh!*
*Schlaf in himmlischer Ruh!'*

Some of the men sitting next to Leopold began to join in,

*'Stille Nacht, heilige Nacht!*
*Hirten erst kund gemacht*
*Durch der Engel Halleluja*

*Tönt es laut von fern und nah:*
*Christ, der Retter ist da!*
*Christ, der Retter ist da!'*

Leopold and Meyer smiled, and Leopold closed his eyes. His mind was cast back to Germany and his family sitting around the Christmas tree, and his younger brothers and sisters opening their presents. He opened his eyes and looked around the room, as more and more of the German men began to sing.

*'Stille Nacht, heilige Nacht!'*

Leopold, Bosch and Meyer joined in,

*'Gottes Sohn, o wie lacht*
*Lieb' aus deinem göttlichen Mund,*
*Da uns schlägt die rettende Stund*
*Christ, in deiner Geburt!*
*Christ, in deiner Geburt!'*

The song finished, and the men applauded the choir and themselves. It was the first time for ages that Leopold felt connected in his new home.

Sarah came over to Leopold and Meyer with her aunt and uncle, and was introduced to them for the first time.

'That was beautiful,' said Sarah. 'I didn't understand the words, but of all the songs they sing, this is one of my favourites.'

'Thank you,' said Meyer. Leopold nodded his head and smiled.

'Is it a German song, or is it an English song that you sing in German?' asked Sarah.

'It's an Austrian song, written by Joseph Mohr,' said Meyer. 'I suppose it's the exact reverse, really. A Germanic song, sung in English here, but it should always be sung in German, I think.'

'Do you sing?' Leopold asked Sarah, admiring her blue eyes, high cheekbones and long, auburn hair; and trying to avoid an awkward moment created by Meyer's comment.

'I do, but not to an audience or in a choir,' said Sarah.

'It's such a gift to be able to sing,' said Leopold.

Sarah's aunt and uncle joined in the conversation, which went from singing to Christmas carols, and on to how Meyer and Leopold used to spend Christmas at home in Germany.

'We listen to a lot of Celtic music,' said Sarah. 'I think the music is very haunting at times, and at other times, it's very cheery.'

Leopold was surprised at first at her comments, as other women he had met in Adelaide seemed to have no opinion at all, and he appreciated the strength of character she showed.

'I'm not very familiar with Celtic music, but from what you've just said, I think I would like it,' said Leopold.

'Would you care to join us for dinner one night?' said Thomas O'Leary to Leopold, keen for his niece to be introduced to a gentleman. 'I could get someone to fill in for me here, and we could listen to some Celtic music. And you can tell us all about your travels, and your adventures here in Australia.'

Leopold looked at Meyer.

'Of course, you would be welcome to join us also,' said O'Leary, hoping that Meyer and Bosch had other arrangements.

Meyer looked at Leopold and Sarah, and then across to O'Leary.

'Thank you, it's a kind offer, but it depends on the date?' said Meyer, not intending to come to the dinner at all.

'Very well, perhaps we could meet next Tuesday? It's usually a quiet night here,' said O'Leary.

'Thank you,' replied Leopold.

'Unfortunately, I'll have to decline your kind offer, as I told my mother I would have dinner with her that night,' said Meyer.

'Me also. I like the offer, but cannot come,' said Bosch, who knew Leopold was keen to see Sarah.

'Very good. Dinner will be at seven then. See you here at half past six, Leopold,' said O'Leary, before heading back to his office to finish some paperwork. Sarah and her aunt went upstairs to their rooms.

Meyer gave Leopold a big smile.

'I didn't think your mother was out here?' said Leopold.

'No, you're quite right. She's still in Germany,' answered Meyer.

'You're a good friend,' said Leopold, and smiled.

# Thirty-Six

Dinner with the O'Leary's began a little awkwardly, as would be expected when a young man is smitten by a beautiful young lady.

'Eat up, Leopold. There's plenty of that if you want some more,' said Thomas O'Leary. 'Irish stew's a good hearty meal for a young man, especially in your line of work.' He paused for a moment to swallow his food. 'Did Sarah tell you her father was a policeman?'

Leopold looked at Sarah and wondered if she was comfortable with her uncle telling him about her father. He waited to see if Sarah wanted to say anything herself about her father, but she remained silent.

'What do the prisoners do all day,' asked her aunt.

'They are kept busy. Some of them work in the prison bakehouse and kitchen, and the others do maintenance work or are cleaners.' Leopold replied. 'They're not all dangerous, so some of them work outside the wall as gardeners or on the olive plantation.'

O'Leary got up from the table, picked up his tin whistle and started to play. Leopold found himself tapping his foot to the music.

'Could you teach me to play the tin whistle some time? I have to agree with Sarah, it's both haunting and very cheery,' said Leopold.

'If we see enough of you, young man, I'd be happy to oblige,' said Thomas O'Leary, hoping Leopold may one day be his son-in-law.

Mrs O'Leary stared at her husband, as a warning not to say anything inappropriate. Then she turned to Leopold and asked, 'What will you be doing for Christmas, Leopold?'

'To be truthful, I haven't given it much thought. Last year, I spent Christmas in Palmerston. I suppose I'm always hoping to get back home to my family for Christmas, so I never seem to plan ahead.'

'You must miss them,' said Mrs O'Leary. 'Do you come from a big family … many brothers and sisters?'

Leopold was trying to think how he would explain it.

'Yes. I have twelve brothers and sisters in all.'

'That's quite a lot for your mother to look after,' she said.

'My mother died when I was young. She was my father's second wife. My father's first wife, Jenny, died shortly after my older half-sister Minette was born … Minette was about seventeen when my father married again, for the third time. In a way, Minette was a bit like another mother to us all at times.'

'Poor little thing, growing up without a mother,' said Mrs O'Leary.

'My mother, Ludmilla, was Jenny's niece. All of my father's wives were von der Recke's. My parents had ten children, but my mother died when I was twelve, and my youngest sibling was only two.'

'Oh. Your poor father has known a great many losses,' said Mrs O'Leary, with great sympathy.

'So that's a total of eleven for the first two marriages?' said Thomas O'Leary.

'Yes. When my father married my mother's sister, Emma, they had two more children,' explained Leopold.

'What's a von der Recke?' asked Mrs O'Leary, trying to pronounce it correctly.

'That's their surname,' smiled Leopold.

'It's quite confusing to keep track of,' said Thomas O'Leary. 'Young man, I think we'd like to see more of you in the future, and to learn more about your family and your history. Perhaps you might like to spend Christmas Day with us?'

Leopold turned to Sarah, 'Does that suit you, Sarah?'

Sarah smiled and nodded her head.

'What do you do for Christmas when you're at home?' asked Mrs O'Leary.

'Most of the time it's snowing, for at least a few days before Christmas, although, sometimes it doesn't snow at all; but when it does, it's so beautiful. My father or one of the staff would go into the pine forest, usually followed by the children, and choose a pine tree to cut down, and then we'd carry it inside and decorate it with waxed candles. The children would make Christmas cards for the family … my mother was very artistic and taught us all to paint. The Christmas cards were always very welcomed.'

'That sounds delightful. What about dinner? What do you eat?' said Sarah, 'If you don't mind me asking?'

'We celebrate Christmas on the eve, and then eat a hearty meal of roasted pork, with sauerkraut, roasted potatoes and pumpkin, and greens,' replied Leopold, delighted that Sarah was interested.

'We go for a picnic beside the River Torrens, in the city, on Christmas Day,' said Sarah. 'It's such fun, and there are so many other families around, which makes it so much more enjoyable. The thing I don't like about Christmas is the heat and the bushfires.'

'I can't say that I'm used to Christmas being so hot, even the ground is hot. It's all so dry and crisp. Not like sleet and snow. And, of course, we have deer wandering through the forest, and Christmas wreaths on the door, and Christmas carols,' said Leopold.

'Well, that's set then,' said O'Leary.

'What are you talking about, Thomas?' asked his wife.

'It's all set. Leopold will have Christmas with us this year. Isn't that right, Leopold?'

'Yes. I look forward to it. Thank you for your kind invitation. I also look forward to the lessons on the tin whistle,' said Leopold as he smiled.

# Thirty-Seven

'Remember Sarah, a lady never tolerates rudeness, crudeness, indifference or ignorance, to or from another human being. Remember to be positive in everything you say,' said Sarah's aunt. 'Oh! And think before you speak, and never gossip. And if he compliments you, accept gracefully.'

Mrs O'Leary liked Leopold and hoped that his meetings with Sarah would be successful and lead to marriage. Christmas together had been a great success, and so had been the chaperoned dates between Christmas and Valentine's Day. Sarah was twenty years of age now, and her aunt and uncle were keen to see her married and not end up an old maid.

'Auntie, do you have anything blue I could borrow?' asked Sarah.

'No, I don't usually wear blue,' said her aunt, not understanding the inference of borrowing something blue.

'What about something old?' said Sarah, dying to tell her aunt the good news.

'I'm sure I've got something old, I haven't bought myself anything for a ... Sarah,' said her aunt, 'are you saying what I think you're saying?'

Sarah smiled. 'Yes, Auntie. Leopold asked Uncle for my hand in marriage last night, and he agreed. He was so happy that he got out his tin whistle, Leopold told me, and started to play a jig.'

'How come no one told me?'

'I am, now. We're getting married, and I'm so happy!'

Sarah's aunt gave her a big hug. 'Your mother would be so proud of you. I know I am. I'm so happy for you.' And they hugged again. 'Have you decided on a date?'

'We thought that May or April would be a good time, before winter.' Sarah noticed a serious, thoughtful look on her aunt's face. 'Auntie, are you alright? You look like something is bothering you.'

'I just thought of something. What was that poem we all used to say about what month you should be married? Do you know it? It starts like:

'Marry when the year is new, always loving, kind, and true.
When February birds do mate, You may wed, nor dread your fate.
If you wed when March winds blow, Joy and sorrow both you 'll know.
Marry in April when you can, Joy for maiden and for man.

'What was the next part? Marry when the year is new. Da da da. That's it:

'Marry when the year is new, always loving, kind, and true.
'When February birds do mate You may wed, nor dread your fate.
If you wed when March winds blow, Joy and sorrow both you 'll know.
Marry in April when you can, Joy for maiden and for man.

*Marry in the month of May, you will surely rue the day.*
*Marry when June roses blow, over land and sea you'll go.*
*They who in July do wed Must labour always for their bread.*
*Whoever wed in August be, many a change are sure to see.*
*Marry in September's shine, your living will be rich and fine.*
*If in October you do marry, Love will come, but riches tarry.*
*If you wed in bleak November Only joy will come, remember.*
*When December's snows fall fast, Marry, and true love will last.*

'It's an Irish verse. They're such a superstitious lot, the Irish. Your uncle included.'

'April it is then,' said Sarah's aunt, delighted for her niece.

'I'm not sure that we can, Auntie. Leopold's a proud man and he wants to contribute to the wedding, so we might have to wait until the middle of the year.'

'He's not expected to, Sarah. I'm sure we will be able to pay for it ourselves.'

'I know, Auntie, and I'm very grateful, but I think it's important to Leopold. Do you mind?'

'This will be a new start for you both, so if it is important to Leopold, then we must accept it.' Mrs. O'Leary paused for a moment. 'Now, what about something old, something new, something borrowed, something blue and a sixpence for your shoe.'

'I didn't know about the sixpence?' said Sarah. 'Is it important? What does it mean? And why do you have to have all those things?'

'I imagine you'll have a lot of questions over the next few months? The something old is about continuity with your family.

That you remember us and don't go to his family only ... The something new is about change. Because you'll go from being a single lady living at home to a married woman in your own home, it symbolises a new start. Now what was the something borrowed for?'

Sarah shrugged her shoulders.

'Oh yes. That's for ... now what was that for? Oh yes. I lost the thought for a minute. I'm so excited. Now, the something borrowed. It can be anything, and you usually ask someone for something to borrow who is happily married, so the good luck rubs off. I remember when your uncle asked me to marry him. It was the typical Irish way of asking someone to marry them. He didn't ask, would you marry me. It was more like, would you like to hang your washing next to mine.'

They both laughed.

'What if I don't have all those things for my wedding day?' asked Sarah.

'Your uncle wouldn't have it. No Irish man would let one of his own walk down the aisle without them. It may be superstitious, but we wouldn't want to test it, would we?' said her aunt. 'Besides, I quite like the idea of these good luck things. The something blue ... that is for fidelity or faithfulness, and the sixpence is to wish you prosperity.'

'It's going to be so exciting,' said Sarah, still smiling.

# Thirty-Eight

A year to the day before Leopold and Sarah's wedding, three hundred and seventy-three pounds had been spent on renovations at the Congregational Church in Hindmarsh Square.

It was the year Eighteen seventy-five, a time of change for Leopold and Sarah, and for Adelaide: men were now only working an eight-hour day; trade unions were being recognised legally; and the University of Adelaide was preparing to start teaching.

'They who in July do wed, must labour always for their bread.' It had been a wet July, with heavy rains, but the third of July, the day of the wedding, the sun shone.

'If the sun shines on Sarah, it'll bring her good luck,' Thomas O'Leary said to his wife.

'I think you're more superstitious than I am,' she replied.

It was a small wedding, with just a few friends and family intimately gathered to hear Pastor Heinrich perform the ceremony.

Sarah looked beautiful in a white, silk wedding gown, covered in hand-made lace, a copy of the French designs she had seen in magazines. She wore white, hand-made silk shoes to match.

Thomas O'Leary walked down the aisle with Sarah on his arm. As they approached Leopold, the soon-to-be new husband and son-in-law, Leopold smiled at Sarah.

Thomas stepped next to Leopold, and gently took Sarah's arm from his and placed her hand into Leopold's hand.

'You look beautiful,' whispered Leopold.

The preacher recited prayers over the couple and asked them to take an oath to love and to honour each other, and for Sarah to obey her husband.

'Yes,' they both said.

'It was such a wonderful idea to come here for the celebration, Uncle,' said Sarah. The Hamburg Hotel was filled with music and laughter; there was delicious food, and Thomas O'Leary played the tin whistle.

The bride and groom were looking forward to a new life together, and would soon move into a four-room house together that Leopold had managed to furnish with the few pounds he had from Schönebeck.

Leopold had felt mortified at not being able to provide for his new wife the way he had intended. Someone other than Meyer and Pustkuchen had been entrusted to invest Leopold's money for him, and rather than invest the money in various stocks, as he had been directed by Alhard, the investor put all of Leopold's money into bank shares, which were lost as a result of an economic downturn after the gold rush and poor planning.

'Thank you for allowing me to marry your beautiful niece,' Leopold said to Thomas O'Leary. 'I will do my best to care for Sarah and to provide a good life for her, and I promise the same for the children we will have in the future.'

# Thirty-Nine

Leopold was given more police work, which suited him well, now that he was married and was feeling much better again physically. His strength was improving every day since contracting yellow fever.

He was given a case where the body of a baby was found in a bed of seaweed on the beach at Glenelg. The baby had been wearing a nightgown and had been discovered by a member of the public who had been riding his horse along the beach.

Footprints in the sand leading to the large bed of seaweed possibly left by the baby's mother, Joanne Sullivan, had been found.

It had seemed as though the body of the baby had been thrown into the water and had landed in the seaweed. The only mark was a bump to the back of the baby's head, but they were uncertain whether the baby had been hit on the head and then tossed into the water or had hit its head after being tossed.

Coroner Ward thought the baby had most likely died from suffocation by drowning, and may have been in the water for up to twenty-four hours.

Leopold found listening to the evidence of the various witnesses difficult. He was interpreting for Bertha Schumann, the landlady of the house where the child was born. She was being questioned by the Coroner.

'What can you tell me of Joanne Sullivan's whereabouts on the third of July?' asked Coroner Ward.

Leopold interpreted for her. 'She was at home, Your Honour.'

'Was the said baby healthy, as far as you are aware?' asked Coroner Ward.

'Yes, Your Honour, he was always nice and plump, except for his legs. They were crooked, and bandages were used to straighten them, Your Honour.'

'Can you tell me about the events that occurred on the seventeenth of July?'

Leopold looked at Bertha with a comforting smile. She had been answering questions now for some time, and her nervousness was starting to show. 'Just answer the questions as you know them to be in your heart,' said Leopold in German. Bertha was twisting a handkerchief around her index finger.

'It was a Thursday; I know that much … because every Thursday I do the front garden. A bit of weeding and trimming … She left the house with her baby, saying that she was going to take him to the bay to some people who would nurse it. She didn't come back until about eight o'clock, I think it was,' said Bertha.

'How do you know it was eight o'clock?' asked Coroner Ward.

'I'd done too much gardening that day, so I went to bed early. I'd just lit the wick in my lamp, and was closing my curtains, when I saw her. I waved at her, and she waved back.'

Bertha continued without waiting for the next question. 'She told me that she'd have to pay eight shillings a week for three months for the woman to look after her baby, and, after that, ten shillings a week, and she even told me she'd have to pay eight shillings in advance.'

The Coroner could see she was anxious to say more. 'Continue, if you like?' he prompted.

'She was crying a little bit, and she said she'd have to wash the baby's clothes, and take them down to the bay.' Bertha paused, weighing her words, before finally saying, 'I never thought she liked the poor little thing, the way she treated it.'

'You said she talked to you, when she returned home, at eight o'clock that night, yet you also said you waved to her through the window. I'm wanting some clarification around this. How and when exactly did you speak to her?' asked Coroner Ward.

'Well, when I saw her at the window, and we waved to each other, she just stood there, not moving, so I thought she wanted to talk to me, so I went outside,' explained Bertha. 'She was always a sad little creature, and I don't like to see anyone in trouble, so I thought I'd do my bit.'

'You also stated that you thought the mother did not like the child. Could you explain what you mean by this,' said Coroner Ward.

'She used to slap it when it wouldn't sleep. I'd hardly consider that going to help the child, do you? I mean, how would a baby go to sleep when it's getting slapped. Poor little beggar.'

There were no further questions for Bertha Schumann. Next, John Hamlin was called to the stand, and Coroner Ward asked him what he was doing on that Thursday.

'Thursday evening, the same one she was talking about,' he said, pointing to Bertha. 'A woman came into the bar for a nobble of brandy just after the gas was alight. I don't know that I could identify her, but she was in a dark dress with a dark veil with spots on it, and was about the same height and build as

Sullivan, the accused.' He paused for a moment, then continued, 'She looked somewhat nervous and uneasy. I can't remember anything in her arms, like a baby or a shawl, or anything ... it's unusual though for a woman to come in for a drink of brandy.'

As more witnesses came forward to tell their story of the events that took place concerning Joanne Sullivan, Leopold thought to himself, 'Did she kill her own baby? How could she do that, and why? Was it because the baby's legs were deformed, or had Bertha simply thought they were?'

Even though Joanne Sullivan claimed that her child 'took a cold in the train and had died, so she put it away in the beach', she was charged with wilful murder.

The Coroner, in summing up, remarked that the case pointed to one of infanticide. From experience at inquests of late, he had been led to the belief that 'the crime of infanticide was rather increasing in this colony.' The doctor's evidence went on to confirm that death in this instance arose from suffocation by drowning. The child found on the beach had been identified, the mother sworn to, and a variety of circumstances sworn to, which tended to show clearly that child-murder had been committed. The Coroner concluded that 'there was every reason to suspect that the baby was put in the water after receiving a blow on the back of the head by some means not stated.'

After about half-an-hour's deliberation, the jury agreed, from the evidence they had heard, that Joanne Sullivan was guilty of the murder of her male child.

Bail was refused.

# Forty

Leopold and Sarah had settled in well into their home in Kent Town in the Eastern suburbs, an area with a large and growing population. The Council were about to introduce a new form of public transport, horse-drawn saloon carriages. The carriages had plenty of space both inside and out to accommodate passengers.

Sarah was keen to use the new carriages. She had been feeling tired lately and longed for an easier way to travel to the city. The present form of transport was by indifferent omnibuses, which in the hot weather was crowded and uncomfortable, and in the cold weather, the passengers were exposed to disagreeable draughts.

'Could you bring home some more potatoes tonight please, Leo,' asked Sarah. 'I seem to be hungry all the time, and the grated potatoes, with egg, flour, pepper and salt, you taught me how to make, seem to fill that hunger.'

'You've become quite a good cook,' said Leopold, about to leave. 'Have you thought about when we should have our Christmas dinner? On Christmas Eve, like we do in Germany, or on Christmas Day, like most people do here?'

'I thought that before we have children, we could celebrate Christmas on Christmas Day, and then once we have children, we can follow your German tradition, and celebrate on Christmas Eve. What do you think?' asked Sarah.

Leopold smiled and was very happy with her decision. 'I love that idea,' he said and kissed her on the forehead.

'There's only one problem though,' said Sarah. 'This will be our first and last Christmas Day.'

'Why? What do you mean?' asked a naïve Leopold.

'Leopold … I'm having a baby,' said a calm, but tired and slightly nauseous Sarah.

'I'm going to be a father! We're going to be parents! Wait till I tell everyone back home. Have you told your aunt and uncle? Sarah, this is wonderful news.' Leopold stopped to catch his breath. 'Are you alright. Can I get you anything? Maybe you ought to sit down or something?'

'I'm fine; there's no need to fuss. Not yet anyway.'

'I'll see if I can organise to work closer to home next year when the baby's due to be born. I can't continue to be away for weeks at a time, travelling to Edithburgh, Jamestown, Caltowie, Port Pirie, all over the place. I'll just have to work closer to home, like today.

~

Time went fast, and Sarah continued to yearn for potatoes, and lemon drinks and lots of fruit, and Leopold continued to do less and less long-distance travel with the police force.

On July, the fourth, Eighteen hundred and seventy-six, Agnes May was born, named after Leopold's sister.

And in the years that followed, Minette, Wilma, Ludmilla, and little Winnifried were born.

'I would love to have met your sisters, and I know how deeply you miss them, but at least, in a way, naming the girls after them means that they can be with us,' Sarah had said to Leopold one sunny day out walking as a family.

With their home in Kent Town becoming too small for their family, Leopold and Sarah moved to a larger property in Chain of Ponds, in the Adelaide Hills. They felt it would be a good place to bring up their children, away from the city.

# Forty-One

Passing through Port Augusta on his way home from one of his routine checks in Port Lincoln, Leopold decided to stop off at the Wharf to check on the goods being unloaded from the ships and see if the paperwork was in order. Ten adult camels had been delivered and were being shepherded into a makeshift stall, when a fascinating old character by the name of James Heirn came over and introduced himself.

'Ships of the desert, they call them, and they call me James. James Heirn. Pleased to meet you, Officer,' said a friendly James.

Leopold stretched out his arm to greet James, who responded with a firm handshake and immediately started chatting to Leopold as though he had known him for years.

'Better than donkeys or bullocks any day. Don't reckon the Overland Telegraph would've gone down if they hadn't shipped the camels out. I think they might've even transported all the equipment needed for surveying and constructing.'

Leopold thought that, by the colour of his sunburnt, leathery skin, gnarly hands and sun-bleached hair, he must have been about fifty.

'Thought I knew everyone out this way. Where are you stationed?'

'Adelaide. Gumeracha, near Chain of Ponds.'

'Lived there meself not that long ago. Maybe ten years ago,' said James. 'You live on your own, I take it. Otherwise, what'd a young fella like you be doing out here? I better warn you, someone has to. You're not gonna find yourself a wife out here. This place is for men of adventure, like meself. Hope you're a good cook and like your own company.'

'In fact, I'm married, with five little girls under eight,' said Leopold.

'It's expecting a bit of yourself, isn't it then? Leaving your family to come out here?'

'Didn't have much choice. About four months ago I was thrown from my horse and shattered my shoulder. The doctor said it would probably take about a year to mend properly. You see, I was the police photographer, but not easy to do when you've got a broken shoulder. I had to take a few weeks off work,' said Leopold, who stopped and wondered why he was chatting about such personal things to a complete stranger.

'There's something about him that makes it alright,' thought Leopold, and he continued his story. 'So they've got me doing a few things. I interpret, I work as a detective, and go out like this, up north for about five to six weeks at a time.'

'You'll be pleased to get back then?' said James. 'What, say, if it's knock-off time for you, we go over there and have a pint?'

James led the way, past the hungry camels, past the wheat being loaded on to the ships for a return visit to England, along the wharf, to the hotel.

'Had an accident when I was a young fella 'probably about your age I reckon …,' said James, as they sat down at a table. 'Used

*The Second Son*

to be a strong, healthy-looking fella like you, not the crippled-up man you see now. Still a young man in spirit, though.'

'Have you lived up this way all your life?' Leopold asked.

'Not exactly! Come here when I was twelve with me family, though I feel I was born here. Been working the land most of me life ... Since I was sixteen, in fact.'

James continued his story, and Leopold nodded to let him know he was listening. He studied his weathered face and wondered how old he really was.

'Me father was a Pastor, he was. We come out here from England to try our luck at a better life. Big family, we were, coming out here to start over, thirteen of us in all, and of course me parents. Had eight brothers and two sisters. Had a protected life back in Devon, we did, so it was a real shock when we landed here. After being at sea on the 'Cleopatra' for so long, me father got impatient waiting for the small boat to come out and get us, so he paid for someone else to take us in.' He paused briefly, as though reliving the moment.

'His impatience, always wanting his own way, changed our lives that day. Yep, from that day on, I decided I didn't want anyone telling me what to do ... Anyway, the boat capsized coming up the Port River, and me father and me youngest brother, Dennis, drowned, along with five hundred sovereigns that sank to the bottom of the river. You can imagine just how devastating it was for me Ma. Me mother bought some land around Gumeracha, and I stayed with her for about four years, and then went off on me own, with her consent. One less mouth for her to feed, I thought. She didn't have much money for school if there was even a school around, after she bought the land, but she did her best to teach us right from wrong. I used to speak better back then, but hanging round with all the men, making money, I didn't worry 'bout it much. The harder I worked, the more money I got, and the more money I had, the more I could send home to her. But it meant being 'round all sorts of blokes. It was more important to make a living. I'd forgotten what it was like to speak to a well-spoken man like yourself.'

'Hard times for you!' said Leopold.

'I suppose it was. For a couple of years, I went up to Mannum with Captain Randall's brother. Taught me bushcraft and the business of stock raising, while I was with him. I live in Adelaide now. On me way back there in a week or so. I can't do much work now out here. Got all crippled up like this when a cart I was driving tipped over and rolled several times. I almost broke me back, and me knee went out of joint, so I'm not much good to anyone out here. Me faithful old horse escaped with a few scrapes, so we were lucky. Anyways, I better get meself going. Nice to meet a friendly officer.'

'I better get home myself. My wife's been on her own with the children for weeks, and I think she needs me home. We've got a sickly baby, little Winnifried, and she's been so tired and quiet lately. I've been worried about her, and how my wife's managing without me around.' Leopold stood up from the table, and shook James's hand. 'Good to meet you. I haven't had such a good conversation with someone for a long time.'

'You, too, young man. It's been good to have a chin wag with you.'

Further along the mail route, on the way to Coralbignie outstation, Leopold came across three salty wells before finally finding a well with clean, fresh water to drink. It was a particularly dry year, and some of the cattle stations even had to shoot surplus stock due to the lack of water.

Outstations like Coralbignie had made attempts to grow hay but with little success. Every so many years, hay for the horses was brought in from Port Augusta a hundred and twenty miles away.

The landscape was dry and barren. Black oak trees and some scrub were scattered about in small patches, as was edible broom. Out in the distance, on the west side of the path, he could see the remains of an ancient woolshed, hemmed in by masses of red granite. He could also see the top of an underground water tank on the hill. The tank could hold up to five years' worth of rain, which was invaluable in an area that had rainfall as low as seven inches in some years.

Leopold walked his horses over to the well and tied them to the timbers. He picked up one of the many rocks and dropped it into the well, counting off the seconds … waiting to see how long it took for the stones to land … with a thud or a splash.

'Water,' he said, relieved to hear a splash. His horses were much in need of this cool refreshment, as was he.

He used a 'whip-and-bucket' apparatus to bring the water to the surface, which he estimated was about thirty feet down. As he wound the apparatus to bring up the bucket, he hoped it was fresh and salt free. The water was clear, so he scooped his hands into the bucket and drank.

'Ah! No salt,' he said aloud, knowing that even the slightest taste of salt would stop the horses from drinking it. Cows and sheep would drink salty water, but not the horses.

After a short rest, he mounted his horse and headed off toward Nonning Valley, where he was delighted to see shade from the only tree for fifty miles around: an old gum he thought was about two hundred years old. The tree stood as a landmark for travellers. It meant that it would not be long before he arrived at the next outstation along this arduous mail route.

The abandoned shearers quarters, that once accommodated thirty-two men, had been built near the embankment, and behind the sheds was a melon patch. To the right of the sheds flowed a creek for five to six miles northwards.

Leopold watched as a group of men were steering bullocks around the embankment by White Well, attempting to make the dam a little larger. There was already eight feet of water in the dam, but the overflow led into the creek behind the embankment, a place that was difficult for the sheep and cattle to reach, and once the animals came in to drink from the edge of the dam, the water would soon disappear. Leopold could see the importance of the hard work the men were doing.

Rain clouds were forming overhead as winds began to pick up the dust. Leopold watched as the dust swirled in ever increasing circles, and he wondered if the men would finish their work before the rains came.

'At least,' he thought, 'the dust will settle and maybe they can get some crops growing?' He watched as the clouds grew darker and seemed to move quickly across the sky, knitting together, in preparation for the storm.

Kangaroo skins hung on wire fences, the smell becoming stronger as the wind blew up. Some had been shrivelled by the sun over the past week.

The Government had an idea for getting rid of vermin, and it had shown to be effective. Aboriginals were paid one shilling per scalp, not just for kangaroos, but for rabbits as well, and they had proven themselves to be very efficient.

Leopold had to keep moving, so he continued along the mail track. After several hours he reached the Gawler Ranges. The ground was hard, and scattered with stones and spinifex. He was forced to rest the horses more than usual because of the difficult terrain.

Occasionally, he found it necessary to lead the horses by their reins while he walked, to lessen the load. 'Only another hour,' he thought, 'and I'll be home.'

After miles and miles of bushy scrub, Leopold finally walked his horses across the creek at the bottom of his property, at the spot where the children often played and the horses drank. As he looked around at the lush, green environment of his Chain of Ponds home in the Adelaide Hills, with its acres and acres of eucalypt trees and pine, he knew that the hot, dry weeks, looking for wells and negotiating the harsh, stony terrain, were behind him.

Approaching the house, where Sarah and the girls would be waiting for him, Leopold was never more delighted to be at home than at that moment.

# Forty-Two

Leopold was dusty and exhausted. He was keen to settle his horses in for the night and make his way up to the house, where he expected Sarah to be cooking dinner and the children playing chasey.

As he walked along the path to his front door step, he noticed the beauty and colour of the irises, periwinkles, buttercups, jonquils and daffodils, and a few roses flowering out of season.

Leopold opened the wire door and stepped into the kitchen. 'Sarah,' he called, but there was no answer, which Leopold thought was rather unusual.

'Sarah,' he called again, louder this time, but there was still no answer. His heart started to beat fast. It was Tuesday, and Sarah was always home on a Tuesday.

'Sarah,' he shouted, in an alarmed manner as he saw her sitting on the floor near the stove, leaning against the stone wall.

'Sarah … Is … everything alright?'

He was lost as to what to do. He had never seen her looking so unwell before. There were occasions when she had retreated to her room, but she had never looked as sick and pale as looked now.

'Sarah?'

He cast his eyes around the room searching for a sign of the girls.

'Sarah, where are the girls?' His voice seemed to echo in the void. There was no answer. He could feel his heart beating faster in his chest, and his throat was dry and tense.

Sarah neither lifted her head, nor looked to see who had come in through the door of the kitchen; she merely stayed motionless on the floor with her back against the cold stone wall, seemingly staring at nothing. It seemed that light had not entered her Irish, blue eyes for weeks.

The pine kitchen table was littered with breadcrumbs and sticky apricot jam. Flies had crawled into the milk glasses and were buzzing and spinning in circles, their long thin legs like pencils drawing patterns along the side of the glass.

'Sarah, where are the girls?' he asked again.

'Wilma! Minette! *Lieblinge,* wo seid ihr?' he yelled. Sarah did not stir. 'Ludmilla! May!'

From behind the bedroom door he heard a voice, 'Here, Papa.'

The voice was light-hearted and melodic. Leopold breathed a sigh of relief. It was Minette, followed by Wilma carrying Winnifried on her hip.

'Here Papa,' chorused Ludmilla and May.

He squatted down to hug the children, his precious girls. His outstretched arms were a warm retreat for the girls, who had secretly worried that something had happened to their dear papa. Six weeks it had been this time, that he had been away in Port Lincoln and various other towns along the way, isolated from his loved ones.

'Mama's not very well ... so we've been looking after Winnie,' said May, who was seven-and-a-half years old. Agnes May preferred to be called by her second name.

'I've been helping, too, Papa,' said six-year-old Minette.

'She won't eat though, Papa. We tried to give her some soup that Mrs Hobbs brought over, but she wasn't interested.'

'Who won't eat? Winnie?' asked Leopold.

'No, not Winnie, Papa. Mother won't eat, unless we feed it to her,' she replied. 'Or at least she's not interested to cook anything, but we've been making her eat. Mrs Hobbs said, that because Mama's still feeding Winnie, she must eat more.'

'Has someone been here to help you?' asked Leopold.

'Mrs Hobbs has been coming, but she wanted us to go and live with her ... We don't have to, do we, Papa?' asked Ludmilla, who had recently started school. 'We've been so very hungry and May couldn't reach the food, even with a chair, so we've just been eating porridge, and bread and jam.'

'We decided we wouldn't go for help again after that,' said May. 'What if you have to go away again, Papa? What will happen to us?'

'Firstly, as kind as it was for Mrs Hobbs to invite you there, you'll be staying here with us,' he replied, still feeling breathless. 'We need to stay together as a family.'

'How long has your mother been like this?' asked Leopold, as he cast his eyes over the girls' dirty white cotton dresses, the ones his mother had sent as a gift from Germany. As he was about to approach Sarah again, he heard a knock on the door and the words, 'Sarah, Leopold ... anyone home?'

Ludmilla opened the door. 'Hello, Doctor—'

'Leopold. Good to see you're home,' said Doctor Holthouse.

Leopold beckoned the doctor to come outside with him so he could discuss his wife's condition in private.

'Leopold, Sarah has completely withdrawn into herself over the past few weeks,' said Doctor Holthouse, who had been a friend of Leopold's for ten years.

'It's serious Leopold ... she has developed what we call in the medical profession "Reproductive Instability". She appears to have no interest in the baby, and the girls have had to manage looking after little Winnifried themselves.'

'What does this "instability" mean? What will happen to her?' asked Leopold.

'It can vary, depending on the severity, but she should be well enough before six months is up,' explained Doctor Holthouse. 'There is a belief that the connection between mind and body is unbalanced, but they're not quite sure if it's a physical or psychological problem.'

'Is she safe to be with the girls?' Leopold asked, thinking of how long he had been away from them this time.

'That's not such an easy answer. The children were insistent: telling me that you would not permit anyone else here to look after them. I think they get that from you ... They can at least get Sarah to take Winnifried on the breast even if she's not interested in eating anything herself ... As to whether it's safe to leave her with the girls, I think you've come home just in time ... It's not that she would do anything to harm herself or the girls, but she can't care for them. The girls have managed with help, but they need you here with them.'

Leopold looked across to the line of pine trees and the flag he and his children had made with the Von der Borch family coat of arms on it. The wind was cold, and chilled the back of his neck.

'Leopold ... Leopold,' said Doctor Holthouse, trying to get his attention, 'You'll have to give up work, or someone else will have to look after the children. They've been managing on their own mostly, and the neighbours have been cooking some meals for them, but they can't go on like that, it's not healthy for anyone ... Laura has been coming here with her two boys to sleep at night because your children were so scared.'

Leopold pulled his collar up around his neck, not speaking, and as the flag flickered in the wind, he thought back to his life in Germany: the coat of arms with the three black jackdaws carved in stone, which took pride of place beside the front door at Holzhausen; his sisters' laughter, echoing throughout the house; and workmen out in the fields harvesting.

He thought back to the letter he had sent to his brother, pleading to come home, but that was years ago now, before he was married with four girls, and the twins they had lost, and poor little Winnifried, a sickly baby with a bad heart who was not expected to live long.

'Leopold. You'll have to decide what you're going to do with Sarah and the girls. Some of the neighbours have offered to have the girls, but they can't take all of them. They could each take one child.'

'You're not suggesting I separate them, are you?' said Leopold with a stern, but anxious voice. He felt he was losing control of his family. He ran his hands through his hair and closed his eyes. 'I can't lose another family ... Why does Alhard's God want to make me struggle? Is there no end to the pain I have to suffer to be a part of a family?' he cursed. 'Always it was God's way, no matter whether it was good or bad, he'd always say, "It's God's way."'

'Leopold, I don't think you have a choice,' said the doctor.

They walked back into the house to check on Sarah. Doctor Holthouse lifted Sarah's thin, limp arm and took her pulse. It was slow and regular. She looked up and smiled a little at his familiar face. The dark smudges under her eyes from lack of sleep had become more prominent, and he wondered if she had slept at all the night before.

'Has Laura been giving your mother milk and the beef tea I prescribed?' Doctor Holthouse asked May. He had instructed Laura to prepare the beef tea the day before. It was a messy and time-consuming process, soaking the raw beef in water, then slowly heating it in a saucepan, before pouring it through a gauze-type cloth over a pan and straining the beef from the broth. But it was worth the effort; it was believed by many to be highly nutritious.

'Yes, Doctor Holthouse, I watched her, and she gives her thirty-eight grams of hydrate of chloral, to help her sleep … Laura, I mean Mrs. Doddridge, said I should know what to do in case she couldn't come one day, because she has her own family to look after, and she can't always be here to look after us,' replied May.

'Hydrate of chloral, that's quite a big word for you to say,' said a surprised Doctor Holthouse. 'You're quite a brave girl, May.'

'Papa said I am good with words, and I can speak some German words, too, now.'

May went off to fetch a glass from the cupboard and showed it to the doctor. 'See,' she said, pointing to the piece of tape on the glass, 'Mrs Doddridge put it there for me, so I wouldn't give Mama too much. I'm not allowed to go above the line when I pour in the medicine. She also told me to store the medicine really high, so my sisters can't get it. I'm the only one that can reach it.'

'That's a big responsibility for a girl of your age,' said Doctor Holthouse, amazed at her poise and her courage.

'Thank you, Doctor Holthouse. Papa said that it was our duty to do things even if we don't feel like doing them,' she replied.

Leopold smiled. He was proud of his daughter, even though he had never imagined that May would have to put into practice, so early in life, everything she had been taught.

'Papa, can you take Winnie,' asked Minette. 'She's getting too heavy for me, and she won't get to sleep.'

Leopold looked down into Minette's sweet, little face. Minette lifted Winnifried from her hip and gave her to her father. 'I'm glad you're home, Papa. Please don't go away again. We were scared at night when it was dark, and we could hear the animals, and Mama couldn't help us.'

Winnifried snuggled into Leopold, her legs gripping tightly around his waist, her arms around his neck. It was as though this small baby knew everything would be alright now.

'Holthouse,' said Leopold. 'What will happen to Sarah, now? Will she need to go to hospital?'

'Mama doesn't have to go, does she, Papa?' asked Minette before the doctor could respond.

'No, Minette. I'll organise something with Doctor Holthouse. Come on, girls. Off you go. Doctor Holthouse and I need to discuss things.'

Doctor Holthouse looked at Leopold and wondered if the burden of caring for Sarah and the girls would be too much for him.

'Losing the twins,' he said to Leopold, 'and now with Winnifried being sickly, and what with the isolation … it's just been too much for Sarah. She needs you to be home with her, more than anything else.'

Leopold bent forward and placed Winnifried in Sarah's lap. She looked at the baby, then up at Leopold, and smiled. Winnifried nuzzled into her, ready for a feed. 'She needs some milk, Sarah,' Leopold said.

Sarah leaned forward, away from the cold stone wall, holding on to Winnifried. Leopold took Sarah's arm and helped her up, then led her to their bedroom, so she could feed Winnifried in comfort.

Feeling a glimmer of hope that things might improve, Leopold gently stroked Sarah's cheek with his hand. 'I wouldn't want you to go to hospital,' he said, before returning to the kitchen to chat further with Doctor Holthouse.

'Whether Sarah goes to a hospital, that's your decision to make, Leopold,' said the doctor.

'She lost her mother when she was only nine, and her father remarried and went back to live in New South Wales. It didn't work out for her, so she came back here to live with her aunt and uncle … I don't think she ever felt that she had a home … I think I'm quite able to look after her myself.'

'What she needs is a "rest cure". Continue with the same treatment she's been having, but you stay around, look after the girls and Sarah. I'm sure your neighbours and friends will help with food or anything else you need,' suggested Doctor Holthouse, pausing to consider all options. 'What about Sarah's aunt and uncle?'

'I'm afraid they've been of little use. Not long after we married they moved to New South Wales to take over the Mount

Murchison Hotel, so we see very little of them, and they certainly haven't offered help of any sort, including monetary help,' said Leopold. 'Sarah's spoken to me several times about them moving away after we got married. I don't think it's helped her condition. I sometimes think she feels like they've abandoned her.'

Leopold walked over to peer through the doorway of the bedroom. He looked over to Sarah and let out a sigh. Winnifried had gone to sleep at Sarah's breast and needed to be put to bed.

He gently lifted her up, and a trickle of sticky breast-milk dribbled from the corner of her mouth. He carried her to her cot at the foot of their bed, wiped her mouth with a clean handkerchief, covered her up with a soft pink blanket, and kissed her on the forehead.

'*Schlaf gut, mein Kleines,*' he said.

He walked back into the kitchen to continue his conversation with the doctor, 'Winnie's too young not to have a mother. I was only young when my own mother died, but at least I can remember her soft skin when I kissed her goodnight, and her arms wrapped around me when she hugged us, and her wonderful, cheerful smile.

'And Sarah's mother died when she was a child, so she has no-one to show her how to be a mother, or how to look after the house and the children … I don't think I have a choice … I'll have to make arrangements to take time off work from the police force. I have no idea what I'll do for money, apart from the money that comes from Germany, but if all else fails, I can go to one of those money lenders,' said Leopold, trying to come to terms with an unknown future.

'Not the money lenders, surely, Leopold?' said Doctor Holthouse, alarmed. 'They've been known to charge fifty percent interest!'

'Desperate times can make a man try anything,' answered Leo.

# Forty-Three

It was a full moon outside. For what seemed like hours, Leopold watched the shadows from the willow tree cast odd shapes across their bed and across the room to their wardrobe. He was memorised by the dancing shadows, the flickering of light, and the curtains blowing into the room. The only sound he could hear came from the curtains as they floated back and forth with the breeze, scraping against the corner of the trunk that he had brought with him from Germany.

Leopold could hear Winnifried move about in her cot, her little legs stretching out beneath the blankets. He propped himself up on his elbow to see if she was alright, and saw her little legs curled up close to her body. She quickly settled herself and went back to sleep.

Leopold then turned to Sarah lying next to him. She looked relaxed, free from the tension and anxiety Leopold had seen in her face earlier in that day. As he looked closer, he noticed her sleeping eyes moving beneath her closed eyelids, they began darting about, as though she was searching for something that had eluded her … and then her eyes were still again. How peaceful she looked lying there.

As he continued to watch Sarah, he wondered where she disappeared to in her mind during the day when she sat in silence, disconnected from the world, from him and the children ... and now lying next to him, he wondered if she travelled to that same place at night, while she slept.

Leopold had asked Doctor Holthouse what it took to go mad, but there was no answer that satisfied him, especially the doctor's explanation that she was a woman, and that they were prone to 'reproductive instability'.

'She gave birth to four other girls before Winnie, so why didn't this happen before,' he thought. 'Why now? I suppose the other girls were healthy, and she hadn't yet lost the twins ... but I'm still not convinced.'

'What is it that starts madness, and, more importantly, what is it that stops it?' he had asked Doctor Holthouse, but still no answers were forthcoming. He thought that if being under too much pressure, or feeling lost or alone, brought on madness, then maybe he, too, would be waiting for it to visit him.

It's a result of an 'overindulgence of the imagination', he could almost hear his father say, a man he certainly loved, but not a man he considered interested in exploring creativity. Leopold wondered if his sense of wonderment and creativity came more from his mother's family.

Suddenly, the wind outside picked up, and he felt the hairs on the back of his neck stand up. It felt as though something, or someone had slipped into the room uninvited, interrupting his train of thought. He tried to brush the feeling away with his hand, much like when a mosquito buzzes around your face on a warm summer night. The sensation reminded him of the feeling he had felt at Minette's, when he had seen an unknown figure at the gate, the person who had run off when Leopold shouted out 'hello'. He hoped everything in Germany was alright.

Leopold whispered to Sarah, 'I'm just going out to the kitchen to heat some warm milk with honey and nutmeg. I'll be back shortly.' He was unsure if she was asleep or not, but if she was awake, and she heard him, she would know he was nearby.

Leopold went over to the *armoire,* to search for an envelope he had been looking for before he went away to Port Lincoln, the envelope had held photographs his mother had sent him from Germany.

'That's strange. It wasn't in this spot, where I originally thought it should have been, before I left, yet it's here now?' As he took the envelope in his hand, Leopold noticed some papers partially hidden under a soft woollen blanket that seemed to have been roughly folded up and plonked on top of some clothes.

He unfolded the papers and looked at them. 'I wonder who wrote this. It's a letter,' he said, but it was unrecognisable in the darkness. He decided to take it with him into the kitchen where he would have more light to read by.

He leaned over and kissed Sarah on the forehead before leaving the room as quietly as he could.

As he walked passed the girls' bedroom and looked in on them, tears fell from his cheeks. His precious girls. He wondered what would become of them all. He longed to be home with his family, to share his life with them. He wanted his children to know his mother, and for her to be able to cuddle them and walk through the beech forest with them, to set up the easel and paint with them, to be a grandmother to them, to tell them her stories of 'The Musicians of Bremen', and to collect brightly-coloured wild flowers. They could meet his relatives and walk through the local village of Nieheim, where generations of other families had lived. And he wanted to tell Sarah how much he loved her, and that everything would be alright. He wanted to take her in his arms. For now, it all seemed impossible.

Guided by the light of the moon, he entered the kitchen and sat at the table. He removed the glass dome from the lantern, turned, and poked a long, thin stick into the fire burning behind the enamelled doors of the stove, and lit the lantern's wick. He moved the envelope with the photos of his family to one side, and unfolded the letter.

*Dear Leopold,* it started. The handwriting was Alhard's and was dated some months ago, and yet he had not recognised it, nor had he read it before. He certainly could not remember seeing it when he was in the bedroom the last time he was looking for the photos. Folded inside the letter was another one, signed 'Sarah', but the handwriting seemed to bear little resemblance to that of his wife's. As he read the letters, he began to realise that Alhard's letter appeared to be a reply to Sarah's. But before he could finish the one by Sarah, he stopped, furious. 'Who wrote this rubbish to my brother?'

*If you could send the money to me I would be most grateful. Leopold's drinking and gambling have gotten worse, and I don't think my beautiful, well-bred children should have to go without …*

'Leopold's drinking and gambling … Leopold's drinking and gambling!' he said aloud. 'Who has written these lies to my brother? What on earth must he think of me?' Leopold felt like his head would burst. 'I'll never get home if Alhard believes such rubbish.'

He could hear someone stirring in their bedroom, and he stopped rustling the paper to listen. The noise stopped, so he continued to read. He could not believe what was in the letter. 'If this is Sarah's writing, why would she do this? And how did Alhard know what was written? He doesn't speak or read English. And Sarah doesn't speak German, so how would she be able to read Alhard's reply?'

'Is this part of what the doctor called "reproductive instability"?' thought Leopold. 'Perhaps she's not herself at all. Even the handwriting is not the writing of the Sarah that I know.'

In a fit of anger, Leopold screwed up Sarah's letter and threw it across the room. He took Alhard's letter and held it closer to the lantern.

*Leopold can certainly not afford to be indulgent, and to drink to this extent, nor gamble, when he has a family to care for.*

He was trying to contain his disbelief. 'You have no idea, Alhard,' he said to himself, 'what my life has been like over the past few years. And as for drinking and gambling? If I were going to do that, I had the perfect opportunity while I was in Palmerston, so far away from everyone, and had no-one to lean on when I was so sick, and nearly died … and where is your God? I haven't found him here anywhere, helping me, or does he only reside in Germany, where life is easy?'

He left the table to go in search of a quill and some ink. He began writing in earnest.

## The Second Son

Dear Alhard,

Sadly, you have been taken in by someone other than Sarah. Sarah, at this moment, is asleep in bed, very unwell. Indeed, I am not certain of her future, nor mine, nor the children's.

It occurs to me that I have not told you of the difficulties we have experienced over this past year or so, and perhaps that is my fault.

Be assured, I do not have a drinking or gambling problem.

It also occurs to me that a number of people in this community are aware that I receive money from Germany, and I think someone has taken advantage of Sarah and her illness, and is asking for money for themselves.

Last year, Sarah was pregnant with twins, and at about twenty-three weeks into her pregnancy, as determined by the doctor, Sarah lost them, and almost haemorrhaged to death. I ran a mile to the doctor's to fetch him, as it was quicker than trying to find the horse and saddle him. Sarah was alone in the house with the girls. We have four other little girls under the age of seven. They were sound asleep and oblivious to Sarah's pain and suffering. You can imagine my heartache and worry, running as fast as I could, breathless in the dark, trying to navigate the quickest way to the doctor's house. My poor baby, Winnifried, is now almost five months old, and is a weak child, who we have been told might not make it to her first birthday.

I will have to give up my job for I don't know how long, to take care of my wife who the doctor says suffers from 'reproductive instability.' I don't know what it is, but it seems to be a type of madness where she just sits and stares, and is disinterested in her girls.

I will have no money coming in except for what I'm able to get through from Schönebeck. I have been relying on friends to help, *and they have been generous with what little they have. I don't know how I can ever thank them?*

*Be assured, I do not have a drinking or indeed a gambling problem, and that I love my wife and children dearly.*

*Your loving brother*
*Leopold*

Leopold blotted the paper and blew on it to help the ink dry. He looked across at the letter signed Sarah, that was still lying crumpled on the floor, and gently shook his head from side to side.

'Who would do such a thing?' he said. 'Surely it wasn't Sarah, even with her state of mind? I will never believe that she would've done it, even the way she is now. It is not in her sweet character to do such a thing, so who *did* write to Alhard?' pondered Leopold.

He looked across to the family photos sticking out of the envelope, but his interest to look at them had faded. He placed them carefully back inside the envelope, blew out the flame in the lantern and put the letter and envelope back in the *armoire* where he had found them, before he went to bed.

Sarah and Winnifried were still asleep, and the moon had dimmed a little more.

Leopold laid his head on the pillow, and put his hands together behind his head, his elbows sticking out like large triangular ears. He began to think of his situation, when suddenly he remembered the crumpled letter still on the floor out in the kitchen. He quietly got up, grabbed the letter, smoothed it out, and put it in the trunk that he had brought out from Germany and that was sitting under the window in his bedroom. 'It should be safe there,' he thought, as he went back to bed. 'Everyone knows they're not to touch my personal things in there.'

The shadows and flickering light had disappeared, and was replaced with a soft glow. Leopold turned his head and looked out through the window and out to the sky. In the distance, he could hear the distinctive hoot of an owl, and he could hear the wind rustling through the leaves. It was as though he could hear for the first time. It was crisp and uninterrupted … no other sounds to distract him from his thoughts.

He could very much feel his own presence in the softened, dark space that filled the room.

'It's up to me now,' he said aloud.

# Forty-Four

Leopold continued to weed around the rose beds, on either side of the front steps leading to the path, trying to be careful not to pull the violets out with the handfuls of soursobs that seemed to have grown overnight.

'These things,' he said, holding the soursobs, 'grow so fast …'

Sarah was in the kitchen, at the table, and had begun to read aloud from the newspaper. It had been months since her confinement, and life had begun to return to normal.

'It says, "the following directions for Typhoid, Measles, Diphtheria and Scarlet Fever …",' she called out to Leopold.

'I can't hear you, Sarah … Come outside … and then I can keep gardening,' he shouted back.

He could hear the girls playing in the creek, and splashing around, throwing clods of dirt into the water, and laughing aloud when they got splashed. The creek ran along the downhill side of their property, beyond the front of the house. At night, as they drifted off to sleep, they could hear the frogs croaking.

Sarah came outside with the paper and sat down on the wicker chair to read it.

'I don't suppose you feel like making a hot pot of tea?' pleaded Leopold. 'And maybe we could have some of those melting moments you made, too?'

Sarah looked at him, and smiled at the patches of dirt on his forehead and cheek, where he had wiped his sweaty face with his arm.

It was a hot day, and Leopold was determined to have the garden looking beautiful for the Sports Day they were having at their place in a week's time. A thank you for the kindness and generosity shown to them by their neighbours during Sarah's illness.

'How many people are you expecting to come, Leo?' asked Sarah.

'Could be up to two hundred people from the local district.'

'Two hundred,' she said, surprised, and got up to make the tea. As she put the paper on the table, the wind blew up and caught it, sending it flying all over the front garden, as far away as the creek. The children squealed with delight as they chased the papers, and each other, around the front garden, between the house, and along the creek.

'Here, Papa,' said Minette, and she handed him a screwed-up pile of papers.

'Thank you, Minette,' said Leopold. 'I might give these to your mother to sort out. She's much better at jigsaw puzzles.'

'Oh! Papa,' said Minette, and laughed as she raced back to join the other children.

Leopold stood up and wiped his hands on the seat of his pants.

'That's starting to look much better,' he said, looking at his hard work in the garden.

'It does,' said Sarah, standing behind him. 'Tea and biscuits are ready. Come and sit down.'

'Girls ... Minette, Ludmilla, come now. Mama has some treats for you. Wilma, May, you, too.'

The girls were wet to the knees from playing in the water, and their beautiful dresses told a story of their days' adventures. 'Dirty marks, muddy splotches, all a mark of a successful and imaginative day,' thought Leopold.

'Thank you, Mama,' the girls chorused.

'Wilma, would you go into the kitchen and fetch the extra jug of milk, please,' requested Sarah. 'Second thoughts,' she said, looking at splashes of mud on Wilma's feet and legs. 'Wash your feet under the front tap first, and dry them with this,' she said, passing Wilma a towel that was hanging over the back of the wicker chair.

'Yes, Mama,' replied Wilma. In no time, Wilma had washed her legs and face and had prepared the tray to bring outside.

Leopold poured milk for the girls, and they each took some biscuits and sat on the edge of the verandah, swinging their feet back and forth, gently tapping the verandah step with the back of their heels.

'When we finish, let's make a daisy chain,' suggested Ludmilla.

'Or a soursob chain … then we can eat them, too,' said Minette.

'Not me, they're so sour,' said Ludmilla.

'Come on, let's go,' said Minette.

Sarah and Leopold sat on the verandah, in their wicker chairs, and looked out across their front garden, beyond the creek, to the pine trees in the distance.

'This is the sort of day that reminds me of being back home in Germany,' thought Leopold. He looked across at the girls who were now pulling soursobs stems from the garden and making daisy chains, and smiled at the delight that children take in simple things.

'This reminds me of when I was a little boy at home, sitting out the front with my brothers and sisters, looking across to the pine trees that lined the driveway to the Big House,' said Leopold.

The girls came up to the verandah, with soursob daisy chains around their necks and on their heads.

'Here, Mama, this one's for you,' said Wilma, as she carefully placed a daisy chain on her head. 'Do you want one, Papa?'

'Could you place mine on the table, I wouldn't want it to fall off while I'm weeding,' replied Leopold.

'What was your home like, Papa, when you were our age?' asked May, the eldest daughter, who had recently started to ask questions about Germany and if they could go and live there one day.

'Did you have a verandah like ours, and did you have any pets?'

As he tried his best to answer May's flurry of questions, Leopold thought to himself, 'I love this … sitting with Sarah and the girls as a family once again, just chatting and laughing. I don't know if I could ever go through Sarah's illness again. I'm so glad she's back to her old self, and the girls are so happy.'

Winnifried was getting restless sitting still for too long, so Leopold picked her up, put her on his lap, and gave her a spoon. She pretended to feed herself, often missing her mouth. The girls laughed at her attempts to coordinate the spoon.

'Is it a very big house, the house in Germany, or more like ours?' continued May.

'Our house here would fit in the front verandah … I can't even remember how many rooms there are,' said Leopold.

'How can you not know how many rooms there are?' said Wilma.

'Let's see. There's a basement with about eight rooms, then there's the ground floor and first floor, and two more floors of attics,' said Leopold, as though everyone lived in a big house like Holzhausen.

'I'd love to have a basement,' said Minette. 'Is it haunted?'

'No, but we do have a haunted wishing well,' replied Leopold.

'I'd love that,' said an excited Minette. 'Why is it haunted?' The girls came over and stood next to Leopold to listen to his story. Ludmilla lifted herself up onto Leopold's lap, next to Winnifried, and tickled Winnifried's tummy.

'You know, Minette, I never did find out. I just know that most of it was covered in ivy, and when you looked down into the well, there seemed to be no end to it … I used to wonder if it was a secret tunnel that led into the house, under the moat.'

'Did you ever try to climb down to find out,' asked Minette.

'No. But I wanted to,' answered Leopold. May interrupted.

'Would our lives be the same in Germany as they are here, Papa?'

'Life in Germany is very different to here. You would be speaking German, and you would have a governess and she would teach you lessons from home … and the staff would bow their heads when they greeted you, and let you walk through the doorway first,' said Leopold.

'Even us … even though we're children?' asked May.

'Yes, May,' said Leopold. 'And you would have had riding lessons, and if there were any boys, they would learn how to hunt.'

'I always wanted my own horse. A chestnut horse. Oh, could we have one, Papa,' pleaded May.

Leopold looked at Sarah and then to May. 'Wouldn't it be wonderful if we could,' he said.

'Would we use our titles, Papa?' May continued. 'Would they call me Baroness?'

'Yes, and you could use your title here, too; only, people don't really trust the Germans, and using a title would make people uncomfortable or more suspicious of your loyalty to your country,' said Leopold.

'Well, what if we lived in the city?' asked Ludmilla.

'Dear Ludmilla. When I say "country", I mean Australia, not out from the city, where we live, here in Chain of Ponds,' smiled Leopold.

'Why?' asked May.

'I don't know why. I suppose people are often suspicious of new people who come here, and we're not English,' said Leopold.

'But that's not fair, Papa,' replied May.

'Yes, I agree, and I think in the end, we should all be measured by our own efforts, and by the way we treat others, rather than making a judgement simply based on a person's nationality, or position in life. My mother, your grandmother, used to say to us when we were growing up, that people can't help the circumstances they grow up in, and that at any time, our circumstances could change, too, so we must be kind to people.'

'Papa is just saying that, sometimes, people are just nasty and make it difficult when they don't have to,' explained Sarah to the girls, as she watched the children chat with their father. 'We need to be kind to people, and think about what it might be like to live their lives.'

Over the past few months, Sarah had grown more confident again, and loved being with her children, cooking together and teaching them how to read. But being out on the verandah, watching them play, with Leopold at home, was what she most loved.

'It will be getting dark soon,' said Leopold. 'Let's chat later, girls. I want to finish the weeding before the sun goes down, or we won't be finished before everyone arrives in a couple of days.'

Ludmilla hopped off Leopold's lap, as Leopold got up from his chair and put Winnifried on Sarah's lap. Sarah kissed Winnifried on the top of the head, and then cuddled into her. Then she leaned over and gave Ludmilla a kiss, too.

'But I still don't know how many rooms there are in the Big House?' said May.

'Maybe, one day, we can all go together and count them, May,' said Leopold. 'Perhaps you can help me weed, and we can continue chatting about Germany?' he suggested, as he walked down to the patch of weeds on the path.

The girls raced each other to see who would be first to reach their father.

'I won,' said Ludmilla, who was the fastest runner at school.

'I'm second,' said May, and next came Wilma, followed by Minette, who had stopped to look at a caterpillar.

'The soursobs are easy to pull out, but there are so many. Maybe you,' he said to May, 'and you,' he said to Ludmilla, 'can weed the garden bed next to the creek and the other two can stay with me?'

'But I'm the one that wants to know how many rooms there are, Papa,' said May.

'Me, too,' said Minette.

'Very well. Minette and May can weed with me, and you two can weed the garden by the creek,' said Leopold, pleased that the girls were interested to ask questions.

'Thank you, Papa,' May and Minette chorused.

'And Ludmilla and Wilma can do some work with me another time, and we can chat then,' said Leopold, as Ludmilla and Wilma skipped off to do their weeding.

By the time the girls were organised with hessian bags to put the weeds in, and had worked out who was going to weed where, the discussion about the number of rooms at Holzhausen had been forgotten.

Sarah held on to Winnifried as she got up from the wicker chair and headed off in the direction of the kitchen. She opened the door and then returned to get the tray. 'I'll be inside, giving Winnie her bath; it's nearly bedtime for her,' she called down the path to Leopold, who waved to acknowledge that he had heard her.

'Did you do anything silly when you were a little boy?' asked May.

'I'm sure I did, in fact I did several silly things ... remember when you asked me about climbing down the well, and I said I wanted to? That's probably the silliest thing I can remember doing. I must have been about eight years old, and I thought the wishing well might actually be a secret tunnel, with an opening that went under the moat and into the cellar,' laughed Leopold.

'And was it?' asked a curious Minette.

'I never found out,' Leopold replied.

'But that's not silly, Papa. Maybe it was.'

'The silly thing is how I tried to prove my theory ... you see, one day when my parents had gone out to Hagen to visit relatives, I sneaked away from the governess, and went out to the stable. I took a small piece of cloth that the staff used to polish the saddles ... I also took a sandwich and a small stick of *Wurst*, and some bread, in case I got lost wandering through the tunnel,' said Leopold.

'What was the cloth for?' asked May.

'Well, I had taken some small coals from the fire in the from one of the rooms on the ground floor, and put them on a plate. I thought I'd light the piece of cloth with them, to help show the way once I was inside the well and going through the tunnel,' explained Leopold.

'That's a good idea,' said May.

'Mm. That's what I thought, but you see, the cloth I'd taken from the stables had some sort of oil on it, and when I held it over the small coals, it caught alight very quickly, and the flame ran up the cloth and burnt my hand … I got such a fright that I threw the cloth away, and it landed next to the well …'

'And then what happened?' asked Minette.

'Luckily, the stable hand had been watching me and had been curious as to why I wanted the cloth, because he knew I didn't like polishing saddles, and he saw what happened and put the flame out … and forbid me ever to try it again, or he would tell my father.'

'But that's so unfair, Papa. Did you ever go back when no-one was looking?' asked May.

Wilma had got bored with weeding down by the creek and wanted to know what Leopold was talking to May and Minette about, so she came up and joined them.

'Just once. I was on my way back from visiting the family cemetery, and it had been a cold, windy day. The big oak trees on Eichen Allee were making spooky sounds, a bit like … an owl with a squeaky cold,' said Leopold.

'Oh, Papa, nobody knows what an owl sounds like when it's got a squeaky cold,' said Minette, whose imagination failed her for the first time.

'I don't like spooky things,' said Wilma.

'Sshh! What then, Papa?' asked Minette.

Ludmilla in the meantime, had found some white bird feathers and was making a pattern with them on the path.

'No-one else was around,' said Leopold. 'Everyone was inside, out of the weather, and so no one noticed I was walking slowly down the path, waiting to sneak over to the well and look inside. I picked up a few stones along the way, and dropped them down the black, black well and waited to hear them plonk into the water at the bottom.' Leopold could see that the girls were enthralled with his story telling.

'And did it go plonk?' asked May.

'No, that was the thing ... I didn't hear anything. Nothing at all. I wonder why that was?' he asked the girls.

'Maybe ... someone was down there and caught it?' suggested Minette.

'Or ... maybe, there is no bottom, or it's so deep, that you couldn't hear it land?' suggested May.

At that moment, Sarah called out from the house. 'Leopold, could you come here for a moment. If I don't tell you now, I'll probably forget.'

'You keep on weeding the garden, girls. I'll be back shortly. I'll go up and see what your mother wants.'

'But, Papa,' the girls chorused.

Leopold stood up and stretched. 'I think I'm getting too old to do this, girls. I think you'll have to finish it.'

The girls cast their eyes around the acre of land that needed to be weeded in the front garden, and sighed.

'It's quite alright, girls, I'll be back,' laughed Leopold.

As Leopold walked up to the house, he admired the view. Sarah had bathed Winnifried and put her to bed, and was in the kitchen peeling potatoes for dinner. When he walked through the doorway, she looked at him and smiled.

'I just went in to check on Winnie, and I suddenly remembered,' said Sarah.

'What did you remember?' asked Leopold.

'I forgot to tell you that the doctor thinks I'm pregnant again!' said a delighted Sarah.

'Are you sure?' asked an excited, but surprised Leopold. He walked straight up to Sarah and gave her a kiss, and then squeezed her tight. He was so delighted.

'We need some good news,' he said. 'A new beginning. A new life, and soon I'll go looking for a new job. This is the best news we've had for a long time. I'll go and tell the girls. They'll be so happy.'

'No, Leopold. Let's wait a little longer,' said Sarah, who was a little apprehensive about having another baby. 'I'm a bit nervous.'

'There's no need to worry.'

'I'm sorry, I can't help it. I suppose I'm worried that something might be wrong with this one, too. I don't think I'll ever completely get over losing the twins, and Winnie isn't a strong baby. What if something happens to this one?'

'You'll be fine, I promise. You're stronger now, and there's no reason to think anything will go wrong. We'll get through this together. *Ich liebe dich,* Sarah,' he said as he kissed her again. 'Try not to worry. This is wonderful! I'll be weeding at double the speed now.'

Sarah laughed, and Leopold went back outside to join the girls.

'Papa, we need to know about the haunted wishing well,' said May, insisting on hearing the rest of the story.

'Where were we up to?' asked Leopold.

'The black, black hole and you couldn't hear the stone land anywhere … not even a splash, Papa?' said Minette.

'That's right. And that was the thing that made me curious. Why couldn't I hear a splash? It had been raining. It did have a slate roof on it like the house, but thinking about it now, surely some water would have got in there?' said Leopold.

The girls looked at their father, eyes wide open, waiting for him to continue.

'I never found out why there wasn't a splash; although, once when the men were cleaning out the moat, they found a large sculpture of a man and a woman that had been thrown in there by Napoleon's soldiers,' said Leopold. 'It was this high.'

The girls watched as Leopold measured the height of the statue against the height of Minette.

'It was about two and a half feet high … and it was intact. Imagine, Napoleon's soldiers storming into the house and throwing it out of the second story window into the moat, and it didn't break!' said Leopold, still amazed. 'My father, and now your Onkel Alhard, keep it in the library, upstairs.'

'It could still be a tunnel then, couldn't it, Papa. If nobody knows for sure, then it could be,' said Minette, who had a wonderful imagination and loved to think that all things were possible.

'Could we have a haunted wishing well here, please, Papa?' asked Ludmilla.

Leopold looked at the girls' faces, and the delight they showed wondering at the possibility of the well being haunted. It provoked their imaginations, which he loved.

'I don't see why not. Let's keep weeding and tidying up the garden for Sports Day and the picnic, and once that's over, we can concentrate on the wishing well,' said Leopold.

# Forty-Five

Leopold handed the *Kapunda Herald* to his wife.

'What's this for?' she asked.

'A typhoid outbreak. There's been another outbreak, and this is to let people know what they need to do to avoid it, or if they have it, how to treat it,' replied Leopold.

Sarah read it aloud, as though seeking confirmation from Leopold, who had recently been appointed Health Inspector by the Governor:

1. *When a case of any of these diseases occurs in a family, the sufferer alone should be placed in a large, aired room, provided with a fire place and windows; part of the window should be kept open day and night.*
2. *All superfluous furniture, carpets, curtains, clothing etc. should be removed from the room.*
3. *A small fire, even in summer, should be kept alight in the fireplace to promote the circulation of the air.*
4. *The door of the room should frequently be wiped with a cloth, moist with a solution of chloralum, the clothes, wet with the same solution of Condy's Fluid, may be hung about the room.*
5. *No person should enter the room except the doctor, nurse and clergyman. The nurse should as soon as possible be clad in cotton*

or linen garments; woollen articles more readily retain and disseminate the germs of contagious diseases.
6. The chamber utensil and bed pan should always have in them about a pint of the solution of sulphite of iron. The utensils, immediately after use, should be covered up, carried away from the room, and their contents buried away from the house, and not emptied into a pan used by other members of the family; after rinsing them well with water, a fresh pint of the solution should be placed in the vessels.
7. Instead of handkerchiefs or towels, pieces of clean old soft cotton rags should be used for wiping the mouth, blowing the nose and removing the discharges; immediately after use, burnt. Sheets and body garments removed from the patient should not be retained in the room, but at once be steeped in boiling water.
8. All the other members of the family, except those in attendance of the sufferer, should keep away from the room of the sick one, and should avoid risking neighbours, and attending school or church. This is especially necessary where it is a case of scarlet fever, measles, or diphtheria.
9. All ashpits, closet pans, and other receptacles for offensive matters, should frequently have a supply of the iron solution applied to them. The drains should also be treated with the iron solution and kept well flushed with water.
10. The water and milk supply of the house should be carefully looked into; and it would be the safest plan never to drink any water not previously boiled, nor any milk not previously scalded. All water tanks should be from time to time emptied and cleansed. The sale of milk from the house must be at once discontinued.

11. Should the patient die, the body should be immediately washed with the solution of chloralum. It should not be laid out in any other room or placed in a church, but be conveyed direct to the grave with the least possible delay, and the funeral be attended by as few friends as possible.
12. After the recovery or death of a patient, fumigate the room, the bedding, etc. with burning sulphur. All doors, windows, fireplace, and crevices should be closed during fumigation, the brimstone being placed on an iron vessel resting on a pair of iron tongs, over a tub of water. The room should not be open for twenty-four hours, and then the doors and windows should be kept open day and night for several days.
13. It is advisable, especially in a case of typhoid fever, and where the above directions cannot be thoroughly carried out, and where efficient day and night nursing cannot be provided, that the sick patient be removed at once to the hospital.

'This sounds serious, Leo,' said Sarah, shocked at what she had read.

'It *is* quite serious … and I must admit, I do worry about the girls, now they are back at school …'

'Imagine losing a child and then having to bury them so quickly, and not have many friends or family there to say goodbye to them. That would be so sad, Leo.'

'I can't imagine the pain,' said Leopold, who went over to Sarah and gave her a hug.

'We lost our own little twins … and I still remember the sadness, and I nearly lost you … but to lose a child that you've cared for, and watched them grow up … taught them how to walk, and laughed at their funny little ways … I can't imagine it, and hope I never have to … that we never have to face something like that,' said Leopold.

'Have you ever wondered what keeps us strong, Leo?' asked Sarah. 'After all, we came from such different worlds, you and I, and we've been through a lot over the past few years …'

'That's true … but I've always thought that the one thing that has kept us together is that we've both known sadness … the kind of sadness that a child feels when they lose a parent, and we both lost our mothers at a young age … I was twelve and you were only nine-years-old … not very old … and as much as others try to understand that loss, they haven't experienced that emptiness, of lying in bed at night sobbing and not wanting anyone to hear you … and of trying to cope because the parent that's been left behind has changed, and they're trying to adapt to things, too, which is a difficult time for them, but in a way, it feels like we've lost both parents. I think it makes us stronger … we know that life can be harsh, and that we can get through those difficult times. I don't think you ever take anything for granted after something like that.'

'I'd never thought of it that way, but you're right … You were so caring the way you looked after me, after I lost the twins, and earlier this year when I couldn't cope … I think that was love, but also understanding.'

'Maybe I was sent here just to meet you?' said Leopold. 'I can't imagine my life without you, and the beautiful girls you've given me … and a new little one on the way.'

'I know you still wish you could go home?' said Sarah.

'Yes. Often … I dream of that journey and all of us meeting the family and going to live at Schönebeck. The children playing in the lake and running barefoot in the beech forest. Although, if we lived there, life would be much more formal, and the children would never be seen without shoes.' Leopold kissed Sarah on the forehead.

'Germany ... Holzhausen ... It's a part of me: a part of what makes me tick ... I'm like a German cuckoo clock that has been made in Germany and exported somewhere else ... I keep perfect time in Germany, I manage well, but out here, my tick is a little out of rhythm sometimes and runs a bit slow, and other times a bit too fast, and I wonder if I'll ever tick the same as the other cuckoo clocks.' Leopold paused for a moment. 'I don't want to let go of my dream to go home ... if I did ... it would kill me, I think, bit by bit ... One day, I hope we can all go back to Germany ... all of us.'

'Maybe you should write to your family more often,' said Sarah.

'I think that, too, at times. I often get the writing set out of the *armoire*, and sit down to write at night by the light of the oil lamp, when everyone's asleep ... but it makes me feel sad. So, I pack it away, and promise myself I'll write tomorrow,' Leopold explained.

'But if you wrote, maybe the family would write to you more often?' Sarah suggested to her husband.

Leopold was distracted. 'I have never asked her about the letter to Alhard,' he thought to himself.

'Writing makes me remember I'm not at home with them,' he said. 'I can't put into words how that makes me feel ...'

He knew, at some point, he had to ask Sarah about the letter. Maybe there would never be a better moment than now.

'Can I ask you something, Sarah? he said tentatively. 'It's about a letter someone wrote to Alhard. A letter that seems to have been written by you.' It felt wrong as soon as he had uttered the words. He was the last person who would want to upset Sarah, let alone accuse her of such a thing.

'What letter, Leopold? I've never written to Alhard. You know I don't speak or write German, and why would I write to him?' Sarah was puzzled. 'Leopold?'

'When you were unwell, I was looking for the photos my mother had sent me, and I found a letter to Alhard, signed by you … or, how should I say it, it was signed with your name. And inside that letter, folded up, was one from Alhard. I can't understand it,' said Leopold. 'It doesn't make sense.'

Sarah was shocked, and immediately took Leopold's hands in hers. 'I swear to you, Leopold, I have never written to Alhard or any of your family. What did the letter say?'

'Whoever wrote the letter was asking for money, and they also—' Before Leopold could finish, Sarah gasped.

'Money! Who would do such a thing? Do you still have the letter? I want to see it.'

'I can show you tonight. The worst thing they said in it was that I was gambling and drinking.'

'Oh, Leo! Whoever could have done such a thing! It all sounds so preposterous. Alhard is your brother; surely he wouldn't believe such nonsense.' Sarah paused to think. 'Of course, you know me well because I'm your wife, and we have been married for several years. But your brother doesn't know me; we have never met. To him, it must have seemed like a frantic plea from a desperate wife.'

'I only chanced upon the envelope when I was looking for the photographs that were in the envelope Mama sent me. The only thing I can think of is that someone wrote to Alhard, and he thought it was from you, so naturally he put our address on it when he replied. Someone, and I don't know who, must have picked up the mail when you were sick and popped it on the table with some of your other things, and in their haste to tidy up, put it away in the *armoire* with some of your clothes, not knowing what was inside.'

'I can't remember for certain who came here, apart from Laura and Doctor Holthouse, and I'm sure we can trust them. But I have a feeling there were a few other people who came in to help, but my mind's a bit of a blur, and I'd rather not think about it,' said Sarah.

Leopold hugged her. 'You know I'm not accusing you, don't you? It's just such a baffling thing to have happened. I'm so happy I married you. I knew it couldn't have been you.' And he kissed her forehead.

'What are you going to do about it?'

'There's nothing I can do, other than what I've already done, and that was to write to Alhard and explain. I only hope he believes me.'

'Of course, he will. He's your brother.'

'I guess we will never know who was behind that letter,' Leopold thought to himself, still vexed by the whole thing. As a former police officer, his urge was to bring the person to justice, but as a married man, he knew it was best to forget about it and concentrate on the wonderful things in his life, such as the new addition to their family that Sarah would be giving birth to soon.

'I can see the sadness in your eyes sometimes, Leo,' said Sarah, interrupting her husband's thoughts. 'It must have been very difficult for you. Leaving all your family and not knowing if you'd ever see them again.'

'At first, I think I thought of it as an adventure, but after contracting yellow fever, when I thought I might die and never see any of them again, something inside me changed. That was a difficult time for … trying to find work. And yet, a great opportunity came of it, the opportunity to work as a photographer for the police; that would probably never have happened if I hadn't been so ill,' said Leopold.

'Mama, we're ready,' said Minette.

'Well, I suppose I better take the girls to school now. I didn't realise it was getting so late. You know I love you, don't you, Leo. Very much,' said Sarah.

'And I better get going, too, or I'll be late for work. Don't forget to keep the piece about typhoid, will you?' said Leopold.

'As long as you don't forget you have a family here that loves you very much,' said Sarah with a smile.

'Bye,' said Leopold, relieved he had finally spoken to Sarah about the letter.

# Forty-Six

'Good morning, Miss Phillips,' chorused the children of Millsbrook public school.

'Good morning, children,' replied their teacher, a young spinster of twenty-two years of age.

'Remember, children, to always wash your hands before you eat, and after you've been to the toilets. It's very important,' said Miss Phillips, who had been given notification about the various diseases such as typhoid and diphtheria.

Olivia Phillips was of English descent, with long blonde hair, which was tied back, pale blue eyes and a fair complexion. She was about average height and had a small, shapely body.

Miss Phillips had no distinguishing features to set her apart from anyone else, but she was treated differently, and her life was often tedious, with restrictions, because she was an unmarried, female teacher. She knew the Teachers Creed off by heart. It restricted her life so much that she wondered why she had taken up teaching.

*I promise to take vital interest in all phases of Sunday School work, donating of my time, service, and money without stint for the uplift and benefit of the community.*

*I promise to abstain from all dancing, immodest dressing, and any other conduct unbecoming a teacher and a lady.*

*I promise not to go out with any young men, except in so far as it may be necessary to stimulate Sunday School work.*

*I promise not to fall in love, to become engaged, or secretly married.*

*I promise not to encourage or tolerate the least familiarity on the part of any of my boy pupils.*

*I promise to sleep at least eight hours a night, to eat carefully, and to take every precaution to keep in the best of health and spirits, in order I may be better able to render efficient service to my pupils.*

*I promise to remember that I owe a duty to the townspeople, who are paying my wages, that I owe respect to the school board and the superintendent that hired me, and I shall consider myself at all times the willing servant of the school board and the townspeople.*

The school desk was old, and had been well used by previous staff members, with bits of paint scratched off the legs. Her chair, in spite of the slatted wooden seat and curved back, was comfortable.

An ink pot and a quill with a nib on the end of it, took pride of place, resting in the groove at the top of the desk, along with a line of lead pencils, an eraser and some blotting paper. A vase of white daisies and sword fern, were placed on her desk each week, to remind her of home.

Behind her desk was a chalk board with information about any upcoming events, such as the Sports Day to be held at Leopold and Sarah's, in gratitude for the care their community had shown them during Sarah's ill health. A portrait of Queen Victoria hung on the wall to the left of the chalk board, and was always tilted to one side, a reflection of how often Miss Phillips knocked it with her hand when she vigorously rubbed the day's work off the board. On a side wall, were two chalk boards, one for how many pennies equalled a pound, or how many eggs made up a dozen, and for algebra equations, and the other board for work written up for the children, under the headings of Grade Three, Grade Four, and Grade Five.

A third chalk board was for the teacher to write on during her daily lessons.

On the opposite wall, hung a huge map of the world, with light blue to represent the ocean, and light orange and darker shades of orange to mark out the mountains. Next to the map was a large Australian flag.

Book shelves were tucked away in the back corner of the room, under the window, opposite the door.

'Christmas holidays in two weeks,' said Miss Phillips.

'And Sports Day at our place this weekend. It will be so much fun,' said May, who had forgotten to put her hand up.

Miss Phillips raised her hand, 'Remember, children, if you want to speak, please raise your hand like this.'

May knew about the rule of raising your hand, but she was too excited at the prospect of the whole community coming to her place for a picnic and for Sports Day to remember.

'Everyone's invited, children, so you can all put your hands down.'

The children's faces lit up at the thought of a picnic and games at the von der Borchs' home.

'Did my mother give you a list of things for the other families to bring?' asked Wilma.

'You see the way Wilma put up her hand to ask me a question?' said Miss Phillips. 'That's what I expect everyone with good manners to do ... Yes, she did, Wilma, and I gave them to the appropriate persons, yesterday.'

'Thank you, Miss Phillips,' said Wilma.

'The picnic will be down by the creek, because the water's nice and fresh and clean, so if anyone needs a drink or gets too hot, they can cool off,' said an excited May, who remembered to put her hand up to get Miss Phillips' attention.

'Yes, Robert,' said Miss Phillips.

'Well. I was just thinking about it, and I want to know what games we'll be doing?' he asked.

'May, would you like to answer this question,' said Miss Phillips, who was yet to read the information.

'Three-legged races ...,' she said, trying to think of the other games. 'Egg and spoon races; what's that one where you have to get in a bag and jump to the finish line?' she asked Wilma.

'The sac race?' she said, unsure if that was what May was thinking.

'Yes, the sack race ... that's so funny to watch,' said May.

'And the men and boys can do the horseshoe throw,' said Ludmilla.

'Why can't the girls do it?' asked one of the girls in the class.

'Because it is unseemly for a young lady to participate in such things,' said Miss Phillips.

'Because they make the shoes for the horses, so they are the only ones allowed to throw them,' answered Minette, trying to find an explanation for why the boys were allowed to do everything while the girls were restricted. 'And the men and the boys can play some cricket, too, after the picnic, and we can watch.'

'I'd like everyone to come back to order now, and do some work,' said Miss Phillips, who was actually annoyed that she was expected to attend the picnic, instead of being able to spend the day with her family.

The day passed quickly, with the children from ages seven to twelve studying their times tables and English, with some time spent outside playing in the yard.

At lunch, all the von der Borch girls liked to take their shoes off, but today, for some unknown reason, Miss Phillips decided they must keep them on.

'Girls, I cannot have this any longer. You must wear your shoes at all times,' snapped Miss Phillips.

The girls looked at their teacher and then at each other.

'Why Miss Phillips?' they asked innocently.

'Because I am your teacher, and I want it to be so,' she said.

As the girls were about to do as they were told, Ludmilla couldn't resist saying, 'But my feet are Australian.'

'What do you mean, Ludmilla? That makes no sense at all to me,' said Miss Phillips.

'Well, Papa said that we always had to dress nicely, like we would in Germany, but because we live here, we had to have something that was Australian, and Australian children have bare feet. So, our feet are Australian,' Ludmilla answered. She thought Miss Phillips was such a wonderful, knowledgeable person. When she grew up, she thought, she would like to be a teacher just like Miss Phillips.

Miss Phillips had no answer, just smiled and went back to class.

It had also been a frustrating day for Minette who had been asked by Miss Phillips if she believed in fairies, after she had seen a drawing of Minette's.

'Yes, Miss Phillips, we have some in our garden, in some of our gerberas, and they're so tiny you can hardly see them,' she replied.

Miss Phillips was horrified, 'You cannot believe in fairies ... in fact it's almost sinful to believe in something you can't see!' she snapped at Minette. 'And do you believe in God, Minette?'

Minette thought carefully, and decided that she was not going to be caught out again by saying she believed in something she could not see.

'No, Miss Phillips, I don't believe in God.'

Miss Phillips was even more horrified, and told Minette she should never say she did not believe in God, even if she could not see him.

'I think I will have to speak to your father about this,' said an officious Miss Phillips.

'I think you need to speak to him, too. Somebody's made a big mistake,' mumbled Minette to herself, sure that Miss Phillips was wrong.

School was dismissed promptly at three thirty in the afternoon.

# Forty-Seven

Saturday had arrived and brought with it beautiful weather and a cool, southerly breeze.

The neighbours had been up early, and had come over to help Leopold and Sarah. They had set up the trestles for the picnic under the gumtrees behind the house.

'There should be enough shade for everyone for most of the day,' Sarah had suggested to Leopold. 'As the sun moves around later in the day, we might have to move the trestles; although, we would have had lunch by then, so it could be alright. We'll have to wait and see.'

'Very well,' said Leopold.

'For us, and for anybody who doesn't bring any food, I've cooked roast beef, and roasted four chickens, and we have the pies and pasties, and Wilma helped me bake some bread, and the other girls helped with the potato salad,' Sarah informed Leopold, who had spent the previous evening outside, cleaning up, and had no idea what they would be eating.

'I also made a couple of large plum puddings we can eat cold, if anyone's still hungry,' she said.

'I think you should take it easy,' said Leopold, referring to Sarah's pregnancy.

'Where are you going now?' asked Leopold. 'That should be

plenty, Sarah … everyone's bringing something to share.'

Sarah was looking for the girls, who were already getting ready for the picnic.

'Don't get dressed yet, girls, I still need your help,' said Sarah, as she walked into the girls' bedroom.

'May, could you look after Winnie for me. You just have to watch that she doesn't get into mischief or crawl outside on her own. She was awake on and off during the night, so she's a bit tired and grumpy. Perhaps the rest of you could take the porcelain plates and the cups and saucers for your father to put on a trestle table for me please.

Sarah was very good at delegating jobs. Leopold often laughed at the thought that perhaps Sarah was really from German stock, and not English and Irish. 'After all, they are known for being organised,' he would say to her.

'All we need now are the clean hessian bags for the races … I boiled the eggs last night, but I can't find them. Does anyone know where they are?' asked Sarah, starting to feel a bit rushed, as people would be arriving within the hour.

'I put them outside on the trestle table with Papa. He said he'd look after them for the race,' said May.

'Very well. Thank you, May … What else do we need, girls?'

'Can we get dressed now?' asked Minette. 'We've finished putting all the plates and things on the trestle table.'

Just then, Sarah's friend and neighbour, Laura, came up to the house. 'Anyone home,' she sang out.

'Inside,' replied Sarah in a loud voice, pleased to see her.

'The boys will come a bit later. I thought I'd come and help you with any last-minute things,' announced Laura.

Just then, Leopold came inside, 'What can we do with the tablecloths?' he asked.

'What do you mean? Aren't they clean enough?' said Sarah.

'Yes, but the wind's blowing up a bit, and the tablecloths are flapping up and onto the table.'

'Have you tried to put some small rocks or something on the corners?' suggested Sarah.

'Yes, but they look quite ugly.'

'Well, remove them, and we won't have tablecloths … maybe we can be more like everyone else, and not fuss about those things so much, Leo,' said Sarah, becoming anxious.

Leopold raced outside to remove the tablecloths, becoming worried that he was running out of time to change out of his gardening clothes.

'Now, where were we, Laura. Oh, yes, if you'd like to make a pot of tea, that would be lovely … if you'd like to have one with me … Now, let me think for a minute. Cold beef, chicken all cut and ready to eat … could you cut some slices of bread for me, that'd be a help, Laura.'

Laura got up to make the pot of tea and tried not to get in Sarah's way.

'Wilma, when you're dressed could you come in here and help me put the potato salad in bowls,' said Sarah.

'Yes, Mama … do you still want me to help with the plates?'

'I'd forgotten about the plates. Maybe do that first … no, perhaps we'd better finish the salad.'

'What if I help with the salad,' suggested Laura. 'And Wilma can finish putting the plates out and then get dressed. The girls have been looking forward to this day so much, and they need to feel pretty in their dresses. Are they wearing the ones your mother-in-law sent them, with the beautiful handwork?'

'Yes, they are; and you're right, they need time to dress. Thank you.'

'Is that alright then, Mama?' said Wilma, seeking confirmation.

'Yes, off you go,' said Sarah.

'Back again,' said a cheerful Leopold. 'That's much less frustrating now, and doesn't look so ugly.'

'What doesn't look so ugly?' asked Sarah, preoccupied with getting the food ready.

'The tablecloths,' replied Leopold.

'Yes, of course; thank you. You'd better have a quick wash, before everyone starts arriving.' Then, looking up at Leopold and smiling, Sarah said, 'You've got bits of the garden all over you.' And they all laughed.

'Did Sarah tell you our news?' Leopold asked Laura.

'No. No … are you?' said Laura.

'Leopold!' scolded Sarah.

'They're starting to arrive, Mama, lots of people,' yelled out Ludmilla. 'I think there are even people we don't know. How exciting!'

'Yes, we are,' said Leopold to Laura. He thought Laura should know, especially because she had been such a supportive friend to Sarah.

'Thank you, Ludmilla,' said Sarah, untying her apron and hanging it up behind the kitchen door.

'I'm sure Laura would have sensed something about you soon enough, Sarah,' said Leopold, trying to defend his decision.

## The Second Son

Horse carriages and people on horseback continued to arrive at the creek at the bottom of the property, where everyone continued on foot across the small bridge. They made their way up to the trestle tables, which had been clearly marked with a big WELCOME sign. The sign had taken the girls two days to complete.

Leopold had placed small, various-coloured flags around the property to mark where the races would be held. He had also marked out the lines for the sack race.

'Oh, Papa, this is so exciting,' said May.

'Isn't it,' agreed Leopold. 'It reminds me of being back home.'

'I'd love it back home then, Papa … Let's go sometime … all of us,' suggested Minette. 'Maybe we could visit the wishing well … or maybe—'

'No time for wishing wells now, Minette,' interrupted Sarah. 'We have to greet our guests, and Papa isn't even washed and dressed yet.'

Leopold darted out of the room. 'I'll be as quick as I can!'

May was holding Winnifried, who was asleep, on her hip.

'Take a blanket with you, May, and then she can lie on that and sleep if she wants to … but in the shade, of course.'

'Yes, Mama,' answered May, and grabbed a blanket before she went off to greet everyone.

'Please, don't say anything about my having another baby,' Sarah pleaded with Laura. 'I'd like to keep it a secret for a bit longer.'

'Of course. But I can't resist saying, congratulations to you,' said Laura, wondering how Sarah must be feeling.

'Before you run off, Wilma. Are Minette and Ludmilla ready?' Sarah asked.

'Yes, Mama, I helped them with their buttons and their shoes,' replied Wilma.

'You're such a wonderful help to me,' said a smiling Sarah.

'*Hallo,* Leopold,' Doctor Holthouse called out as he came up the front steps of the house.

'He'll be with you in a minute. He's almost ready. You could come in, but I'm afraid we don't have much room in our little kitchen,' said Sarah.

'That's quite alright,' said Doctor Holthouse. 'I might just take a seat on one of the wicker chairs out here on the verandah, and light a pipe, if you don't mind.'

'Please, do,' said Sarah.

Soon after, Leopold was outside chatting to Doctor Holthouse and other guests that had come up to the house.

The men chatted in German for a while and then converted to English, so as not to appear rude.

'I thought I would come and say hello, and see how Sarah is coping with the pregnancy,' said Doctor Holthouse privately to Leopold.

It was time to begin the day's events, and it was Leopold's duty to call everyone together. The sports started with the usual running races: with boys competing against boys, and girls competing against girls; then any family members joined in, competing against other families, playing as a tag team for three times the length of the race. There were no prizes and no ribbons, just the fun of being together.

May bought Winnifried over to her mother, and asked to be relieved of her duties for a while.

'Of course. Thank you, I can take her now,' said Sarah.

May went over to watch the sack races, and laughed equally as much as Minette at the boys trying to stay upright and move forward without falling over. The boys had various techniques: some of them held their bags up under their armpits, like trousers they were trying to keep up, while others pulled the bag in tight to their wastes.

'Hello Sarah,' said Doctor Holthouse. He looked at her flushed cheeks, and at Winnifried's pale complexion. 'How are you both? It's quite a big day for someone in your condition,' he said in a whispered tone.

He secretly hoped that her flushed cheeks were from rushing to get things done, and not due to high blood pressure. He was also a little concerned about Winnifried's pinkish-blue lips.

'She's a bit quiet today,' said Sarah, about Winnifried who was seated on her lap, 'but otherwise, we're all doing well.' Then, trying to moderate her excitement, 'I can feel the baby moving, I think; you know, that popping sort of feeling.'

'I might come over tomorrow after lunch to see how you are,' said Doctor Holthouse, who was a little anxious about Winnifried, but did not want to alarm Sarah. 'I'll be out this way to check on somebody else nearby.'

'Yes, thank you. If you'll excuse me, Doctor, I promised to help the girls with the egg and spoon race, and then I need to start preparing the tables with food.'

'Can you look after Winnie for a little while please, Leopold,' said Sarah, as she passed Winnifried across to her husband.

'I'll come, too, to watch the girls in the race,' said Leopold to Sarah. Then, turning to the doctor, 'Coming, Holthouse?'

Once the children were at the starting line, with spoons

tightly held between their teeth, they waited excitedly for Sarah to place the eggs.

'On your marks, get set ... go,' announced Sarah, watching as the children tried to navigate their way to the finish line, tilting their heads just enough to see where they were going. Two of the children dropped their eggs, and one was trodden on by one of the other contestants.

'Sorry, Timothy, you can take my egg and finish the race,' said Robert.

The crowd cheered the children on, and everyone applauded when they finished the race.

'I think May won,' said Leopold to Sarah, quietly.

'Time for lunch, everyone. Please share everything we have,' announced Leopold, as loud as he could so everyone could hear him. Almost two hundred people from the community had gathered, spreading their rugs and opening their wicker baskets, to begin sharing their food.

The children quickly ate some food and headed off to play in the creek, splashing and squealing with laughter.

After everyone was settled and relaxed, Leopold picked up a pot and banged it with a wooden spoon to get everyone's attention. As he did so, his mind caught a fleeting memory, of tapping a glass to get everyone's attention when Alhard was about to make a speech after their father died.

'I just wanted to thank everyone for coming here today. Sarah and I are so very grateful to all of you for your kindness and help during a difficult period in our lives. I cannot begin to tell you, how much that means to us, and I hope that if you ever need our help, you will allow us to return the favour. I hope you are all enjoying yourselves as much as we are, and will continue to enjoy the rest of the day.'

Smiles from the community filled Leopold and Sarah's hearts.

As Leopold went back to sit with Sarah, Winnifried awoke, just long enough to crawl over to her mother, cuddle up with her, and go back to sleep.

For the next two weeks, Winnifried slept a great deal.

# Forty-Eight

Leopold stood at the foot of the tiny grave, on a hot December morning, and wept. Tears rolled down his cheeks as he turned to Sarah, who stood motionless, still in disbelief. He took her hand in his, and gently squeezed it to let her know he was there for her.

The Blumberg Catholic church of Saint Matthew's was only small, and its public graveyard sparse, but the community was warm, and giving, and caring.

The last time Leopold attended a family funeral was his father's. This sad occasion took Leopold back to that painful day, and of the separation from a man he loved and admired. He looked up from Winnifried's grave, to the harsh, dry, landscape that surrounded him: the brown hills, scraggly gum trees with bark peeling away from their trunks, and the dry ground devoid of any welcome or comfort. Ants were crawling over small stones as though they were mountains, on their way to a small fruit bat that lay dead under a nearby tree. Leopold had an urge to go over and remove the small bat, to protect it from the ants, but it was just a momentary distraction from the importance of being with Sarah and paying tribute to his precious baby girl.

He watched as a current of air moved across the grass, like a hand brushing over a piece of velvet, and felt comforted by its strength.

'You should be buried in Germany, my little one, with our family, my dear little Winnie. Not here amongst strangers ... There are no souls here to look after you,' thought Leopold, as tears continued to roll down his cheeks. He looked at Sarah and thought, 'Where is Alhard's God now?'

*'The Vons always seem to die in December,'* he could hear his father say.

As they placed the small white coffin into the ground, Sarah put her hand on her pregnant stomach and sobbed. Sarah felt a little hand slip into the palm of her hand. She looked down at Minette's little face and squeezed her hand. Minette cuddled into her side as she watched the ceremony. May, Wilma and Ludmilla went to the other side of their father, each holding the other's hand.

One of the women in the church had collected rose petals from Sarah's garden, so that the girls and friends of the family could gently release them and watch them fall into the grave.

May, Wilma, Ludmilla and Minette were the first to walk over to Winnifried's grave, in their matching white dresses: the same as the one Winnifried was buried in. The same dresses they had worn on the day of the picnic. As the petals fell, they prayed to God to look after their baby sister.

Not a dry eye could be seen.

The priest said some prayers of guidance for Winnifried as she entered Heaven, and after the service was finished, the friends went on their way so that the family could grieve in silence.

Leopold and Sarah stayed by the gravesite.

'I made a daisy chain, Winnie, so that you'll look pretty when you see God,' said Ludmilla.

'We'll miss you, Winnie,' chorused the girls, who left to wait for their parents by their horse carriage with Laura.

Leopold looked at Sarah's face, stained by the tears she had shed over the past few days. The loss of Winnifried would leave a gaping hole that would stay with their family for the rest of their lives.

Leopold wondered how Sarah would cope with the death of Winnifried and the birth of another baby in just a few months. And he hoped above all else, that the baby would be healthy and that Sarah would not suffer from 'reproductive instability' again.

'If she does, I have no idea how the children and I will cope. I won't be able to leave my new job,' he thought. 'At least I have some money coming in monthly from Schönebeck, which will help … so much more expensive here … if only we'd been able to go back to Germany … with my family. I hope they don't forget me. I think I would have coped better with family around me … I don't think I'll ever understand why what I did should have cost me so dearly … can't let Sarah know I'm not feeling well again,' thought Leopold, still suffering from his life-long problems with his kidneys and liver after contracting yellow fever in Palmerston. 'And I'm getting older … don't think about it … it'll work out … I just hope Sarah will be alright,'

He brought his thoughts back to the moment. 'Let's just cope with now. Poor little Winnie … her dear little face, and her smiles … and her cuddles … I can still feel you cuddled into me, with your little head turned away looking at the others playing. I will always love you and hold you close in my heart … *Ich werde dich immer lieben.*'

Leopold was still holding Sarah's hand. 'I suppose we'd better go,' he said, as he put his arm around her. His heart was beating fast, and he could feel his throat tighten. He could feel a physical connection to Winnifried, as she was being pulled away from him.

'I don't want to leave you here, *Liebling,*' he said to himself. 'This is by far the most difficult thing I have had to do in my life. I'll just have to be strong and walk away. I'll need to be strong for Sarah.' He picked up a shiny white stone and put it in his pocket to put with his collection of things he cherished.

'We're here, Papa,' said May.

'We'd better go, Sarah,' said Leopold, trying to delicately help his wife, who was still frozen at her child's grave. 'Winnie will be alright.'

'*Schlaf gut,* Winnie,' he said as they walked away.

# Forty-Nine

'It's a boy!' Doctor Holthouse shouted out to Leopold, who was in the kitchen pacing back and forth. 'It's a boy, and he's beautifully healthy,' he added, pleased that Sarah and the baby boy were both well.

'How's Sarah doing?' asked Leopold, a little tentative, as he stood in the doorway of their bedroom.

'You can come in if you like ... might be good for you, and the girls, to meet the new baby. If I were to guess at his weight, I'd say at least eight pounds, but the midwife will tell you when she comes to check up on you tomorrow. I think having this little one around the house will bring you all a lot of joy.'

Leopold looked at a rather tired Sarah, as she was holding their baby boy.

'Are you sure it's a boy, Holthouse?' asked Leopold. He loved his daughters more than anything in the world, but was pleased that he would have someone to take on his role.

'Yes, unless you doubt my credentials ... it's a boy,' laughed Holthouse.

The girls came in one by one, and stood around the bed, looking at the baby.

'Can I touch him, Mama?' asked Minette.

'All things considered, I think we can make an exception this time,' said Doctor Holthouse. 'But then you mother will need her rest. Perhaps one of you could pull the curtain across to keep the light out of the room. Remember Sarah, resting the mind and body is important, so no reading for three days, and let the others look after you for the first five to nine days. Depending how you feel.'

'He is strong and healthy, and he'll stay with us forever,' said Sarah to the girls. 'Doctor Holthouse says he's perfectly healthy.'

'Is that true, Doctor Holthouse? Will he be alright?' asked May.

'Yes, as far as I can be sure of anything, this little fellow will be perfect,' answered a caring Doctor Holthouse.

'We need to let your mother rest now, girls,' said Leopold. 'I'll come in a minute, and we can all help get dinner ready together. You can all come back and say goodnight when you go to bed.'

Minette gave her mother a big hug. 'Thank you, Mama, for my new little brother.' She leaned over and gave the baby a gentle kiss. 'He looks a bit like an angel, doesn't he, Mama? Do you think Winnie will see him from Heaven?'

'I'm sure she will. Maybe Winnie sent him to us?' answered Sarah, holding back her tears.

'This will be a new beginning,' thought Leopold. 'The children have seen enough of sadness over the past few years.'

*'Maybe one day you'll have a son, and you'll walk with him around the estate on your shoulders, teaching him what I have taught you,'* Leopold remembered his father telling him. *'Teach him to be strong and resilient. Teach him that family is important, and share our stories. Teach him good manners and the importance of giving back to the community, and teach him not to explain himself*

*to anyone. Remember, it's how we do things in life and how we treat other people, that makes us truly decent people. It's expected of us.'*

'He's beautiful, Sarah, and he does look like an angel, just like my sister, Amalia, did,' said a proud Leopold.

'What do you want to call him?' asked Leopold.

'Shouldn't you name him; after all, he's our first son?' said Sarah.

'I think you should have the pleasure of naming him, and I'll name the second son,' replied Leopold. 'You named the first-born girl, and I know you named her after my sister for me ... so name the first-born boy, too. But this time, a name of your choice, regardless of my family. You've been through so much. I want you to name him. I love you, *Liebling,'* Leopold said.

'Then let's call him Lionel,' said Sarah.

Leopold had no idea where she had heard the name, and he knew of no-one else with that name, including relatives. He liked it. It was different.

*'Hallo Lionel, ich bin der Papa,'* said Leopold, feeling sentimental about his first son. He held Lionel in his arms, and was comforted by the baby's arms and legs wriggling around beneath his warm blanket.

'He's a strong baby, Sarah. He'll be alright. We'll all be alright ... and he has nice pink lips,' he said, and handed their son back to his wife.

'If there is a God, please let us keep this one and make him strong,' thought Leopold.

As he turned to leave the room, Leopold said, 'I've asked Laura to come in and help for the first two weeks, so you can get your strength back ... We will get through this together. Lionel

## The Second Son

is strong, I can tell by his cry. He's a real von der Borch—they like to be heard.'

Lionel seemed to agree, making a little gurgling sound. Sarah looked at him with a loving smile. Leopold gently shut their bedroom door and went to help the girls prepare dinner.

# Fifty

'It's been such a dreadful time for all of you,' said Laura.

'It has. We always knew Winnie was a weak baby, but I don't think we were prepared to lose her. Not when we did ... I thought if she could make it to one, she would be alright,' said a saddened Sarah.

'I'm so sorry, Sarah. You and Leopold have certainly been tested over the years. But now you have this dear, healthy, little boy.'

Lionel was sound asleep in his wicker basket.

'He's so precious, and Leopold is so happy to finally have a son,' said Sarah. 'He loves his daughters, too, but to have a boy he can teach how to fish, and go for walks ... makes him so happy. I come into our bedroom sometimes, and I can hear him talking to Lionel, who's fast asleep, but it doesn't stop him. He tells him about Gut Holzhausen, and of his aunts and uncles, and what they did as children. It's very touching to see a grown man being so gentle. It's one of the things I love about him.'

'I don't think there was ever question about his love for the children and you. Look at when you were sick and he gave up work for you and the girls. I sometimes wonder if my own husband would have done that for me and my boys?' said Laura.

'He hasn't had it easy. I did question whether he married me for love, or out of loneliness, when we first got married,' confessed Sarah.

'What makes you say that?' asked Laura.

'Well, you know how he got so ill, up north in Palmerston, and nearly died?'

'Yes, he's spoken about it a few times.'

'Well, the very next year he lost all his money on bank shares, well, not him really, but someone else's doing, and with the economic depression, times were very difficult … and that was around the time he met me,' explained Sarah. 'And he desperately wanted to go back to Germany, to be with his family, but he had no money: so, I wondered if he thought he would just make a family of his own here, and married me?'

'Never, never would I think that,' said Laura.

'He'd lost everything, and I didn't have anything to offer,' answered Sarah.

'There you are, that proves it must have been for love!' said Laura. 'What did your uncle do?'

'Nothing to help. He and my auntie moved, just after we married, and went back to New South Wales. I think they were pleased to get rid of me. I know they love me, and I love them, too, but it must have been a burden for them to take me on.'

'You shouldn't say that about yourself, Sarah. Leopold is very lucky to have you, and your aunt and uncle wouldn't have taken you in and looked after you if they hadn't wanted to. You're one of the sweetest people I know … and Leopold certainly must have loved you then as he does now.'

'Thank you, Laura. I know you're right. And I don't question it anymore. He's proven his love for me over and over again … and I truly love him.'

'I think we all question ourselves about whether we were in

love with our husbands when we married. I know I did,' said Laura. 'But time helps, and if we didn't love them when we married, I think most of us fell in love with them after time.'

'My father was a police officer. Did I ever tell you that?'

'No,' replied Laura. 'Maybe that was another reason why you fell in love with Leopold?'

'I've wondered that myself. In the end, I decided that it didn't matter why we got married. The fact that we love each other and have a beautiful family is all I could have hoped for.'

'For him, too, I think,' said Laura.

# Fifty-One

Leopold was awake early. The relentless heat, and the mosquitoes buzzing around his head, night after night, while he tried to get some sleep, had left him feeling tired and grumpy. The air was hot to breathe in, and his skin was sticky and felt uncomfortable.

'How long before a cool change,' Sarah asked, standing next to Leopold on the verandah.

'It think it will rain soon,' said a confident Leopold. 'Last night there was a small, rainbow-halo around the moon, and it always rains within a day when it's like that.' He paused for a moment. 'Are the children still asleep?'

'Yes, or at least they were when I came out here,' said Sarah.

The sunrise awakened long forgotten memories for Leopold. *'I see you as the one to keep the family together and to help the girls find suitable proposals of marriage,'* he remembered his father saying.

'Why don't you come inside, and I'll make you a pot of tea?' said Sarah, noticing that Leopold was deep in thought, probably visiting his distant past again.

*'As a boy, when you couldn't get to sleep, you'd always wander down to the kitchen to find something to eat … I'd hear you get up, and I would follow you down to see if you were alright. Then we'd both get something to eat, clean the dishes so no-one knew we'd been up, and then I'd carry you upstairs on my shoulders back to bed.'*

'Thank you. Give me a minute and I'll be in,' said Leopold.

He sat in one of the wicker chairs and looked up at the scattered stars in the darkness, high above the pink of the sunrise, and remembered his journey out to Australia on the George Shotten, and of the storm that blew up, and the claustrophobic feeling of having to stay below deck and ride out the storm. He felt somewhat like that today.

*'If anyone comes looking for me, don't tell them where I am,'* he had said to his father so many years ago. *'I fear for my life. Ever since I went to court, I have heard from friends that when the conmen get out of jail they will come after me. You are right, going to Minette's might help me to hide from them for a while. Hopefully, they'll give up and get on with their lives for the better.'*

Leopold had Lionel now, a son who would be heir to Gut Holzhausen and Schönebeck if his brother, Alhard, had no heirs. Yet, here he was, still in Adelaide, so far away from his rightful place of birth.

'Papa,' said Minette, who surprised her father, 'can I sit on your lap?'

'Certainly, *Liebling*,' he said, as Minette made herself comfortable on his knee. 'Look up there to the stars. Aren't they beautiful?'

'They're so twinkly, Papa.'

'Do you see that very bright star, above the sunrise?'

'No. Where?' asked Minette.

Leopold pointed. 'There. Do you see it?'

'Oh, yes, now I do. It's the brightest one in the whole sky. Why is it so bright?'

Leopold decided not to explain that it appeared brighter because it was a planet and not a distant star. Like his mother, he was imaginative, and wanted his children to have a life filled with stories and make-believe.

'Well, when any of our family members die and go to Heaven, that's where they go, up to that star, which is bright, so we can find them.'

'Is that where Winnie is, Papa? Up there with all those other twinkly stars?'

'Yes, Minette, your sister would be up there; she would be with my mother and father, your Opa and Oma, and they would be looking after her.'

'Were you very sad when Opa and Oma died?' asked Minette.

'Yes. I still miss them ... I'll let you into a secret. If I feel lonely or sad, I talk to them, or think about the times we used to do things together. A bit like people do when they say their prayers. I don't know if they can hear me or not, but it makes me feel better; and when I can see that big bright star, I don't feel so lonely, or miss them so much.'

Minette looked up at the star. The light of the morning sky lit up her face, and Leopold watched as she closed her eyes. A moment later she opened them and gave her father a hug.

'What was that for?' he asked.

'I talked to Winnie, and asked her if she was alright, and if she got the daisy chain,' said Minette. 'Do you think she might have heard me?'

'I can't really say. Did it make you feel any better?'

'I think so,' said Minette, still thinking about the concept that Winnifried was up in that beautiful, bright star. Then, suddenly, she jumped off her father's knee. 'I'm hungry. I think I might go inside and have breakfast,' she said.

Leopold began thinking back to the time when he was told that his mother had died, and of the conversation he had heard, that 'only the good die young.' He remembered thinking, 'If that is the case, then I'm never going to be good.'

Minette opened the door for her mother, who was carrying a tray with a pot of tea and a plate of porridge on it for Leopold. Sarah had made the porridge just the way he liked it, served with a few dobs of butter, and some sugar and cinnamon.

'Look, Mama, up there,' said Minette, pointing. 'That's where Oma and Opa are. Up there on that star. And Winnie's up there, too. And Oma and Opa are looking after little Winnie, aren't they, Papa?'

'That's beautiful, Minette. If that's what Papa says, then it must be true,' said Sarah, as she put the tray on the wicker table and touched her daughter tenderly on the cheek.

'Such beautiful stories you are telling our girls,' she said to Leopold. 'Minette, show me again, where exactly are they all?' Sarah looked up into the sky, following Minette's pointing finger to a star that was fading into the colours of morning.

Minette kissed her mother and father. 'I'm going in to see what the others are doing.'

Leopold and Sarah watched as ants busied themselves on the front path, looking for crumbs of food, and hurriedly criss-crossing to get back to their nest before the change in weather came.

'The wind's starting to blow. We'd better lock the chickens in, and close the doors on the stables. I think we're going to be in for a storm,' said Leopold, a little alarmed by the suddenness of grey clouds building up in the distance.

'My goodness, it is coming on fast, Leopold. I'll take the tray back inside, and then check on the chickens.'

Big splotches of rain began to fall, as Leopold checked on the horses. He breathed in, and sighed. 'I love that pungent, damp, earthy smell that comes with the rain,' he said to himself. 'There's nothing like it after hot weather. Just hope it doesn't get too stormy out here.'

'I checked the windows, and brought in everything that was lying about outside when I checked on the chickens,' said Sarah as Leopold entered the kitchen. 'Just making breakfast for the girls now. Will the horses be alright?'

'Yes, they'll be fine. They may get a bit spooked if there's thunder, but they've been through worse.' Leopold looked out the window. 'That wind is really picking up, and the darkest clouds are heading right in our direction.'

Wilma, Ludmilla, May, and Lionel joined the family in the kitchen.

'I'm hungry, Mama. Can I have Powwidge?' asked Lionel.

'Por-ridge, Lionel. You try it,' said Leopold.

'P-o-w-w-i-d-g-e,' repeated Lionel, with a big smile. 'I did it.'

Leopold and the girls smiled.

'He didn't say it, did he, Papa,' whispered Ludmilla. Leopold shook his head. 'No, but he made a good effort to do so.'

The rain started to pound down on the roof, an intense hammering sound. The children were silent.

'It won't hurt us, will it, Papa,' said May.

'No. It might sound loud, and that might scare us a little, but it will stop; it never lasts long,' said Leopold. 'The storm will always pass over, and sometimes we need to have a storm, so we can appreciate it when the sun shines.'

'Why does it do that?' asked Ludmilla.

Before Leopold could answer, they heard a loud banging noise coming from the stable. Leopold jumped up to see what was causing it.

'What is it, Papa?' chorused the girls.

'The stable door has come open. I'll be back in a moment.'

As Leopold grabbed his jacket and flew out into the pounding rain, the candles in the kitchen blew out.

Sarah began to re-light them. 'There are more candles in the kitchen drawer, May. Could you get them for me, please?'

'Yes, Mama,' said May, walking over to drawer.

A clap of thunder echoed through the surrounding hills, and a flash of lightning lit up the sky.

'I don't like the big noise it makes,' said Lionel.

'I'm worried about Papa getting struck by lightning,' said Wilma.

'Your father will be quite alright,' said Sarah. 'He'll be back in no time at all.'

The girls looked out through the window to watch Leopold, while Lionel continued to eat his porridge.

'Here he comes,' said Ludmilla.

When Leopold reached the verandah, he took off his coat, shook it vigorously, and placed it over one of the wicker chairs. Then he opened the door and almost jumped inside to escape the wind.

'Brrr. It's suddenly so cold outside. Feel my hands,' Leopold said to the children. He then went over to Sarah and put his hands on her face.

'Leopold!' said Sarah, scolding him.

'Did you like storms when you were little, Mama?' asked Minette.

'No, not very much,' said Sarah. 'When I was very little, I used to hide under the blankets.'

'What about you, Papa?' asked May.

'I never liked the *Donnern und Blitzen*,' said Leopold.

As they finished breakfast, the storm began to subside.

'Can you tell us a story?' asked May, who was always fascinated that her father's childhood had been so different to theirs, and that he had mixed with real princesses, and rode in beautiful carriages, and had once had his clothes made for him by a tailor.

'You don't have very long. It's a school day today, don't forget, and the storm has almost passed,' said Sarah. 'And Laura will be here soon.'

'Yes, the rain's just about stopped now,' said Leopold. 'What's say you all get dressed and then we can have a quick story together before Laura arrives to take you to school?'

The children jumped up from the table.

'On your way back, Wilma, could you get the photograph album I gave your mother when Lionel was born?' asked Leopold.

Leopold poured another cup of tea for Sarah and himself, as Sarah began clearing the table.

'Thank you, Wilma,' said Leopold, as she returned with the album and handed it to him. The album was a maroon-coloured, leather-bound book with gold leaves around the edges, and it was held tightly closed by a silver, triangular-shaped lock.

'It's beautiful,' said May.

'What is. Let me see,' said Lionel, struggling to fit between his sisters.

'Say "please", Lionel,' encouraged his mother.

'Please, let me see,' he corrected himself.

'Is everyone settled?' asked Leopold.

'I want to see who I look like,' said May.

'Me, too,' chorused the other girls.

'I don't want to look like anybody,' said Lionel, not really sure what they had been talking about.

'Who's that man,' asked Lionel.

'That's my brother Alhard,' answered Leopold, looking at Alhard's deep set eyes, high forehead and neatly trimmed beard and moustache.

The children started turning the pages, asking who everyone was, but not giving their father enough time to answer before continuing to turn the pages.

'I think we might let your father turn the pages,' said Sarah, nervous that they might damage the book.

'Your mother's right,' said Leopold. 'That's my father and mother, your Opa and your Oma,' he said, pointing.

'Why has he got a stick and a hat,' asked Lionel.

'And a pair of gloves in his hand?' said Ludmilla.

'It's the way a gentleman is meant to dress. If I was in Germany, I'd be dressed just like him,' said Leopold.

The children started laughing. 'Would you really?' asked Ludmilla. 'But you'd get so dirty doing all the jobs in the garden and in the chicken shed.'

'If we lived in Germany, I would have the life of an aristocrat and we would have staff to do all those jobs,' he answered.

'Why has he got a funny beard?' asked Lionel.

'It's called a goatee,' said Leopold.

'Look, how big her dress is,' said Minette. 'She couldn't come through the doorway, it's so big.'

'I love her parasol and her hat,' said Ludmilla. 'I think she looks beautiful. And her hair's been plaited. Can I have my hair like that?'

Leopold smiled at the interest the girls and Lionel showed in his family.

'Time to get ready to go to school, children,' said Sarah.

'I don't want to go today. I'd rather stay here and look at the photographs,' said May.

'Unfortunately, school is compulsory,' said Leopold, 'and it has been for some time, even before your mother and I had all of you.'

'Well, I don't think it's a good rule. You've always said to us, Papa, that if you can read, you can educate yourself. And we can read …'

'Part of a good education is learning to obey rules and learning discipline, and going to school teaches you that,' said Leopold, who surprised himself with his comment.

'But we didn't get time to see who I looked like, Papa,' said May.

'Laura's here. I can see her at the front gate,' said Sarah, looking out the window.

'The photographs will still be here when you get home tonight,' said Leopold. 'Off you all go.'

Leopold and Sarah kissed the children goodbye, and watched them walk down the path to meet Laura at the gate.

After the children had left, Leopold turned to Sarah and placed his hand on her pregnant hump. 'Not much longer,' he said.

# Fifty-Two

Over the next few years, Sarah gave birth to two more healthy baby girls, first to Wanda, then Olga. With each pregnancy, Sarah grew more confident, and Leopold did not worry about her 'reproductive instability' any longer.

Leopold was outside with Lionel, walking around the property, before work, checking on the garden and the chickens and horses. Wanda and Olga were staying with friends, as a new baby was due anytime now. The older children had left for school.

'Leopold,' Sarah shouted from the verandah, bent over. 'Leopold!'

Leopold looked up.

'Go and get Laura or Holthouse. The baby's coming.'

She held her stomach, unable to move for a moment. She breathed out, hoping that the contractions would slow down a little.

Leopold rushed up to help her. Lionel followed.

'Let me help you inside,' said Leopold, trying to stay calm.

He lifted Sarah up and carried her into the bedroom. 'Maybe I should stay?'

'No. Go and get Laura or Holthouse. I don't think the baby will be here just yet. Leave Lionel in the kitchen with some things to play with … You'll be faster without him.'

Leopold ran to the stable, put the bridle on the horse and rode bareback to get Laura, who he knew would be home.

Meanwhile, Sarah was trying to breathe in deeply and relax herself. She knew, as this was her seventh baby, that it would arrive very soon.

'What are you doing, Mama?' asked Lionel.

'I am taking big breaths to keep me relaxed. Off you go, back to the …' Another contraction came. This time, stronger than the last, '… kitchen.'

'Can't I stay with you?' asked Lionel.

'No …' The contractions were coming closer together and were stronger. 'Go back to the … kitchen.'

Lionel walked back to the kitchen, wondering why his mother was so grumpy.

*Hallo.* Mama is so grumpy,' said Lionel to Doctor Holthouse, who had just arrived after seeing a nearby patient. 'And she won't let me stay with her, and she's breathing all funny.'

Doctor Holthouse went directly to Sarah's bedroom.

'I'm so glad to see you. I think the baby's almost here,' said a relieved Sarah.

'It is,' said Holthouse, pleased to have arrived in time. 'Where's Leopold?'

'He just rode off to get Laura, and then to look for you.'

Just then, Leopold walked in the kitchen door, quite breathless, with Laura. 'Is Mama alright?' he asked Lionel.

'No, she's really grumpy,' answered Lionel.

'I'll explain shortly. Stay here,' said Leopold.

Laura picked Lionel up on her hip. 'What can I get you, young man? Would you like some porridge, and a glass of fresh milk?'

'Yes, please,' answered Lionel.

Minutes passed and all Leopold could hear was Sarah breathing fast and hard. Then a big sigh.

'It's a boy,' shouted Doctor Holthouse from their bedroom. 'It's a boy!'

Lionel was a bit confused by everything that morning. 'Why does he keep saying there's a boy? Where is that boy?' he asked.

'Come in here, Lionel. Mama's got something to show you,' said Leopold, who was over the moon with delight.

Leopold picked up Lionel, and carried him into the bedroom.

Lionel looked at his mother, who was in bed, and then at the baby. Leopold walked closer and put Lionel on the floor next to the bed.

'This is your little baby brother, Alhard Christopher Rudolph,' said Leopold.

Lionel looked at his father, and then to his mother again. He was silent for a moment, a bit overwhelmed.

'This is your new little brother, Lionel. What do you think?' asked Sarah.

'Where did you get him?' asked Lionel.

'We'll explain later,' said Leopold.

As Lionel bent forward to smell the baby, Alhard's light blonde hair tickled his nose. Lionel rubbed his nose and then started to laugh. 'He's a funny baby, isn't he, Mama?'

# Fifty-Three

'Papa, can you lift me up higher,' asked Lionel.

Leopold held Lionel around the waist and lifted him as high as he could, so that he could pick an acorn from the oak tree.

Lionel struggled to reach the acorn, and twisted and stretched in Leopold's hands.

'Got it, and its hat stayed on,' said Lionel. 'When I'm bigger like you, I'm going to climb right up to the top.'

'I'm sure you will. You will be quite the adventurer, won't you! These acorns remind me of something we used to do when I was about your age, back in Germany.

'Where I lived,' explained Leopold, 'we had very old oak trees, in the Eichen Allee near the Big House; and friends and family would ride through the Eichen Allee on their horses and carriages, and they would look up at the huge oak trees, trying to see to the very top of them. In one very special tree, in the trunk, my sisters and brothers and I found a hollow, and we would play and hide in it. And just like you, we were fascinated by the acorns and their little hats. What would we would do was to take the hats off the acorns and make them into little boats, and then we would float them in the water around the moat.' Leopold was delighted to be talking about his favourite trees and of home.

'What's in it? It's all rattly,' asked Lionel.

'A seed, and if we plant it, it might one day grow into a big oak tree like this one.'

'Let's just keep it and make a boat … and put it in the creek,' suggested Lionel.

With Lionel still on his shoulders, Leopold walked back to their house along the various ponds that joined together to make a creek. As they walked past the trees, Lionel reached out and tried to grab at the leaves. He laughed aloud when leaves and little pieces of twigs broke off and fell onto his father's head and shoulders.

'Let's do it again, Papa,' said Lionel.

'I've got a better idea, let's go a bit faster,' said Leopold, as he started to walk faster, and jumped over small rocks. He held firmly onto Lionel's hands.

'Let's go,' said Lionel, imagining he was on a large horse. 'That was fun, Papa. I like it when we can have fun together.'

'Can I hop down now?' he asked. Leopold put him down and with that, Lionel started to run towards the house. 'I can beat you, Papa.'

Leopold started to run after Lionel, making it look as though he was trying very hard to win. 'I won,' said Lionel, with a big smile on his face.

Leopold pretended to be puffed out. 'So you did,' he said.

Sarah was on the front verandah, shelling peas for dinner, with Ludmilla and some of the other girls eating them almost as fast as Sarah could scrape them out of their pods. 'Leave some for dinner, girls,' she said, smiling.

May and Minette came out onto the front verandah, with a

handful of items that made Leopold wonder what they had been up to.

'What are these, Papa?' asked Minette, and held out some of the items.

'Where did you get those?' asked Ludmilla.

'They were in Papa's trunk under the window in the bedroom,' replied May.

'Did you ask your father if it was alright to look through his trunk?' said Sarah, disappointed to think the girls would have done such a thing.

Leopold looked at May, knowing how curious she was about his life in Germany. 'It's alright this time, May, but you must ask for my permission to do such things.'

'Oh! While I think of it, a letter came for you today,' said Sarah, as she pulled the letter out of her apron pocket and handed it to Leopold.

'Thank you. I'll read it a little later. I've told May for a while that I'd talk to her about home, and Germany, and I always seem to run out of time, so now is as good a time as any.'

'What do you have, *Liebling?*' asked Leopold.

'This,' she said, and handed him a medal. 'It's very shiny, and it looks important. Is it yours?'

'Yes, it is mine. Can you read the date on it?' Leopold asked.

'Yes, Eighteen hundred and sixty-six,' she said.

'The Austro-Prussian war,' said Leopold.

'What did you get it for, Papa?' asked Ludmilla.

'Let me see it, too' said Lionel, interrupting while trying to squeeze his way between his sisters, as usual. 'They always won't let me see things.'

'I fought in a war once, back when I was about twenty. It was just a quick war, as far as wars go, but unfortunately a lot of people lost their lives. I was in the Forty-fifth Infantry Regiment—' but before he could finish, the girls started asking more questions.

'Did you kill anyone, Papa?'

'What's a Forty-fifth Regiment?'

'Do you still have a gun?'

'Were you the only one who got a medal?'

The questions kept coming, and Leopold sat back to think how he would answer them all.

'The Infantry Regiment means that I was on horseback really. Let me say, though, that I believe a war never really changes anything. Too many people lose their lives, often fighting for something they didn't necessarily believe in.'

'I don't know what he said,' said Lionel. 'Was he talking Germany again?'

'Your father doesn't believe in fighting wars,' explained Sarah.

'Oh,' said Lionel.

'The medal was made from the cannons Austria used against us. The Germans melted down the metal from the cannons and made medals for all of the soldiers … and this is one of them,' Leopold said.

'What's this?' asked Ludmilla, looking at a lock of hair.

'And this?' asked May.

Wanda sat quietly, taking it all in.

'That's a piece of my hair, when I was about four years old. It was tradition in some parts of Germany to cut the boys' hair, and then tie it up with ribbon, like this, for a keepsake,' said Leopold.

'Your Oma sent it out to me about a year ago, when she sent more photographs of my family.'

'But it's a different colour?' said May.

'A lot of the children in our family are blonde until they are about five or six years old, and then our hair changes and becomes brown,' said Leopold. 'Some of you are getting darker. You might notice it more as you get older.'

The girls looked at their mother and at each other. 'Is that right, Mama?' they asked.

'It's true, just as your father said. And when some of us get really old, our hair turns lighter again, and some of us can lose all our hair colour and it becomes white.'

Minette came over and stood on her toes next to May, and tried to stretch up so that she could put her head next to her.

'What are you doing, Minette, you're stepping all over my feet,' said May.

'I'm just trying to get my hair next to yours to see if it is changing yet?'

'Mama,' said May.

'It looks much the same, Minette, now off you go so we can hear what Papa has to say,' said Sarah. 'Why don't you read the letter, Leopold, it could be important, and I'll go and make a pot of tea.

'I think we can chat some more later, girls. Put the things back for now, please, and next time you want to look at something, ask your father first.'

As the girls and Lionel followed their mother inside, Leopold heard Alhard crying from the bedroom. 'Must be hungry, dear little fellow,' he thought.

As Alhard fell silent, Leopold knew that Sarah must have begun feeding him. While he waited for Sarah to finish feeding Alhard, he began reading the letter.

*Dearest brother,*

*It appears that your son Lionel may inherit the estates when he is older, and if he decides to renounce his inheritance, then let your second son, Alhard, inherit. It will be important for your sons to learn German when they are living here. And I am organising a Governor to come to Adelaide to teach your sons what will be expected of them when they come to Gut Holzhausen. His name is Gottfried. I shall write further, when I have made the arrangements.*

*I fear you may never return, as your health has given you some problems, but that will be up to God. You wrote that your eyesight is starting to fail, and I wish for you that it does not fail completely.*

*Love as always*
*Alhard*

'I'd forgotten I had written to him of my eyesight,' thought Leopold. 'I haven't told Sarah or anyone else over here.'

Sarah came out and put Alhard in Leopold's arms. 'Can you take him, and I'll get that pot of tea I was going to make for you half an hour ago.'

'Can you open the door for me, please, Lionel,' Sarah asked. And then turning briefly to Leopold, she said, 'Did you read the letter, Leo?'

After he held the door for his mother, Lionel ran to his father. 'Can I sit on your lap, too, Papa?'

Leopold moved Alhard a little so that Lionel could also fit

on his lap. Lionel snuggled into his father and looked up at him. *'Ich liebe dich, Papa,'* he said.

*'Ich liebe dich auch,'* said Leopold.

As soon as Sarah had returned with the tea and made herself comfortable, Leopold handed Alhard to her and said, 'I've read the letter, and I'm just mulling over the ramifications of it.'

'You look worried, Leo. What does it say?'

'Well, it appears that this little fellow,' said Leopold, talking about Lionel on his lap, 'is most likely to inherit the family's estates when he's older, and if he doesn't wish to take on the responsibility for them, then Alhard will be next in line.'

Sarah put down her cup. 'What do you mean? I thought your brother, Alhard, had a son, and *he'd* be the heir?'

'You're correct. The eldest sons inherit, and then their sons, or their brothers and then their sons. There can also be other factors that come into play, but that's basically how it works.'

Sarah was unusually quiet. Leopold reached over to hold her hand. Sarah looked at him and at their boys and smiled.

'Everything I've been through out here,' said Leopold, 'and now this letter comes saying that Lionel or Alhard might inherit … it means more to me than you can imagine. I finally feel I've been forgiven for my misdeed … and for such an innocent mistake. I knew in my heart that my children would all be welcomed at Holzhausen, and this confirms it.'

'What happens next?' asked Sarah.

'Alhard has a chap by the name of Gottfried, who he will send over to educate the boys, so that they will be ready to fulfil their expectations, including learning German. All the children need to learn German, actually,' said Leopold.

'But, Leopold, he's too little,' said Sarah.

'Not now. It would be much later. Much, much later,' replied Leopold.

Sarah and Leopold sat drinking their tea, with not a word said for several minutes.

'It's too much to take in,' said Sarah, cuddling Alhard as she looked across at Lionel.

'This could be the start of a better life, and the girls could dress in beautiful attire and meet eligible young aristocrats and have such a different life,' said Leopold. 'I would still need to save money for the fares, and with another child on the way, I can't see how we can get us all over there, at least not straight away.'

'A Governor! I have no idea how to act in front of a Governor … when is he coming?'

'As I said, my brother will let me know. It will take some time to organise.'

'Yes, sorry, you did say that. It's just all a bit sudden. To even think that my dear little Lionel would be a baron of the von der Borch's estates. I know he's already a baron, and has inherited titles like the rest of the children, but he would be the residing baron. It seems unreal, Leopold. I suppose, if it's what you want, then we would all have to get used to it.'

'It's his right,' answered Leopold. 'It's difficult to explain, but I feel like we belong again.'

'It would be an adventure.'

'It would be so much more than that, I promise.'

Leopold hugged Lionel. 'We might be going to live in Germany, Lionel, and you'll have the Big House Papa grew up in. The one with the moat.'

'And can we make little boats out of the acorns, Papa?' asked Lionel.

'As many as you like.'

'And if Lionel decides he doesn't want to do it when he grows up, then Alhard's next in line, did you say?' said Sarah.

'Yes, then Alhard will inherit the estates. Like me, he is the second son.'

Sarah smiled, as each of them cuddled the child in their arms. 'A new beginning, with opportunities for all the children. As long as nothing is rushed, and I have time to catch my breath. We'll need time to adjust. It could be a wonderfully different life!'

'A truly wonderful life,' said Leopold.

# Afterword

My great-grandfather, Baron Leopold Friedrich Carl Gotthard Herman von der Borch, lived a full and fascinating life, one of contrasts and courage.

As he grew to old age, his eyesight began to deteriorate, and he could only make out light from dark. He relied on one of his German friends to continue writing his letters to his brother and to read the letters he received from Alhard. His health in general also deteriorated, and at one stage he was hospitalised for a time. The Jesuit priests cared for him and showed him kindness and in doing so motivated Leopold to convert to Catholicism.

After the birth of Alhard, their second son, Leopold and Sarah had four more children: Curt; Erwein, my grandfather; Marjorie, who lived to be a hundred years old; and Rudolf, known as Rolf.

Leopold and Sarah's first son, Lionel, married and had a son named Max in 1914. Max died at the age of five months, followed by the death of Lionel's wife the same year. Several years later, Lionel married again, but had no further children.

Alhard, founder of the Australian Philharmonic Society, was next in line. He married and had three children. He passed his entitlement on to his eldest son, Leo, who was born in 1923, and named after Leopold, Alhard's father. In 1930, Alhard visited the family estates and met with Alhard and Elisabeth, who were to adopt Leo. In a letter that Alhard wrote to his family in Adelaide, he said,

*I feel that darling father will be happy if he knows I am here amongst the haunts of his childhood, where all who knew him loved him as dearly as we do ... by the way, in the room next to mine, the name Leopold is scratched very neatly on the window pane by father with some sharp instrument. Aunt Agnes pointed it out to me with glee.*

At the age of ten, Leo went with his mother to Germany to inherit Schönebeck. Before Leo's departure, Aunt Elisabeth wrote from Germany to his family in Adelaide,

*We are very happy to get this Leopold here as our child and future hopes ... I wish father Alhard could see him coming here and uncle Leopold ... God bless his little soul. I am looking forward to his coming so very much.*

Leo's mother stayed with her son for a few weeks in Germany, before leaving to return home to Adelaide to be with her husband and her other two children, Rudolph and Katrina. The family were meant to eventually move to Germany to be with Leo, but that never eventuated.

My own belief is that the question of German citizenship came into play. When Leo was adopted, he gained German citizenship, whereas Leo's father and his mother and siblings may not have been considered German citizens at the time, as Leopold, Leo's grandfather, would have been obliged to become a South Australian citizen when he was a young man, so he could work in his position in the South Australian police force.

Leo never saw his parents again, but was reunited with his brother and sister as an adult when he returned to live in Adelaide around 1952.

Diana von der Borch-Garden

∽

Leopold died in 1919, at the age of seventy-five, before his grandson Leo, the heir to Schönebeck, was born.

Leopold and Sarah had twelve children and fifty-four grandchildren. The large von der Borch family in Australia are all descendants of Leopold.

In Alhard's last letter to Leopold, Alhard wrote,

*... That you should return to your homeland in your old age seems to be unlikely, especially as you have lost your sight. Still, if should be possible for you, I will receive you with open arms, and be delighted to see you again. May God grant us that happiness if it be his holly will.*

Diana von der Borch-Garden has a degree in English and Drama. She was a freelance writer for a children's television show, *Kid's Only*, and workshopped a couple of episodes of an Australian television series, *A Country Practice*. She is also a published poet.

Diana works as a rehabilitation counsellor, and has worked in the disability area for a number of years. More recently, she studied art psychotherapy, which she now combines with her work as a rehabilitation counsellor in her area of interest in chronic pain management.

Diana has a son, Alexander, and lives in Adelaide.

www.ingramcontent.com/pod-product-compliance
Lightning Source LLC
Chambersburg PA
CBHW032025290426
44110CB00012B/672